"This book widens the horizon of international studies by highlighting the rise of networks. This is particularly interesting since in recent years we spoke more about global disorder, witnessing attacks on multilateral organisations and declining resilience to financial crises, but also health emergencies. Reaching out to taxation, science diplomacy as well as anti-crime cooperation, this volume highlights a new dimension, with particular attention to the role and potential of European actors."

László Andor, *Secretary General of the Foundation for European Progressive Studies.*

GLOBAL NETWORKS AND EUROPEAN ACTORS

This book examines the ability of the EU and European actor networks to coherently and effectively navigate, manage, and influence debates and policy on the international stage. It also questions whether increasing complexity across a range of critical global issues and networks has affected this ability.

Engaging with the growing theoretical and conceptual literature on networks and complexity, the book provides a deeper understanding of how the European Union and European actors navigate within global networks and complex regimes across a range of regulatory, policy cooperation, and foreign and security policy issue areas. It sheds light on how far they are able to respond to and shape solutions to some of the most pressing challenges on the global agenda in the 21st century.

This book will be of key interest to scholars and students of EU/European and global networks and more broadly to European and EU studies, Global Governance, International Relations, International Political Economy, and Foreign Policy and Security Studies.

George Christou is Professor of European Politics and Security at the Department of Politics and International Studies, University of Warwick, UK.

Jacob Hasselbalch is Assistant Professor at the Department of Organization, Copenhagen Business School, Denmark.

Globalisation, Europe, Multilateralism Series

With the institutional support of the Institut d'études européennes-Université libre de Bruxelles

The series offers an interdisciplinary platform for original peer-reviewed publications on the institutions, norms, and practices associated with Globalisation, Multilateralism, and the European Union. Each published volume delves into a given dynamic shaping either the global-regional nexus or the role of the EU therein. It offers original insights into: globalisation and its associated governance challenges; the changing forms of multilateral cooperation and the role of transnational networks; the impact of new global powers and the corollary multipolar order; the lessons born from comparative regionalism and interregional partnerships; as well as the distinctive instruments the EU mobilises in its foreign policies and external relations.

Series Editor: *Mario TELÒ, Université Libre de Bruxelles, Belgium, and LUISS-Guido Carli, Rome, Italy.*

International Editorial Board

Amitav ACHARYA, American University, Washington
Shaun BRESLIN, University of Warwick
Ramona COMAN, Université libre de Bruxelles
Marise CREMONA, EUI, Florence
Louise FAWCETT, University of Oxford
Andrew GAMBLE, University of Cambridge
Peter J. KATZENSTEIN, Cornell University
Robert O. KEOHANE, Princeton University
Christian LEQUESNE, IEP-Paris
Nicolas LEVRAT, Université de Genève

Leonardo MORLINO, LUISS-Guido Carli, Rome
Tamio NAKAMURA, Waseda University, Tokyo
Yaqing QIN, CFAU, Beijing
Ummu SALMA BAVA, JNU, New Delhi
Vivien SCHMIDT, Boston University
Leonard SEABROOKE, Copenhagen Business School
Karen E. SMITH, LSE, London
Anne WEYEMBERGH, Université libre de Bruxelles
Michael ZÜRN, WZB, Berlin

Series Manager: *Frederik PONJAERT, Université Libre de Bruxelles, Belgium.*

Supranational Governance at Stake
The EU's External Competences caught between Complexity and Fragmentation
Edited by Mario Telò and Anne Weyembergh

China and Multilateralism
From Estrangement to Competition
Yuan Feng

Regionalism and Multilateralism
Politics, Economics, Culture
Edited by Thomas Meyer, José Luís de Sales Marques and Mario Telò

Theorising the Crises of the European Union
Edited by Nathalie Brack and Seda Gürkan

The Unintended Consequences of Interregionalism
Effects on Regional Actors, Societies and Structures
Edited by Elisa Lopez Lucia and Frank Mattheis

Towards a New Multilateralism
Cultural Divergence and Political Convergence?
Edited by Thomas Meyer, José Luís de Sales Marques, and Mario Telò

Global Networks and European Actors
Navigating and Managing Complexity
Edited by George Christou and Jacob Hasselbalch

GLOBAL NETWORKS AND EUROPEAN ACTORS

Navigating and Managing Complexity

Edited by *George Christou and Jacob Hasselbalch*

LONDON AND NEW YORK

First published 2021
by Routledge
2 Park Square, Milton Park, Abingdon, Oxon OX14 4RN

and by Routledge
605 Third Avenue, New York, NY 10158

Routledge is an imprint of the Taylor & Francis Group, an informa business

© 2021 selection and editorial matter, George Christou and Jacob Hasselbalch; individual chapters, the contributors

The right of George Christou and Jacob Hasselbalch to be identified as the authors of the editorial material, and of the authors for their individual chapters, has been asserted in accordance with sections 77 and 78 of the Copyright, Designs and Patents Act 1988.

All rights reserved. No part of this book may be reprinted or reproduced or utilised in any form or by any electronic, mechanical, or other means, now known or hereafter invented, including photocopying and recording, or in any information storage or retrieval system, without permission in writing from the publishers.

Trademark notice: Product or corporate names may be trademarks or registered trademarks, and are used only for identification and explanation without intent to infringe.

British Library Cataloguing-in-Publication Data
A catalogue record for this book is available from the British Library

Library of Congress Cataloging-in-Publication Data
Names: Christou, George, 1973- editor. | Hasselbalch, Jacob, editor.
Title: Global networks and European actors: navigating and managing complexity/edited by George Christou, Jacob and Hasselbalch.
Description: Abingdon, Oxon; New York, NY: Routledge, 2021. | Series: Globalisation, Europe, multilateralism | Includes bibliographical references and index.
Identifiers: LCCN 2020054951 (print) | LCCN 2020054952 (ebook) | ISBN 9780367720827 (hardback) | ISBN 9780367720803 (paperback) | ISBN 9781003153382 (ebook)
Subjects: LCSH: European Union–Decision making. | European cooperation. | European Union countries–Foreign relations.
Classification: LCC JN32 .G57 2021 (print) | LCC JN32 (ebook) | DDC 341.242/2–dc23
LC record available at https://lccn.loc.gov/2020054951
LC ebook record available at https://lccn.loc.gov/2020054952

ISBN: 978-0-367-72082-7 (hbk)
ISBN: 978-0-367-72080-3 (pbk)
ISBN: 978-1-003-15338-2 (ebk)

Typeset in Bembo
by Deanta Global Publishing Services, Chennai, India

CONTENTS

List of figures ix
List of tables xi
List of contributors xii
Foreword xv
Acknowledgments xviii

Introduction: Networks, complexity, and the global order 1
George Christou and Jacob Hasselbalch

PART 1
CONCEPTUALISING NETWORKS IN THE FACE OF COMPLEXITY 15

1 Networks, transnational networks, and global order 17
  Claire Godet and Amandine Orsini

2 World politics as a complex system: Analyzing governance
  complexity with network approaches 34
  Philipp Pattberg and Oscar Widerberg

3 Controlling governance issues in professional-organizational
  networks 51
  Lasse Folke Henriksen and Leonard Seabrooke

PART 2
CASE STUDIES IN GLOBAL NETWORKS AND EUROPEAN ACTORS 69

4 Ruling in a complex world: Private regulatory networks and the export of European data protection rules 71
Guillaume Beaumier

5 Navigating an emerging knowledge structure: Where does the EU stand on sustainable finance? 90
Andreas Dimmelmeier

6 The rise of the EU in international tax policy 110
Rasmus Corlin Christensen

7 Transnational networks of the sovereign debt restructuring regime 127
Nicholas Haagensen

8 Environmental governance networks: Climate change and biodiversity 147
Claire Dupont

9 Global complexity, civil society, and networks 163
Manfredi Valeriani

10 Multi-level diplomacy in Europe in the digital century: The case of Science Diplomacy 181
Luk Van Langenhove and Elke Boers

11 European Union networking against transnational crime 197
Anja P. Jakobi and Janina Kandt

12 Conclusions: Global complexity, networks, and the role of EU and European actors 213
George Christou and Jacob Hasselbalch

Index 223

FIGURES

Figure 2.1	Global forest governance triangle (final update February 15, 2017). Modified from Abbott and Snidal (2009a, 2009b), Abbott (2012), and Keohane and Victor (2011)	43
Figure 2.2	Visual representation of the network by nodes	45
Figure 2.3	Degree distribution in the forestry regime complex	46
Figure 3.1	Professional-organizational two-level network. Source: Henriksen and Seabrooke 2016, 726	56
Figure 3.2	Issue professionals in a hybrid network. Source: Henriksen and Seabrooke 2017b, 296	59
Figure 3.3	Trajectories of issue control. Source: Henriksen and Seabrooke 2017b, 288	62
Figure 4.1	Cumulative number of active private codes of conduct on data protection in the Transatlantic area (Source: Author's data)	80
Figure 4.2	Evolution of transatlantic private regulatory networks on data protection 1997–2003 (Source: Author's data)	83
Figure 5.1	Concept network: nodes scaled by degree	104
Figure 7.1	Network diagram of connections between EU/European actors and PCG and GoT and the Creditor Committee coordinated to negotiate with the Greek government	134
Figure 7.2	Main legal professionals embedded in various expert networks on the issue of sovereign debt restructuring	141
Figure 9.1	Yearbook of International Organizations – number of NGOs 1951–2017	165
Figure 9.2	Mapping the Alliance network	172
Figure 10.1	Multi-level, multi-actor diplomacy	189

TABLES

Table 2.1 Approaches towards modeling political networks based on Cranmer and colleagues, 2017; see *also Robins and colleagues* (2012)   41

Table 5.1 Overview of selected documents commissioned directly by the EU institutions. Chronological ordering (month of publication considered, when published in the same year)   97

Table 5.2 TOP 10 texts of co-publication network by degree   98

Table 5.3 Top 10 documents by overall citations   99

Table 5.4 Problems and policy recommendations with more than two mentions   103

Table 9.1 Challenges and network solutions   168

CONTRIBUTORS

Guillaume Beaumier is a Marie Curie doctoral fellow currently doing a joint PhD program between the University of Warwick and Université Laval. Prior to starting his PhD, he completed a postgraduate degree in international studies and worked at the Canadian embassy in Washington. His work broadly focuses on the global regulation of new technologies and its trade policy implications.

Elke Boers was a researcher and project manager for the Horizon2020-funded project EL-CSID, at the IES in Brussels and UNU-CRIS in Bruges. She is undertaking her PhD at the University of Groningen, where she works on intervention missions and the role of civil-military relations.

Rasmus Corlin Christensen is a Postdoc in International Political Economy at Copenhagen Business School, researching international taxation. His work has appeared in journals such as the *Review of International Political Economy, Regulation & Governance* and *Global Networks*. He has also been recognized as a leading individual in international taxation by the *International Tax Review*.

George Christou is Professor of European Politics and Security at the Department of Politics and International Studies, University of Warwick. His research focuses on various aspects of the European Union's external relations and security and cybersecurity and Internet governance. His latest monographs include: *Global Standard Setting in Internet Governance,* Oxford University Press (2020, with Alison Harcourt and Seamus Simpson), and *Cybersecurity in the European Union: Resilience and Adaptability in Governance Policy*, Palgrave Macmillan (2016).

Contributors **xiii**

Andreas Dimmelmeier is a doctoral candidate at the University of Warwick and Copenhagen Business School. His research focuses on the expert networks in the emergence of sustainable finance and the role that economic paradigms played in this process.

Claire Dupont is Assistant Professor of European and International Governance at the Department of Public Governance and Management, Ghent University, Belgium. Her research focuses on the EU's internal and external climate and energy policies. She is the author of the book *Climate Policy Integration into EU Energy Policy: Progress and Prospects* (2016, Routledge), and has published her work in international journals including *West European Politics, Politics and Governance* and *Journal of Contemporary European Research*.

Claire Godet is a PhD fellow at the ARENA Centre for European Studies at the University of Oslo and a researcher for E3G, an environmental think tank. She is part of the PLATO project, a European training network (MSCA-ITN) focusing on EU's legitimacy after the crisis. She works in particular on EU's climate policies, mainly its Emissions Trading System. She holds an MA in European Politics from the University of Bath and Humboldt Universiteit Berlin and a complementary Master in Human Rights Law from Université Saint-Louis-Bruxelles.

Nicholas Haagensen is a PhD fellow affiliated with Université Libre de Bruxelles and Copenhagen Business School on the GEM-STONES project, which looks at the complexity of the global systems resulting from the proliferation of international institutions. His research is part of the work package looking at how networks determine the EU's capacity to rationalize complex regimes. Specifically, his research focuses on how socio-legal actors in Europe dealt with the Euro-crisis.

Jacob Hasselbalch is Assistant Professor at the Department of Organization, Copenhagen Business School. His research focuses on the interaction between sustainability, innovation, and bureaucracy, in the EU and elsewhere. His research has been published in the *Review of International Political Economy, Journal of European Public Policy*, and *Journal of Professions and Organization*.

Lasse Folke Henriksen is Associate Professor of Sociology at Copenhagen Business School. His research has focused on how professional networks shape transnational institutions. He is currently also working on rising global inequality and issues pertaining to climate crisis governance.

Anja P. Jakobi is the Chair of International Relations at the Brunswick University of Technology (TU Braunschweig, Germany). Her research focuses on different aspects of global and transnational governance, with a research emphasis on different aspects of global crime governance. Among her monographs are: *Crime, Security and Global Politics. An Introduction to Global Crime and its Governance* (2020, Palgrave) and *Common Goods and Evils? The Formation of Global Crime Governance* (2013, Oxford University Press).

Janina Kandt, MA is a PhD candidate at the Chair of International Relations at the TU Braunschweig. Her research interests are crime governance, migration politics, and the European Union.

Amandine is Professor of International Relations at the Université Saint-Louis – Bruxelles. She is a specialist of global and European environmental politics, international institutions' interactions and non-state actors. She has co-authored, among others, *Essential Concepts of Global Environmental Governance* (Routledge 2014, 2nd edition in 2020), *Global Environmental Politics: Understanding the Governance of the Earth* (OUP, 2020) and *EU environmental governance: current and future challenges* (Routledge, 2020).

Philipp Pattberg is Professor of Transnational Environmental governance and head of the Environmental Policy Analysis Department at the Institute for Environmental Studies, Vrije Universiteit Amsterdam. His research theorizes and empirically investigates the complexity of global governance.

Leonard Seabrooke is Professor of International Political Economy and Economic Sociology at the Department of Organization at the Copenhagen Business School. His research focuses on transnational governance and professional networks, with a focus on tax, finance, and demographic issues.

Manfredi Valeriani is a GEM-STONES Marie Curie PhD Fellow at Universität Hamburg and LUISS Guido Carli in political science and international relations. His research interests revolve around global governance, transnational networks, and civil society organization, management, and action. His work often employs mixed methods strategies, social network analysis in particular.

Luk Van Langenhove is Research Professor at the Institute of European Studies at the Vrije Universiteit Brussels and Associated Senior Research Fellow at the United Nations University institute for Comparative Regional Integration Studies (UNU-CRIS) in Bruges.

Oscar Widerberg is Assistant Professor at the Institute for Environmental Studies at the Vrije Universiteit Amsterdam. His research focuses on how transnational actors and institutions engage in global environmental governance.

FOREWORD

The notion of networks: A preface to the transnational architecture of contemporary governance

Diane Stone

CHAIR OF GLOBAL POLICY, SCHOOL OF TRANSNATIONAL GOVERNANCE,
EUROPEAN UNIVERSITY INSTITUTE, FLORENCE

Nowadays, networks are ubiquitous. A century ago, large hierarchical organizations and their bureaucracies dominated the landscape of governance. Nation-states consolidated their territorial sovereignty by hardening their borders, building public sector organizations, and strengthening the architecture of regulatory control and bureaucratic oversight. These types of hierarchical organizations continue to exert their power today. Yet, they are increasingly complemented, and sometimes challenged, by many different forms of networks.

Cross-border networks – both formal and informal – cannot be said to be a new phenomenon. Trading networks have been prevalent for centuries. For generations, diaspora communities have maintained informal connections to their home communities. As civil society organizations have expanded internationally over the past generation or so, associational life has become increasingly networked across borders. Likewise, the professions and other expert or scientific communities have shared their knowledge and practices to form an array of specialized networks that provide forms of policy coordination, "soft" regulation, and other standard-setting functions that not only help make policy "tick" but also help legitimate network forms of policy practice.

Indeed, the authors contributing to this volume are themselves forming a network – an informal research network. Their ideas and analysis, captured here, are in some way indirectly "world-making" of the network modality of governance. The burgeoning scholarship on network governance is expanded and elaborated by the chapters in this volume. The authors contribute to a general trend of collective "puzzling" around network notions. This is "world-making" in substantiating the idea that transnational networks are not only shaping the global order but are also helping to govern it.

Each of the chapters addresses different kinds of networks that have merged around transnational policy problems of crime, environment, finance, and so forth, with many of the authors recognizing that they are only scratching the tip of the iceberg by focusing their analysis on just a few exemplary cases. Examination and evaluation of these quite diverse and unruly network phenomena helps make the term "transnational network governance" socially meaningful and politically salient. Such writing and publication helps to turn that idea into a social "fact" that is recognized in a shared world of ideologies and interests. Not only scholarly concepts about "professional networks" or "private regulatory networks" but also the policy narratives constructed by governments and international organizations about a "networked Europe" are at work in creative processes that build identities, order phenomena, systematize data, or construct versions of what is increasingly seen today as a networked world order.

The European Union is already a densely networked realm where networks perform an important role in fostering integration and socializing the elites in the relative absence of strong institutions and regional governance organizations. In a world of states, "Europe" spreads itself out into this world most successfully through its networks. This spreading out and interconnection is via different types or categories of networks.

Transnational networks are a broader category. Such networks incorporate non-state actors such as elements of civil society as well as private sector corporations and business that cooperate and collaborate with official or governmental actors in governance.

Transgovernmental networks, by contrast, are a more specific category of international collaboration among the agencies of national governments and international organizations. These are the networks of official actors and public agencies. Transgovernmental networks help to preserve the identity of Europe, or more precisely the European Union, as a union of states.

But these two types of networks are not de-linked. Instead, they are traversed by what one chapter calls "issue professionals". These are individuals who are particularly important in how issues are treated and governed transnationally.

Whether transnational or transgovernmental – both categories of networks are frequently represented as more efficient or flexible in delivering public services, regulation, or policy coordination than the rule-bound bureaucracies of government departments and international organizations.

This volume brings to light two types of transgovernmental networks. First the dense network of intra-European networks. Studies of this type have brought out in high detail the complicated character of multi-level European regulation and governance. By contrast, more infrequent are studies of those networks that unfurl EU collaboration with not only international actors but also transnational actors based in business, civil society, or the professions. The chapters in this volume are a very important contribution in rectifying this imbalance in scholarship on European and EU networks.

Today network notions have become an intellectual centerpiece of our global era. Transnational network governance challenges traditional modes of organization conducted through the architectures of the state. Even so, networks can also be a complement and bolster the state's policy powers. State agencies often seek to delegate to networks, to bargain with them, or to use them as instruments of collaboration. Thus networks can be regarded as one type of instrumentation in the tool box of governments and other governing authorities. Networks are not necessarily repositories of power in their own right.

It is not only real-world manifestations of networks that exert governance and control through their professional codes or epistemic authority that have been outlined in this volume. Power also resides in network notions. That is, notions of networks – the theories and network concepts, the dissemination of ideas about networks, identifying and evaluating the distribution of resources and status through networks – help construct our everyday realities into a networked one.

As network modalities of organization and governance increasingly become entrenched, it is also necessary to ask whether the network paradigm of governance has become a "model of elites, for elites, by elites". If we obscure questions of network power, or power within networks, or the network paradigm itself, then we hide the distributional and authority conflicts, the lack of consensus or the inefficiencies within networks that are often resolved or, at least, ameliorated by centralization, hierarchical control, or structures of democratic authority.

But there is one important note to end on when it comes to issues of access and equity or representation and responsibility; indeed, what has been called the democratic deficit in governance by network. There are very many networks. Consequently, in the network architecture of governance there is no single center of power. Rather, there are multiple nodes of policy making or standard setting. Some networks, or actors involved in them, are more visible or public, whereas other non-state nodes of power and persuasion are more private and exclusive. This diversity and plurality of networks offers some prospect for civic participation and as an inclusive public sphere of deliberation and negotiation. Yet, as the two editors hint in the conclusion, the question of struggles for access to and then power within and between networks will be a perennial one.

28 December 2019.

ACKNOWLEDGMENTS

First and foremost, we would like to extend our thanks and gratitude to all the authors that contributed chapters to this volume. Without their engagement, commitment, intellectual contribution, and critical feedback throughout the process of constructing and nuancing the aims, objectives, and content of the volume, it would not have been possible to produce a publication of such high quality.

Such feedback was particularly valuable at the two workshops held to discuss the chapters for the volume. The first in Brussels at the University of Warwick office in June 2018 and the second at the University of Warwick premises in Venice (Palazzo Pesaro Papafava), in September 2018. Thanks are also extended to those at: The University of Warwick in the European Strategy Team and the Department of Politics and International Studies; the Institut d'Études Européennes, Université libre de Bruxelles and the Warwick office in Brussels; staff at the Warwick premises in Venice, that helped us organize the workshops as well as to the discussants that attended, in particular Professor Mario Teló and Professor Anne Weyembergh. Both provided invaluable feedback and guidance on the overall focus, coherence and structure of the volume in the initial stages and as it progressed towards the final stages; as did Frederik Ponjaert, joint editor (with Mario Teló) of the Globalisation, Europe, and Multilateralism Series at Routledge.

We are also grateful for the financial support provided for producing this book from the European Commission H2020-Marie Sklodowska-Curie Actions-IF-2014: ITN in the form of European Joint Doctorates (EJD), GEM-STONES, *Globalisation, Europe and Multilateralism, Sophistication of Transnational Order, Networks and European Strategies* (http://gem-stones.eu/).

A special mention is also reserved for the authors in this volume that are part of the GEM STONES project: Nicholas Haagensen, Andreas Dimmelmeier,

Guillaume Beaumier, and Manfredi Valeriani. As PhD research fellows they have not only engaged constructively in the process of producing a chapter for this book but have managed to do this whilst also balancing the many other demands placed upon them in the completion of their PhD theses within the GEM STONES program.

Finally, and most importantly, we would like to thank our respective families and partners for their constant support and understanding throughout the duration of this project.

George Christou and Jacob Hasselbalch

INTRODUCTION

Networks, complexity, and the global order

George Christou and Jacob Hasselbalch

The observation that the world has become increasingly complex across a range of critical global issues and networks, begs the question of how resultant regimes impact on the ability of state and non-state actors to coordinate policies and actions in a coherent and effective way. From the environment to finance and organized crime, such critical issues have emerged as serious threats to society – economically, politically, and in security terms. But how can such complexity be navigated and managed to produce effective solutions and benefits? The more complex global arena for influence and action has expanded the type and number of actors involved and introduced a plethora of norms, ideas, and interests in any given area that are fluid and contested. Engaging with the growing theoretical and conceptual literature on networks, actors, and complexity, this volume seeks to stimulate the debate on action and coherence. More specifically, through providing a deeper understanding of how the European Union and European actors navigate within global networks and complex regimes across a range of regulatory, policy cooperation, and foreign and security policy issue areas, we shed light on how far they are able to respond to and shape solutions to some of the most pressing challenges on the global agenda in the 21st century.

Our focus on networks and complexity is critical. We are in an era where the role of the state is being reasserted in global governance and where the post-war international liberal order is under threat. Indeed, with this threat, the role of transnational actors, experts, networks, and organizations is being undermined by those states that want to reassert a sovereign intergovernmentalism, that is, by those that want the chessboard worldview to become dominant at the expense of obscuring equally important and relevant actors, processes, and landscapes (Slaughter 2017, 7) that have emerged across many salient global issues. A prime example is the US from 2016–2020, under former President Donald Trump. Some of the primary policy objectives of the Trump administration were to "make America great again", and "put America first" through hardening US borders, challenging the multilateral order, reasserting economic nationalism, and side-lining the opinion and role of experts and networks in critical issue areas such as climate change and the environment. Boris Johnson, selected as UK Prime Minister in July 2019, as well as the more hard-line Brexit campaigners in the UK similarly assert a chessboard worldview, making reference to a strong and sovereign UK that can "take back control" and better protect the UK national interest through leaving the European Union.

At a time then, when sovereign single-mindedness and hard boundaries are being reasserted, it is timely that within this complex and fast-changing world that we find ourselves in, we focus on and emphasize the continued importance of the role of networks in the global order. Indeed, Anne-Marie Slaughter (2017, 7) reminds us and underlines the necessity of a web worldview, that is, an international system "not of states but of networks, intersecting and closely overlapping in some places and more strung out in others". Networks, it can be argued, whilst not taking away from the relevance of state competition in the global order, can bring new ideas and processes, more expertise, and greater flexibility to solve problems across and at different levels of action (Keck and Sikkink 1998, 219–220). The web view of the world is one in which Slaughter identifies many of the pressing problems of our time, from climate change to money laundering and terrorism; networks, in this sense, are critical not only in terms of problem-solving but also in constructing alternatives to a challenged global order when the status quo simply no longer works. Moreover, a focus on networks allows us to broaden our field of inquiry across multiple complex policy arenas in order to explore how a plethora of actors are able to navigate, manage, and influence global debates and solutions.

Specifically, this volume seeks to critically assess the value of EU and European networks and actors in global complexity – recognizing both the strengths and potential limitations of the network approach. This introductory chapter will provide a brief contextual analysis of the literature and articulate the contribution of the current volume. It will then outline the central questions and aims of the volume before offering an outline structure and summary of the chapters.

What do we already know about European networks and global complexity?

Networks have been part of the theoretical discussion within International Relations (IR) since at least the 1970s (Victor et al. 2017; see Chapter 1 this volume), but since the publication of Slaughter's (2004) book, *A New World Order*, it has become increasingly commonplace to view the world of international politics as a complex web of government networks, involving many kinds of actors, and not just states acting through official, diplomatic channels. The growing interconnectedness of the modern world has made the component parts of states just as important as their central leadership. In other words, to effectively manage the challenges facing societies today, it requires the cooperation of international networks of regulators, experts, activists, industry representatives, and many others. These networks have increasingly become the targets of analysis in the EU and elsewhere, and with the publication of *The Chessboard and the Web* (2017), Slaughter has brought renewed emphasis to this agenda.

Networks can be analyzed in any number of ways, and it is only more recently that the method and tools of social network analysis (SNA) have actually been introduced into IR and EU studies. If *A New World Order* changed the conceptual frame of international politics, then the publication of *Networked Politics* (Kahler 2009) did much to instigate the methodological move. This edited volume brought together a broad team of political scientists to investigate networks in important sectors of IR, including human rights, security agreements, terrorist and criminal groups, international inequality, and governance of the internet. In many ways, this volume set the scene for taking network *analysis* seriously in IR, identifying a wide range of cases in which the approach provided useful contributions. The language of links, nodes, centrality, closeness, and betweenness as descriptors of network structure and properties has become common parlance in politics and IR (Hafner-Burton et al. 2009; Victor et al. 2017).

Alongside the ascendance of networks and network analysis, and undoubtedly interwoven with the changing assumptions and observations about modern politics, there has been a growing appreciation for the notion of "complexity" in IR and EU studies. There are at least two ways in which complexity has come to light: through the notion of "regime complexes" and through the assumptions of "complex adaptive systems".

Regime complexes (Raustiala and Victor 2004) challenge the conventional idea that individual regimes governing some aspect of international life are decomposable from others – in other words, they contend that the increasing density of international institutions has created collectives of partially overlapping and non-hierarchical regimes. These collective systems of rules are the regime complexes, and they make it increasingly untenable to disentangle and study the effects of one regime without considering the multiple, non-linear ways it interacts with other regimes (Alter and Meunier 2009; Drezner 2009). In the EU, regime complexes have especially been studied in the context of trade and the environment (Oberthür and Stokke 2011; Orsini et al. 2013).

Faced with a world growing in interconnection through the formation of networks and regime complexes, scholars are experiencing the inadequacy of conventional metaphors and assumptions about world politics. This has led some to replace the traditional, mechanical understanding of direct causation and neatly interlocking parts with a biological understanding of complex adaptive systems. Systems that are complex are neither ordered nor disordered – they fall between predictable, determined systems on the one hand, and unpredictable, chaotic systems on the other (Kavalski 2007). Complex systems cannot be wholly understood through the analysis of their constituent parts, but neither are they completely inscrutable to analysis. Complexity promotes a relational and processual style of thinking that stresses organizational patterns, networked relationships, and historical contexts (Bousquet and Curtis 2011). In spite of attempts in recent years to bring complexity into the mainstream of IR (e.g. Cudworth and Hobden 2013a,b; Harrison 2012), it remains on the margins of the discipline.

As for the EU, there is no shortage of scholars commenting on the "complexity" of European affairs, but they mean this more in the sense of things being "complicated" and not complex adaptive systems. This being said, historical debates on liberal intergovernmentalism versus neofunctionalism were not oblivious to the challenges of complexity, but they have tended to view the framework as something that can be used to explain the grey areas where the dominant theories cannot reach or where they lead to unsatisfactory answers (Risse-Kappen 1996; Geyer 2003). Complexity and networks were thus both enrolled as key conceptual tools when scholars turned their attention to the "transformation of governance" in the EU (Kohler-Koch and Eising 1999), which is understood as the growing role for autonomous, yet interdependent governmental sub-units and non-governmental actors working across state borders. One of the many ways that this tradition is being carried forward today is through debates on the European Administrative Space and the role of social network analysis (Mastenbroek and Martinsen 2018).

When it comes to networks and regime complexity in the EU today, recent works can be divided into two categories: most limit their analysis to intra-EU affairs, and only a handful place European actors within a broader, global perspective.

Starting with the intra-European work, network approaches have dealt with a diverse range of issues. A common theme has been to draw on network approaches to make sense of the complicated character of multi-level European regulation and governance. To give a few examples, Marcussen and Torfing (2007), assessing experiences with governance arrangements at local, national, and transnational levels, argue that governance networks are increasingly conceived of as an efficient and legitimate way of formulating and implementing public policy in a complex world. This strand of work emphasizes interaction between public and private actors on the basis of mutual dependencies, institutional incentives, and shared conceptions of problems and tasks. Such forms of interaction are necessary to boost the regulatory capacity of the EU in order to allow it to take on monumental tasks in public policy, such as realizing the Single Market. Mathieu (2016) explores the EU regulatory networks, expert committees, and EU agencies to that end, and the exceptionally large transnational regulatory system which has resulted therefrom. Empirically, he focuses on how regulatory delegation has emerged and evolved in food safety, electricity, and telecommunications. Network building and delegation is thus associated with institutional expansion.

Whereas some work focuses on the effects of networks on legitimacy and institutions, other work analyzes the people who populate internal European governance networks. For example, the work of Georgakakis and Rowell

(2013) leverages network analytic understandings to hone in specifically on the civil servants, Commissioners, and Members of the European Parliament as they go about their daily work in Brussels. Their purpose is to paint a clearer picture of the professionals and work environment in which much of the regulatory action takes place. This attention to the importance of centrally placed policymakers is carried forward in studies of European elites. Best et al. (2012), for example, on the basis of surveys of political and economic elites in 18 European countries, provide a comprehensive study of the values underlying attitudes toward European integration. They also investigate the embeddedness of political and economic elites in transnational networks and their ability to communicate across cultural divides. Other network studies of elites in Europe are considered through an analysis of lobbying and business influence. Bitonti and Harris (2017), for example, provide contributions that take up the issue of lobbying both at the EU level and at the member state level, whilst Schoenman (2015) explores the role of networks between politicians and businesses in governing through the post-Communist transition in Bulgaria, Poland, and Romania. Networks between experts rather than elites tend to be dealt with in issue-specific studies. Hildebrand (2012), for example, proposes that current forms of counter-terrorism policing within the EU should be understood in network terms. Indeed, within this volume there are several examples of such issue-specific studies that highlight the importance of experts.

Networks have also been understood as a useful way to study cooperation on the larger scale, for example involving Europe's regions. Bellini and Hilpert (2013) present a number of different case studies in which cooperation between European macro-regions, Euroregions and other forms of inter-regional, cross-border cooperation create opportunities for economic development. Adshead (2017, first published in 2002) has also presented a network analytical approach to European regional policy to understand the integration process within individual countries. Finally, the issue of complexity has also been treated in an intra-European perspective by Martinico (2013), where the EU legal order is treated as a complex entity which shares some features with natural systems.

What the above intra-European works all have in common is the objective of explaining some facet of intra-European affairs through network (mainly) or complexity approaches. A different collection of works shifts the emphasis toward placing the EU and Europeans more firmly in an international context as actors in *global* networks. Research on this topic is sparser, however.

A selection of edited volumes from Krossa (2012 onwards, nine volumes), question the concept of "Europe" under conditions of globalization. They argue that the analysis of Europe is limited if it is restricted to itself, and that much can be gained from placing Europe in relation to the rest of the world. The focus of this work is on social, interdisciplinary theory, with very little attention given to empirical case studies. Network approaches are often considered, but they are not deemed essential to the broader project of placing "Europe" in relation to "others". We agree that much can be gained from a stronger appreciation of how Europe shapes itself, internally and externally, through participation in global networks and in relation to bodies and problems that lie outside its borders.

That the network alliances of international organizations are absolutely central to their capacity to meet their mandate was demonstrated forcefully by Stone (2013). She addresses the importance of networks connecting international organizations to knowledge organizations. Moving beyond more common studies of industrial public-private partnerships, Stone shows how, and why, international organizations and global policy actors need to incorporate ideas, expertise, and scientific opinion into their policy programs. Access to such experts frequently takes the form of networked modes of organization. This is an important contribution to the field where European actors are considered but are not at the core of the research puzzle.

These ideas can also be found in studies that take their point of departure in the EU's involvement in transnational policy networks. For example, Scott and Liikanen (2011) place network ideas more centrally in asking whether the EU's promotion of cross-border cooperation (e.g. through the European Neighborhood Policy, ENP) is empowering civil society within member states and in neighboring countries such as Russia, Moldova, Turkey, and Morocco. Civil society networks in the ENP are but one type of potential transnational policy network – Kingah et al. (2016) paint a comprehensive picture of how the EU interacts with policy networks in a broad range of fields, including conflict-prone natural resources, health, energy security, migration, human trafficking, combating of terrorism financing, and climate change.

The project we are advancing here seeks to build on both the internally and externally oriented bodies of work we have reviewed here, but we add value in several ways. We place greater emphasis on building and applying network theory on different analytical levels (micro, meso, and macro), and exploring the links in each case study between intra-European affairs and global networks. We also place greater importance on the concept of complexity, especially in terms of how complexity presents both a condition facing policymakers and a feature of their policy responses. The volume presents a number of empirical case studies in a wide range of sectors that overall help us shed light on the capacity of the EU and European actors to attain policy coherence and effectiveness through networked forms of action.

Central questions and aims of the book

The central aim of the edited volume is to assess the EU's and European actors' networked capacity to contribute toward greater policy coherence on the international stage. The common and overarching question that it will seek to address is:

How has increased regime complexity in the global order impacted on the ability of the EU and European actor networks to navigate, manage, and influence debates and policy?

Overall, the edited volume will explore if and how – in the face of increasing regime complexity across a range of regulatory, policy, and foreign and security issue areas – EU and European actor networks have facilitated effective action. To this end, the volume's shared independent variable is the rising complexity of the global system, and its shared objects of study are the various international networks in which the EU institutions and European actors are involved. In this sense, we are not limiting our analysis to a single set of actors, but rather broadening it out to include a multitude of stakeholders from the public, private, and third sector and across a variety of professions.

While driven by an ever-changing, fragmenting, and contested global environment, the global system's growing complexity is a shared factor across a variety of policy fields as it is fuelled by two structural evolutions: the broadening of the number and types of actors involved, on the one hand, and the emergence and diffusion of contested norms, ideas, interests, and paradigms of effective regulation and governance, on the other. The dependent variable in all empirical chapters will look at the policy networks that EU institutions and European actors are involved in, as the increased complexity challenges us to think more critically about the consistency and efficacy of these networks.

To tackle this shared research focus, the edited volume's various contributions will mobilize network theories articulated at the global, intermediary, and actor-specific levels. At the macro-level, the volume will explore whether networks have allowed the EU and European actors to respond to a global order involving an ever-growing number of relevant players. At the meso level, it will assess whether networks have seen the EU and European actors effectively manage the growing number of regime complexes in which it is involved. At the micro level, it will crystallize whether EU and European actors – at the level of expertise and professionals – have effectively impacted the networks they sponsor. Each of these levels of analysis will be set out in the volume's theoretical section.

The volume's empirical scope is to cover several symptomatic policy fields involving a variety of policy networks which are to be unpacked in light of: (1) the developments shaping the complex regime, its importance, and the relative position of the EU and European actor networks within it; (2) the shifting interactions and relationships that the EU and European actor networks entertain through the complex regime (which includes contestation, cooperation, competition); and (3) the relative outcomes of EU and European actor actions associated with the complex regime.

The objectives of the volume are to innovate in three ways:

1. Through providing an outward-looking perspective that takes increasing global complexity as its starting point
2. By providing increased and differentiated scope through a focus on not only EU but also European actors across and in a broad range of global networks and regime complexes
3. Through offering a state-of-the-art conceptual and theoretical platform to inform our understanding of EU and European actor action

Structure of the book

The volume is divided into two parts. In Part 1, the first three chapters provide a theoretical foundation for dealing with networks and complexity on the macro, meso, and micro levels, respectively. In Part 2, this menu of theoretical concepts is mobilized in a number of case studies that explore the EU, European actors, and global networks in all manner of issue areas. To be clear, Part 1 is not meant to serve as a prescriptive tool for engagement, but rather, given the rich variety of cases, a state-of-the-art review of debates in which authors can locate their cases through utilizing relevant frames, theories, and concepts in response to the central research question outlined above.

Part 1 opens with *Chapter 1 by Godet and Orsini* on networks and global order. This chapter represents the *macro* view on networks in global and European affairs. The chapter reviews network thinking in the social sciences, distinguishing between network analysis and network theory. Network theory aims to explain social and political outcomes through relational accounts rather than by appealing to intrinsic characteristics held by actors or variables. Network analysis, on the other hand, is a methodological tool. Godet and Orsini cover some of the basic concepts and assumptions of network thinking, and address the question of whether it constitutes a new way of looking at the world. Here, they also review several waves of network-oriented scholarship in IR. They conclude that network theory and analysis is a promising route to challenging state-centric approaches but that network approaches have their limits and blind spots.

Chapter 2 by Pattberg and Widerberg engages with networks on the *meso* level. This chapter explores the theme of complexity, suggesting that network approaches are useful tools to deal with and unpack complexity. Pattberg and Widerberg understand complexity as the emergence of multiple and overlapping actors and architectures in global governance. They begin by discussing the state of the art relating to fragmentation and governance complexity. They then proceed to argue that these conditions can be conceptualized as complex adaptive systems, going on to explain the key characteristics associated with such systems. To unravel this complexity, they argue that network theory and relational ontology is central. The chapter closes with an illustration of their arguments, drawing on a case study of complexity in global forest governance.

Chapter 3 by Henriksen and Seabrooke turns toward networks on the *micro* level. In this chapter, the discussion moves to questions of how actors navigate *within* complex network structures. Henriksen and Seabrooke argue that complexity does not necessarily lead to lack of cohesion in social systems, and actors are able to adapt to complexity, to develop ways of dealing with it, and even exploit it. Their chapter conceptualizes two-level networks of professionals and the organizations within and between which they move as a social space for action within complex systems. The focus is on how interactions within these spaces can explain how professionals and organizations come to exert their control over issues within global governance. They introduce the notion of the "issue professional" as a category of professionals that are particularly astute at organizing transnationally in order to control issues. After describing how the structure of and actions within two-level networks can be understood, they conclude by providing examples of six different strategies through which issue professionals establish control over issues in global and transnational governance.

Part 2 begins with *Chapter 4 by Beaumier* on private regulatory networks and the export of European data protection rules. Beaumier analyzes the role of private actors in the regulation of the digital economy. Private actors own a significant share of the infrastructure of the digital economy and have been involved in setting up rules to govern their own activities. Private associations have notably developed multiple rules pertaining to the issue of data protection, constituting this field as a complex area of governance. In this contribution, which is oriented toward international political economy, he argues that scholars must look at the role of private regulatory networks to better understand how rules on data protection have traveled across the Atlantic. At the same time, however, he argues that this does not mean that states are in retreat. Far from it. Beaumier shows that the EU contributed to shaping the structure of the private regulatory network at play here, which in turn helped it export its rules on data protection across the Atlantic. This chapter hints at the importance of viewing private regulatory networks as embedded within complex webs of relationships to other state and non-state actors, and their interactions with these are crucial for determining policy outcomes in terms of coherence and effectiveness.

Chapter 5 by Dimmelmeier investigates the role of the EU and European actors in the emerging field of sustainable finance. Dimmelmeier notes that the connection between the financial sector and sustainability criteria relating to, for example, climate change and the environment, has started to receive increasing attention from international organizations, investors and development institutions, among others. With the publication of the *Action Plan on Sustainable Growth* in March 2018, the EU has also put sustainable finance on the policy agenda. This chapter asks how the EU is addressing and conceptualizing this new policy area. To understand this "how" question, Dimmelmeier takes a constructivist approach to look at how EU-sponsored knowledge production on sustainable finance is used. With the help of the analytical concepts of emergence and regime complexes, and with a social network analysis of two dimensions of knowledge production, the position of EU-sponsored knowledge in the broader debate on sustainable finance is located and assessed. The findings suggest that the knowledge produced by different parts of the EU system is very cohesive and that the EU engages heavily with the three communities that have historically shaped the discussion on sustainable finance. Nevertheless, it is suggested that deeper engagement with less prominent actors would be warranted.

Chapter 6 by Christensen examines the rise of the EU in international tax policy. Two decades ago, the EU was a mere talking shop when it came to international tax policy, and the real decisions were coordinated by the OECD. Today, in sharp contrast, the EU has evolved into a vibrant arena for some of the most prominent global policy discussions, and a key challenger to the OECD's historical dominance. In the context of the global financial crisis, EU tax networks have moved from an embryonic, narrow expert context to a highly heterogeneous, contested, politicized, and unstable setting, with a broad public, political, and interest group involvement. Zooming in on the case study of country-by-country-reporting, Christensen charts and compares the evolution of professional-organizational networks in the arenas of the OECD and EU. The actions of issue professionals, such as those working through the Tax Justice Network, were instrumental in transforming European policy networks into some of the most progressive and active voices within the governance of international tax issues. Yet, Christensen notes that the increasing politicization of the issue has also made its future trajectory more uncertain and unstable.

Chapter 7 by Haagensen surveys the transnational networks of the European sovereign debt restructuring regime. As the global financial crisis unfolded into a Eurozone sovereign debt crisis in 2010, the complex question of Greek debt restructuring became particularly acute. Focusing on the social networks concerning sovereign insolvency, Haagensen looks at the degree to which EU and European actors enabled effective action through these networks. Demonstrating that sovereign debt restructuring networks effectively dealt with the complexity of the Greek case, he further points to the central role of legal professionals and their legal networks in controlling the issue of how sovereign debt restructuring should unfold. Furthermore, in the evolution of the sovereign debt restructuring regime following the restructuring of Greek debt, EU actors are noticeably absent from the legal networks. Haagensen concludes that this is connected to them having their own expert committee on sovereign debt and the European Stability Mechanism Treaty having prescribed contractual clauses for Euro area bonds to enable more efficient Eurozone sovereign debt restructurings in the future. Thus, the interaction between intra-European and extra-European networks is key to understanding policy development on this issue.

Chapter 8 by Dupont studies the role of the EU in global environmental governance. Global environmental governance involves a complex web of international, regional, and bilateral agreements covering an ever-widening range of issues: from biodiversity to climate change, from ozone protection to acid rain. In this chapter, Dupont analyses the EU's involvement in international environmental policy networks, by focusing on two cases of global environmental governance: climate change and biodiversity. First, she discusses the evolving role of the EU over time, considering the development of global environmental governance toward greater complexity. Second, she highlights the contexts (stemming from EU internal dynamics and the broader international context) leading to shifts in the EU's role. Third, she analyzes the "effectiveness" of the EU, by assessing the extent to which goals were achieved and by assessing the extent to which coherence was emphasized and obtained. After an initial period of adjustment to the reality of complexity in global environmental governance, the EU is found to have responded relatively effectively. However, challenges to the effectiveness of EU involvement in international environmental policy networks remain, both in terms of the effectiveness of the output of global environmental regimes (decisions) and of the outcome (impact on the state of the environment).

Chapter 9 by Valeriani uses an in-depth case study of an Italian non-profit organization (Lunaria) and the European network of voluntary service organizations in which it operates to make a broader point about the reciprocal relationship between network structure and policy outcomes. Because the civil society sector in general, and voluntary service organizations in particular, are heavily networked, they represent an interesting domain in which to situate studies of network structure and effect. And because Lunaria is a small organization, it makes for a compelling case study of the potential and limits for actors to reach broader social goals within complex network structures. Valeriani draws on interviews with Lunaria and a network analysis of the structure of committees and working groups within the Alliance of European Voluntary Service Organizations in order to conclude that organizations retain a good amount of agency over the networks they participate in, and their strategic choices are influenced as much by their mission and values as by the opportunity structure presented by the network.

Chapter 10 by Van Langenhove and Boers engages with the role of the EU in multi-level diplomacy against the background of increasing digitalization. Their point of departure is that there is little agreement on the shape of the emerging world order that is replacing the former unipolar world. Populism, extreme voting patterns, and the questioning of the liberal worldview is causing considerable changes to the practice and traditions of diplomacy, trending toward a proliferation of diplomatic practices and a "diplomacy of everything". Van Langenhove and Boers proceed by delineating how things have changed from the traditional world of state-to-state diplomacy toward the emerging and more complex world of multi-level diplomacy, mediated by digital disruptions. They then zoom in on the case of science diplomacy, detailing the agenda of this new form of public diplomacy, as well as reflecting on how it is practiced through and enabled by networks. They conclude that these developments, taken together, raise questions about the role of the classic diplomat in the new world order, offering new opportunities for European actor networks.

Chapter 11 by Jakobi and Kandt examines the activities of the EU in the global fight against transnational crime. They start by introducing the global governance of crime, the importance of networks, and the role of the EU in this field.

In further steps, they go on to analyze the role of the EU in two concrete issue areas of global crime governance, namely (a) in networks established to counter money laundering and terrorism financing; and (b) networks established to counter cybercrime. While transnational crime in these fields benefits from the transnational and virtual properties of the financial system and cyberspace, their networks have developed quite differently. Accordingly, the role of the EU in managing complexity differs, too, ranging from an emphasis on policy development in the area of cybercrime to an emphasis on implementation and policing in the area of money laundering and terrorism financing. Jakobi and Kandt's chapter brings us back to the opening chapter by Godet and Orsini, by concluding that the weakening of the traditional Western alliance is likely to result in further divergences in crime policies. This is likely to propel the EU into taking a leading role in global counter-crime policy development.

Chapter 12 will offer final concluding thoughts and reflections in relation to the central question posed in the volume and the main lessons learned theoretically and empirically from the case studies presented.

References

Adshead, M. (2017). *Developing European Regions? Comparative Governance, Policy Networks and European Integration*. London: Routledge.

Alter, K.J. and Meunier, S. (2009). 'The Politics of International Regime Complexity', *Perspectives on Politics*, 7(1), pp. 13–24.

Bellini, N. and Hilpert, U. (eds.) (2013). *Europe's Changing Geography: The Impact of Interregional Networks*. London: Routledge.

Best, H., Lengyel, G. and Verzichelli, L. (eds.) (2012). *The Europe of Elites: A Study into the Europeanness of Europe's Political and Economic Elites*. Oxford: Oxford University Press.

Bitonti, A. and Harris, P. (eds.) (2017). *Lobbying in Europe: Public Affairs and the Lobbying Industry in 28 EU Countries*. Basingstoke: Palgrave Macmillan.

Bousquet, A. and Curtis, S. (2011). 'Beyond Models and Metaphors: Complexity Theory, Systems Thinking and International Relations', *Cambridge Review of International Affairs*, 24(1), pp. 43–62. doi:10.1080/09557571.2011.558054.

Cudworth, E. and Hobden, S. (2013a). 'Complexity, Ecologism, and Posthuman Politics', *Review of International Studies*, 39(3), pp. 643–664. doi:10.1017/S0260210512000290.

Cudworth, E. and Hobden, S. (2013b). *Posthuman International Relations: Complexity, Ecologism and Global Politics*. London: Zed Books.

Drezner, D.W. (2009). 'The Power and Peril of International Regime Complexity', *Perspectives on Politics*, 7(1), pp. 65–70.

Georgakakis, D. and Rowell, J. (eds.) (2013). *The Field of Eurocracy: Mapping EU Actors and Professionals*. Basingstoke: Palgrave Macmillan.

Geyer, R.R. (2003). 'European Integration, the Problem of Complexity and the Revision of Theory', *JCMS: Journal of Common Market Studies*, 41, pp. 15–35. doi:10.1111/1468-5965.t01-1-00409

Hafner-Burton, E.M., Kahler, M. and Montgomery, A.H. (2009). 'Network Analysis for International Relations', *International Organization*, 63(3), pp. 559–592. doi:10.1017/S0020818309090195.
Harrison, N.E. (ed.) (2012). *Complexity in World Politics: Concepts and Methods of a New Paradigm*. Albany, NY: State University of New York Press.
Hildebrand, C. (2012). *Counter-Terrorism Networks in the European Union: Maintaining Democratic Legitimacy after 9/11*. Oxford: Oxford University Press
Kahler, M. (ed.) (2009). *Networked Politics: Agency, Power, and Governance*. Ithaca, NY: Cornell University Press.
Kavalski, E. (2007). 'The Fifth Debate and the Emergence of Complex International Relations Theory: Notes on the Application of Complexity Theory to the Study of International Life', *Cambridge Review of International Affairs*, 20(3), pp. 435–454. doi:10.1080/09557570701574154.
Keck, M. E. and Sikkink, K. (1998). *Activists beyond Borders: Advocacy Networks in International Politics*. Ithaca and London: Cornell University Press.
Kingah, S., Schmidt, V.A. and Yong, W. (eds.) (2016). *The European Union's Engagement with Transnational Policy Networks*. London: Routledge.
Kohler-Koch, B. and Eising, R. (eds.) (1999). *The Transformation of Governance in the European Union*. London: Routledge/ECPR Studies in European Political Science.
Krossa, A.S. (ed.) (2012-). *Europe in a Global Context* (book series). Basingstoke: Palgrave Macmillan.
Marcussen, M. and Torfing, J. (eds.) (2007). *Democratic Network Governance in Europe*. Basingstoke: Palgrave Macmillan.
Martinico, G. (2013). *The Tangled Complexity of the EU Constitutional Process: The Frustrating Knot of Europe*. London: Routledge.
Mastenbroek, E. and Martinsen, D.S. (2018). 'Filling the gap in the European Administrative Space: The Role of Administrative Networks in EU Implementation and Enforcement', *Journal of European Public Policy*, 25(3), pp. 422–435, doi:10.1080/13501763.2017.1298147
Mathieu, E. (2016). *Regulatory Delegation in the European Union: Networks, Committees and Agencies*. Basingstoke: Palgrave Macmillan.
Oberthür, S. and Stokke, O.S. (eds.) (2011). *Managing Institutional Complexity: Regime Interplay and Global Environmental Change*. Cambridge, MA: MIT Press.
Orsini, A., Morin, J.-F., and Young, O. (2013). 'Regime Complexes: A Buzz, a Boom, or a Boost for Global Governance?', *Global Governance*, 19, pp. 27–39.
Raustiala, K. and Victor, D. (2004). 'The Regime Complex for Plant Genetic Resources', *International Organization*, 58(2), pp. 277–309.
Risse-Kappen, T. (1996). 'Exploring the Nature of the Beast: International Relations Theory and Comparative Policy Analysis Meet the European Union', *Journal of Common Market Studies*, 34(1), pp. 53–80.
Schoenman, R. (2015). *Networks and Institutions in Europe's Emerging Markets*. Cambridge: Cambridge University Press.
Scott, J.W. and Liikanen, I. (2011). *European Neighbourhood through Civil Society Networks?* London: Routledge.
Slaughter, A.-M. (2004). *A New World Order*. Princeton, NJ: Princeton University Press.
Slaughter, A.-M. (2017). *The Chessboard and the Web*. New Haven: Yale University Press.
Stone, D. (2013). *Knowledge Actors and Transnational Governance: The Private-Public Policy Nexus in the Global Agora*. Basingstoke: Palgrave Macmillan.
Victor, J.N., Montgomery, A.H. and Lubell, M. (2017). *The Oxford Handbook of Political Networks*. Oxford: Oxford University Press.

PART 1
Conceptualising networks in the face of complexity

1
NETWORKS, TRANSNATIONAL NETWORKS, AND GLOBAL ORDER

Claire Godet and Amandine Orsini

Introduction

Network is a popular concept in hard and social sciences, designating "a set of relations between objects which could be people, organizations, nations, items found in a Google search, brain cells, or electrical transformers" (Kadushin 2012, pp. 3–4). Indeed, networks have been identified in many different academic disciplines such as Biology, Physics, Mathematics, Sociology, Economics, Anthropology, and Computer Science. They label many different relations, such as the ones developed under social media, between business organizations, or across mathematical representations. Since the 1970s, in Political Science and International Relations, scholars have studied networks to better grasp the relationships and the context explaining political behavior and its outcomes (Victor et al. 2017, p. 9). In a period spanning 20 years, technical developments, and especially the use of specialized software, have revolutionized the study of networks, but the core assumption remains unchanged: relationships between actors matter.

Networks are not new. In order to survive within society, individuals have always needed to tie links with each other. International relations are no exception: across time, networks of international actors, known as transnational networks, have spread and gained in stability, some acquiring an autonomous identity such as the G20, a transgovernmental network that became a quasi-intergovernmental organization. Many different types of transnational networks coexist at the global level. Networks can be informal, such as networks of migrants; or can be highly formalized, such as transnational city networks. Networks can be situated at the local, national, or transnational level.

While networks are not new, they have evolved, formalized, and taken changing roles in International Relations. Initially, scholars studied networks as variables only influencing what remained a classical state-centric international system (Castells 2009) organized around international regimes. Progressively, scholars have considered networks as key international actors, bringing by themselves "a new world order" (Slaughter 2004, 2017). Discussions about the European order are illustrative of this shift. In 1993, Moravscik pictured the European Union (EU) as an intergovernmental machine, a set of regimes in the hands of its member states. The only networked forms of governance, according to him, were represented by potentially networked interest groups who were pushing for more regimes within the EU (Moravscik 1995). Yet at the beginning of the 2000s, others have started to describe the EU itself as a networked form of governance, establishing flexible but harmonized policies (Slaughter 2004, p. 11).

This chapter aims at investigating these assumptions on the evolution of the analytical focus from international regimes to transnational networks used to understand global order. It argues that networks do not build a new global order as much as they offer a new perspective on the classical inter-state Westphalian order. The first section clarifies certain definitions in the network literature. The second section presents two different conceptualizations of global order, including networks. The third and fourth sections show, respectively, how a network approach helps change perspective when conceptualizing international relations, and the limits of such a different perspective.

This chapter provides a general definition and overview of a phenomenon, the emergence of networks within the global order, which is replicated at the meso and at micro level of policymaking as developed in Chapters 2 and 3, respectively. While we use illustrative examples to elaborate our analytical discussion, the book then investigates the concrete causes and effects of networks in a diversity of international relations' fields as outlined in the main Introduction. Below we provide general definitions and understandings, on which these concrete case studies are then later developed in the book.

Networks, network theory, and network analysis

It is necessary to explain certain central concepts that come to mind when talking about networks, namely network theory and network analysis. The aim of this section is not to go into detail about these two concepts but rather to give concise definitions that will clarify the discussion.

On the one hand, network theory – also sometimes named social network theory – attempts to explain political outcomes through relational accounts rather than through characteristics that are intrinsic to actors. The theory is based on three assumptions: the behavior of one node in a network is influenced by the other nodes of the network; the links between nodes allow for exchange (of information, ideas, resources, power, etc.); and the combination of links create a structure that can enable and constrain the nodes. The nodes can be any type of actor (individual or collective, formal or informal, organized or non-organized, etc.), and the links can be any type of relationship (deliberate or incidental, strong or unstable, permanent or ephemeral, etc.). From these general assumptions, network theory deducts proposals that can be applied in different cases. For example, several studies have shown that a node with greater centrality in a network has a greater influence potential over the other nodes (Orsini 2013). Other scholars have attempted to design a model that could explain or predict how innovation or norms can be diffused in a network (Zimmerman 2016). Despite some incipient attempts (e.g. Maoz 2017), the different proposals have not yet been collected and systematized into a coherent set that could constitute a widely approved network theory.

On the other hand, network analysis is known as a methodological tool. Again, it is hardly a unique methodology and the concept has been used to define qualitative and quantitative studies with very different aims (e.g. mapping relationships, evaluating power relationships, or explaining a policy's outcomes). In the past decade, scholars have attempted to systematize network analysis by defining "a set of concepts, measures, methods, and ideas that are suitable to modelling interactions between units of all kinds – cells and nerves, plants and pollinators, predators and prey, individuals, organizations, and nation-states" (Maoz 2017, p. 2). The flexibility of network analysis allows a better understanding of complex political processes and outcomes. By rejecting the essentialist notion of social units and by seeing social transactions and processes as fundamental constituents of social reality (Bousquet and Curtis 2011, p. 49), network analysis gives clear methodological and conceptual instruments to disentangle complex social reality (see Box 1.1). It is important to emphasize that a network analysis is not a theory but rather "a toolset and a unified methodological perspective for the study of any substantive area dealing with interactions – social, physical, or natural" (Maoz 2017, p. 3).

BOX 1.1. KEY CONCEPTS OF NETWORK ANALYSIS

In order to study the fleeting relations between nodes in a network, network analysis has developed concepts that describe and explain nodes and network's behavior.

Centrality refers to the number of ties a node has to other nodes. In International Relations, centrality is often used because it relates to power and influence: the assumption is that the higher the degree of centrality, the higher the political influence (Orsini 2013). Other measures can complement centrality: betweenness centrality (how many actors are connected to each other by a given actor?); or closeness centrality (how many ties would it take to get from one actor to every other actor?), for example.

Community detection aims at identifying subgroups in the network: "a community is defined as a subset of nodes within the graph such that connections between the nodes are denser than connections with the rest of the network" (Radicchi et al. 2004, p. 2658). It is also possible to identify cliques defined as "a maximally completely connected subgraph within the network or a group of nodes that are directly connected with each other such that there is no other node to which all of the members of the group are each connected as well" (Patty and Penn 2017, p. 13). The nodes of these subgroups are thought of as having different relations between them compared to with the rest of the network.

Connectivity determines how well two nodes are connected. Is there a path between these two nodes? How short is it? Are there several paths? The answers to these questions help in evaluating centrality, closeness, and community. Bridges are the nodes that, if they were removed from the network, would leave two or more nodes no longer connected by any path.

Embeddedness can refer to structural or relational embeddedness. The latter describes the quality and strength of a tie between two nodes; while the former concerns the network as a whole. Structural embeddedness is about the influence of network configuration, "about the extent to which a dyad's mutual contacts are connected to one another" (Granovetter 1992, p. 35).

Transnational networks and global order: A new way to look at the world?

The study of networks has transformed the way researchers conceptualize the international scene, and therefore, the explanations available to understand it. This section presents historically how scholars have studied networks and how it has modified their conceptualization of the world order.

The early days: Transnational networks Influencing world order

Social actors create links between them and establish a web of interconnected relationships that form diverse networks. Social actors – being individuals, organizations, or informal groups – have always built relationships that could be mapped as networks. In International Relations, the number of transnational networks has dramatically increased in the 1980s with the transnationalization of world politics favored by, among others, the development of communication technology. Transnationalization meant that new actors, in parallel to states, could act on the international scene, including, among others, experts, non-governmental organizations (NGOs), or firms. Since then, networks have appeared either as new types of organizations or as new types of actors on the international scene. In both cases, they have tried to influence classical International Relations. Initially, those scholars that studied them found that they could only marginally change the world order, notably by orientating the intergovernmental agenda.

In the early 1970s, transnationalists discovered a valuable form of organization that supported governments in implementing policies in the shape of transgovernmental networks. Transgovernmental networks were defined by Keohane and Nye as "sets of direct interactions among sub-units of different governments that are not controlled or closely guided by the policies of the cabinets or chief executives of those governments" (Keohane and Nye 1974, p. 43). Simply put, transgovernmental networks are networks of national civil servants who transcend states. Keohane and Nye have shown that transgovernmental relations heightened the interdependence between nation states, contributed to the definition of issues, and promoted coalitions among governmental sub-units (Keohane and Nye 1974, p. 61). They could transcend national borders in order to help states fulfill their missions (Slaughter 2004).

In the 1990s, other scholars identified another key type of network designed to influence politics: epistemic communities. Epistemic communities are defined as "networks of professionals with recognized expertise and competence in a particular domain and an authoritative claim to policy-relevant knowledge within that domain or issue area" (Haas 1992, p. 3). Peter Haas, who coined the term, has shown how these networks of experts have been particularly active on environmental issues, among others between 1985 and 1987, to push for the adoption of an international protocol on the ozone layer, the Montreal Protocol. It is noteworthy to indicate that the Montreal Protocol has been the most efficient environmental agreement so far for solving the ozone hole issue.

Later, Keck and Sikkink identified another kind of network in international relations: transnational advocacy networks (TANs), being defined as "networks of activists, distinguishable largely by the centrality of principles ideas or values in motivating their formation" (Keck and Sikkink 1998, p. 1). TANs undertake lobbying action to support an international cause. TANs put emphasis on the transnational actions of activists and on their implications in world politics. The authors first mapped the relationships between different actors to then discuss the content of these relationships and finally analyze how these relationships could change intergovernmental politics (Keck and Sikkink 1998). Tracing the relationships between actors also helps in understanding how they influence one another (Minhas et al. 2017) or how they change the organization in which they are embedded (Battilana and Casciaro 2012). TANs exist around all sorts of international issues. For instance, a TAN gathering environmental and development NGOs has recently formed on biofuel issues at the European level (Orsini and Godet 2018). Another example is the International Campaign to Abolish Nuclear Weapons (ICAN), a transnational network which has been advocating for a new international treaty to ban the use of nuclear weapons and which received the Nobel Peace Prize in 2017.

In the 2000s, many other studies developed different types of "influence networks" such as within humanitarian military interventions (Seybolt 2009), or local activism (Stevenson and Greenberg 2000), to cite but a few. Slaughter likewise shows that, today, the political decision-making process occurs – at least partially – outside of the state's container. The state is not able to perform all its tasks in well-tightened hierarchical organizations. Therefore, it relies on networks of governmental or non-governmental actors to gather or distill information, to provide services, to implement policies, to harmonize laws, or to address new problems (Slaughter 2004, p. 7; see also Slaughter 2017). Networks, as an organizational form, offer some important benefits to the actors: they can notably foster learning (Newig et al. 2010), enhance an actor's status (Börzel and Risse 2000), offer economic benefits (Podolny and Page 1998, p. 65), and alleviate external constraints (Woods and Martinez Diaz 2009). Networks can be joined by unexpected actors which changes their initial objective. For instance, actor-network theory shows that non-humans (for example, machines, living organisms such as plants, etc.) are also part of policy networks (Bled 2010). Networks can indeed bypass the traditional public arena and create alternative public spheres (e.g. the World Social Forum that annually gathers civil society organizations in order to build an alternative to globalization) where they can be heard, but they also engage with the traditional state actors, including intergovernmental organizations. These actors, whether they are formalized (the G20) or not (e.g. migrant networks) have an impact on world politics. Actors are affected by the structure and the context they evolve in. Networked actors are no exception.

This perspective of networks assumes that networks influence decisions, decisions that are still in the hands of nation states. Actually, states can themselves take part in these "influence networks". The United States administration, especially the Environmental Protection Agency and the US State Department's Bureau of Oceans and International Environmental and Scientific Affairs have been actively participating in the epistemic community on the ozone layer (Haas 1992). In a complex and fast-changing world, networks might bring new ideas, more expertise, and adaptability to solve global, transnational, or national problems (Keck and Sikkink 1998, pp. 219–220). This perspective sees networks as sites for exchange of information, norms, influence, power, goods, and services that take place outside of hierarchical or market relationships (Powell 1990, pp. 296–297). Networks adapt their strategies and actions according to the result they aim at producing. In this sense, networks are no different to any other actors (Marsh and Smith 2000, p. 9).

Additionally, the "influence networks" conceptualization supplements the social movements' literature by explaining how collective action can be organized (Stevenson and Greenberg 2000, pp. 653–654). However, using networks as an organizational form can be limiting: the web of relationships might not necessarily have the expected explanatory power. Empirical studies have established a link between networks and behaviors, but the nature of the causal relationship is still to be determined (Fowler et al. 2011, pp. 438–439). Moreover, it is not always clear that networks are organizational efforts in line with governmental politics. Networks, thus, can also provide for a true alternative to the classical world order.

Getting autonomous: Transnational networks as new global order

The second conceptualization argues that transnational networks are not simply innovative forms of organizations for influence but that they are themselves governance actors with their own agenda, culture, behavior, and interests. This is predominantly so as networks tend to become autonomous through time:

> networks are made up of individual nodes that change, alter and adapt their behaviour. Connections between the nodes are therefore constantly being created and eroded, and fluctuate in nature and intensity. Because of these dynamics, the networks that the nodes are part of are subject to constant change, not only in their structure or geography – with which the nodes are necessarily connected – but also in the type, purpose and form of communication that happens along or within the connections that link the nodes: *Networked individualism is a culture*, not an organizational form.
>
> (Kramer 2017, pp. 29–30, our emphasis)

This conceptualization considers networks as new systems, new loci of identity, new communities that provide security, social order, or resources where the classic institutions have failed to do so (Castells 2009, p. 362). It sees networks not only as structures formed by social relationships but also as *impetus* for creating a new world order. In this perspective, networks have global agency; they constitute "a new form of governance" by themselves (Marsh and Smith 2000, p. 4). The EU includes networked actors that go beyond states. It uses networks to foster integration, socialize the elites (Maggetti and Gilardi 2011, 2014), gain power when the member states refuse to collaborate (Coen and Thatcher 2008; Kelemen and Tarrant 2011), and interact with other actors on the international scene (see also Dehousse 1997; Blauberger and Rittberger 2015).

Thus, governmental and non-governmental networks are a versatile and flexible alternative or complement to classic inter-state politics, IOs, and their rigid bureaucracies (Woods and Martinez-Diaz 2009, pp. 2–3). The diversity of "governance networks" is very high. These networks can be situated at the level of actors. On climate change, for example, city networks have for a long time been active beyond intergovernmental politics (Betsill and Burkeley 2004) and are likely to be more active in the future with the Paris Agreement adopting a bottom-up approach. "Governance networks" can also be made of broader structures such as norms or regimes. Typical examples of networks that go beyond states are regime complexes. Regime complexes are: "network(s) of three or more international regimes that relate to a common subject matter; exhibit overlapping membership; and generate substantive, normative, or operative interactions recognized as potentially problematic whether or not they are managed effectively" (Orsini et al. 2013, p. 29). Indeed, while until the beginning of 2000, international issues were organized around unique international regimes taking the shape of unique international organizations or treaties, with the proliferation of international institutions and the broadening of their scope, no such thing as a unique international regime for each international issue exists anymore. Most international issues are now evolving within "regime complexes". For instance, international problems on genetic resources are currently evolving at the crossroads of the international regimes for agriculture, environment, property rights, and trade (Raustiala and Victor 2004) made up of numerous international arenas such as the Nagoya Protocol, the World Intellectual Property Organization Committee on genetic resources, or the Food and Agriculture Organization International Treaty meetings, to cite but a few. Other examples are human trafficking issues now dealt with by no less than four international regimes on migration, labor, human rights, and organized crime (see Chapter 12) involving a very diverse set of international arenas including, among others, meetings of the International Organization for Migration (IOM) and the International Labor Organization or the United Nations Children's Fund (Gomez-Mera 2016). Regime complexes have emerged in nearly all international issues. The building of such networks is most of the time unintentional, meaning that they can be complementary but also conflictive sites of governance, with respect to intergovernmental politics (see also Chapter 2).

Networks and global order: A refreshing view to challenge state-centric approaches

Networks are a pivotal tool in International Relations and their introduction into the field has brought new answers to old questions. In between regime theory, which predicts cooperation through common institutions, and realism, which sees states as atomized entities fighting for power, the network approach offers a third path to conceptualize the international scene. It brings a new layer to the "state-centrism versus world society" debate. Scholars have not yet been able to settle the discussion about the core organizing principle of international relations: are we living in a state-centric world or in a global society?

The network approach rounds the angles and bridges these two conceptualizations. A state-centric world is defined by horizontal relations between nominally equal entities, sovereign states, in the absence of world government (Lechner 2017, p. 2). The world society perspective, on the contrary, sees the world as a system, with its own socio-cultural norms, that constitutes the framework "defining the nature and purposes of social actors and action" (Boli and Thomas 1997, p. 187). Some authors depict a society composed uniquely of nation states while others highlight the diversity of actors involved in a world society (Brown 1996, p. 4). In both cases, they assume that actors are not isolated from one another; they "conceive themselves to be bound by a common set of rules in their relations with one another and share in the working of common institutions" (Bull 1977, p. 10). The network approach helps refine these two conceptualizations: the world might be hierarchical, but states are also embedded in networks of relationships that constrain their scope of actions and limit chaos.

The world society perspective might account for homogeneity and predictability at the international level, but the constant changes among or within networks of actors can also explain instability. Seeing the world as a set of networks helps to explain both the randomness and the consistency of world politics because it acknowledges the existence of a common structure, even if fluid and permanently changing. "'Society' is increasingly viewed and treated as a 'network' rather than a structure (let alone a solid 'totality'): it is perceived and treated as a matrix of random connections and of an essentially infinite volume of possible permutations" (Bauman 2007, p. 3). The network approach enables us to study complex actors (the EU, legal professionals, environmental institutions, etc.) and their dynamic relationships whether there is a hierarchical bond or not.

Second, the network approach also challenges the classic state-centric perspective by bringing forth new actors. The proliferation of networks has challenged state sovereignty by blurring the borders and by empowering new actors. Transnational networks comprise many types of actors such as governmental bodies, NGOs, businesses, citizens, and IOs as illustrated below and go beyond the dichotomies between types of actors by gathering them around one common issue or interest. Networks bring new challenges to the state-centric approach and empower new actors. These different effects increase the permeability of national borders. Sovereignty can no longer be imagined as a rigid structure but rather as a shared feature (Krasner 2005, p. 70) or even as an obsolete concept that has now lost its operative power (Badie 1999).

Third, the network approach also allows a redefinition of "power". Power has been traditionally understood as a stable attribute determined by one's material, organizational, or ideational resources. On the contrary, power in a networked world is not an ascribed feature but has to be understood according to the relational context: "it is the relational capacity that enables a social actor to influence asymmetrically the decisions of other social actor(s) in ways that favor the empowered actor's will, interests, and values. Power is exercised by means of coercion (or the possibility of it) and/or by the construction of meaning on the basis of the discourses through which social actors guide their action" (Castells 2009, p. 10). Power is relational; it is not an attribute but a relationship that provides the basis of the connection between nodes (Kramer 2017, p. 32). As in any relationship, power is ever changing and fluid. There is no clear separation between those who have power and those who are submitted to it. It is a reciprocal – albeit asymmetric – relationship where one party influences the other, and, in return, where one party complies or resists. This relationship is a social action that relies on the cultural production of meanings to reassert or adapt itself (Castells 2009, pp. 10–11).

The network approach also unties the idea of power from state-centrism. The blurring of borders and de-territorialization of power means the constitution of a global field of power, a network of governments playing strategically in different arenas (Slaughter 2004, 2017). However, the networks themselves are also spaces with their own stakes; they are not only arenas where territorialized powers confront each other (Bigo 2011, p. 254). The European Union is a great example of a network that is both an arena of competition between national powers and a space where "transnational guilds" of experts and bureaucrats claim power (Bigo 2013, p. 122). The network approach grasps phenomena that other perspectives cannot explain, e.g., the fact that some issues have been put on the international agenda by actors usually considered as weak.

Networks also offer the possibility to redefine structure and agency: the network approach sheds light not only on individuals' behavior but also on groups' behavior. Structures go beyond the sum of their units. The network approach emphasizes both the interdependence between units and the dynamism of the structure. Most importantly, agents and structures are in constant interaction and there is no predominance of one over the other. Contrary to many approaches in International Relations, network analysis refuses to consider *a priori* that either the structure or the agent is the main driver of political outcome on the international scene (Gulati and Srivastava 2014). Networks are a bridge between agency and structure that allows us to link methodological individualism and structuralism (Wang 2010, p. 105). Additionally, it assumes that a unit's behavior is dependent on the other units in the networks and that the relations between units, and therefore the structure, constantly evolve according to the type, the intensity, and the regularity of relationships between units. Moreover, one network can also be influenced by actions in other networks. Networks are interrelated even when they are composed of different units. A power shutdown affects not only the electrical grid but also transportation networks, computerized networks, economic transactions, and so forth (Maoz 2017, p. 4). The network approach assumes that relations between units are dynamic and that actions and choices at one level have unintended and nonlinear implications at other levels. The structure that emerges from a set of relations is thus forever changing and cannot necessarily lead to predictable systemic outcomes.

Finally, some normative perspectives on networks see them as a possibility to rebalance power distribution on the international scene. Slaughter, for example, sees networks as a solution for the future; they would solve the governance "tri-lemma":

> We need global rules without centralized power but with government actors who can be held to account through a variety of political mechanisms. These government actors can and should interact with a wide range of nongovernmental organizations (NGOs), but their role in governance bears distinct and different responsibilities. They must represent all their different constituencies, at least in a democracy; corporate and civic actors may be driven by profits and passions, respectively.
>
> *(Slaughter 2004, p. 10).*

Moreover, in her latest work, Slaughter develops her argument further by showing that the world should not be conceived as a chessboard but as a web where networks can help solve international issues. In a world where borders are blurred and private companies are worth more than national states, politics cannot be thought of as a strategy game where states calculate their moves to annihilate the opponents. Instead, in a web-like world, building networks between nation states but also between public and private actors, will allow the resolution of resilience, execution, and scale problems that hinder international politics (Slaughter 2017). Networks are part of the polycentricity paradigm (Jordan et al. 2018), whereby the involvement of all actors is needed to solve complex issues.

The limits of a network approach to conceptualize global order

Networks offer a fresh lens through which we analyze the world, but they cannot be an excuse to focus more on the lens itself rather than on the actual object that is being observed. Focusing on networks might sometimes limit the overall field of vision. Indeed, the network approach acknowledges the dynamic character of social environments, but it does not automatically provide the necessary tools to identify solutions in those environments. This new lens should not hide the fact, for example, that power struggles are not yet settled. Indeed, networks are also sites of power struggles and the distinction between hierarchies and networks is not as clear-cut as it seems. Hierarchies can also be conceptualized as sets of networks. International firms, for example, are highly hierarchical organizations, but they are also analyzed as sets of networks (Grandori and Soda 1995). Networks have also been used to describe NGOs' organizational structures (Wong 2014). One actor's position within a network (as a broker, member of a clique or of a hub, etc.) affects its power capacities. Some scholars investigate how individuals' connections in a network can foster their influence (Minhas et al. 2017); how their embeddedness affects what they learn about policy in the first place (Coburn et al. 2013); how an actor's position in the structure shapes a set of resources that are accessible to actors and makes salient a set of motivations (Gulati and Srivastava 2014). For instance, a Science-Policy recent study of the networked structure of experts within the Intergovernmental Platform on Biodiversity and Ecosystem Services shows how a limited number of dominant actors control the whole network (Morin et al. 2017; see also Chapter 3). Networks do not *per se* solve global issues and might even be new vectors for the reproduction of inequalities at a global scale. Like hierarchies and markets, they are "sites of power and potentiality of exclusion and inequality" (Toope 2000, p. 97). A network approach challenges governance forms but does not necessarily change their content (Hurrell and Woods 1999, p. 25).

Furthermore, networks allow for a more fine-grained analysis of the structure by considering its constant evolution and its internal dynamics, but they do not solve the ongoing debate about the constitution or effects of the structure. While network approaches tend to consider networks as black boxes, several studies have underlined the international politics of networks where actors' attributes matter:

"[a network approach] complements existing structural approaches to international relations that focus on actor attributes and static equilibria ... it emphasizes how material and social relationships create structures among actors through dynamic processes" (Hafner-Burton et al. 2009, p. 560). Networks do not settle the ontological differences between positivist and constructivist approaches about what constitutes structures. Nonetheless, they allow us to escape from the structuralist conundrum that "reif[ies] system structures in a way which leads to static and even functional explanations of state action" (Wendt 1987, p. 348). If structures are seen as primitive units, they are not separated from the activities of agents: "A network approach...defines structures as emergent properties of persistent patterns of relations among agents that can define, enable, and constrain those agents" (Hafner-Burton et al. 2009, p. 561). Networks provide a new way of looking at the structure, but the network approach does not settle all the issues surrounding the topic. Furthermore, picturing the structure as a network does not necessarily lead to drawing a dynamic structure. If theoretically, the network approach is supposed to enhance the idea that structures are dynamic ensembles made of changing social relationships; in practice, the networks analyzed in empirical research are often fixed to facilitate the observation. Leaving aside the history and social genesis of a network is to lose the dynamics and potential tensions that can exist within a network (Pouliot 2013, p. 54).

Moreover, the network approach does not resolve important questions concerning agency. Different units can be considered as agents: a node (individuals, groups, organizations, etc.) or the network as a whole. This gives great flexibility and allows scholars to apply the network approach to many different objects. However, it can also be tempting to consider that all the agents are similar or that they all have the same properties. In networks, it cannot be assumed that all nodes are equals or that they all have the same power or influence. White and Harary (2001) show that two nodes with a similar number of connections which embed in the same network can have different behaviors. In order to remedy these shortfalls, some scholars conceptualize networks as a link between the agent and the structure. In that case, both the relationships within the networks and the individual characteristics should be considered (Wang 2010, p. 105). Because social relations are at the core of social sciences there is a real risk of overemphasizing the importance of networks and seeing networks everywhere. Quantitative methodology and social network analysis consider networks as structures and study their cohesion, structural equivalence, or spatial representation (Knoke 2012, p. 131). This might lead to some confusion because often, the authors use SNA without theorizing further how they relate structure and agency.

When networks became popular in International Relations, some scholars saw this "new phenomenon" as either a promising or a problematic feature of modern society. Networks have been criticized for their lack of accountability, democracy, legitimacy, and representativeness. While networks challenge the state-centric system, they hardly fulfill these criteria required for national states. At the European level, for example, it has been shown that networks of unelected experts influence policy outcomes without being held accountable for their actions (Papadopoulos 2007). If networks could be relevant "to increase citizen participation in decision-making which is of relevance to them and the preservation of small-scale identities" (Jacthenfuchs 1997, p. 12), they also might be exacerbating the democratic deficit because in practice they fail to imply broad citizen participation and the views represented among the networks are limited and partial (Heretier 2003, p. 818; Jensen 2009, p. 4). Additionally, actors within a network would favor accountability to their peers over public forms of accountability (Papadopoulos 2007). On the one hand, the variety of actors in networks could prompt the promotion of the public good since so many interests have to be considered within networks. Networks might broaden the discussion circle by fostering the consultation of societal actors that were not formerly included (Postel-Vinay 2014, p. 33; see Chapter 6 on tax). On the other hand, "this form of accountability is not assured, since power differentials within the network may skew negotiated solutions, and there is no guarantee that all relevant interests will actually have a voice within the network" (Toope 2000, pp. 96–97). Some argue, however, that networks could ensure procedural legitimacy without undermining the ability for effective problem resolution (Skogstad 2003, p. 334). Networks do indeed change the political landscape at every level of governance, but it is difficult to affirm that this modification is creating in itself more or less democracy. The creation of networks is neither "good" nor "bad" in itself. After all, the questions of legitimacy, power, representativeness, and democracy have always been at the core of International Relations studies; and a new perspective can, at best, bring an original understanding but not necessarily solve these issues.

Conclusion

International Relations has always been about relations and, therefore, about networks (Maoz 2010, pp. 4–5). It might thus be an overstatement to affirm that we are witnessing the establishment of a new world order. Nevertheless, the network approach brings a new perspective to International Relations and offers alternative conceptual tools to understand agency, especially non-state agency, and influence, with ideas on how to rebalance power distribution. This volume intends to apply this new perspective to different European and EU actors and networks in order to shed light on how they navigate and manage a multitude of complex global issues.

Because networks in global governance are so numerous and diversified, several research paths are still available for further research. More comprehensive studies could be conducted on networks across international issues, to see if common patterns or actors emerge. One key question, also for policymaking, concerns the degree of control that states and IGOs can have on networked forms of governance: is it possible to manage networks in an increasingly complex world (Oberthür and Stokke 2011)? If so, how?

References

Badie, Bertrand (1999) *Un Monde Sans Souveraineté: Les États entre Ruse et Responsabilité*, Paris: Fayard.

Battilana, Julie and Casciaro, Tiziana (2012) "Change Agents, Networks, and Institutions: A Contingency Theory of Organizational Change", *Academy of Management Journal*, vol. 55, no. 2, pp. 1–41.

Bauman, Zygmunt (2007) *Liquid Times Living in an Age of Uncertainty*, Cambridge: Polity Press.

Betsill, Michele M. and Burkeley, Harriet (2004) "Transnational Networks and Global Environmental Governance: The Cities for Climate Protection Program", *International Studies Quarterly*, vol. 48, pp. 471–493.

Bigo, Didier (2011) "Pierre Bourdieu and International Relations: Power of Practices, Practices of Power", *International Political Sociology*, vol. 5, pp. 225–258.

Bigo, Didier (2013) "Security: Analysing Transnational Professionals of (In)security in Europe", in: Rebecca Adler-Nissen (ed.) *Bourdieu in International Relations: Rethinking Key Concepts in IR*, Abingdon: Routledge, pp. 114–130.

Blauberger, Michael and Rittberger, Berthold (2015) "Conceptualizing and Theorizing EU Regulatory Networks", *Regulation & Governance*, vol. 9, pp. 367–376.

Bled, Amandine (2010) "Technological Choices in International Environmental Negotiations: An Actor-Network Analysis", *Business & Society*, vol. 49, no. 4, pp. 570–590.

Boli, John and Thomas, George M. (1997) "World Culture in the World Polity: A Century of International Non-Governmental Organization", *American Sociological Review*, vol. 62, no. 2, pp. 171–190.

Börzel, Tanja A. and Risse, Thomas (2000) "When Europe Hits Home: Europeanization and Domestic Change", *European Integration – Online Papers*, vol. 4, no. 15. http://eiop.or.at/eiop/pdf/2000-015.pdf.

Bousquet, Antoine and Curtis, Simon (2011) "Beyond Models and Metaphors: Complexity Theory, Systems Thinking and International Relations", *Cambridge Review of International Affairs*, vol. 24, no. 1, pp. 43–62.

Brown, Seyom (1996) *International Relations in a Changing Global System: Toward a Theory of the World Polity*, 2nd ed., New York: Routledge.

Bull, Hedley (1977) *The Anarchical Society*, London: Palgrave.

Castells, Manuel (2009) *Communication Power*, New York: Oxford University Press.

Coburn, Cynthia E., Mata, Willow S. and Choi, Linda (2013) "The Embeddedness of Teachers' Social Networks: Evidence from a Study of Mathematics Reform", *Sociology of Education*, vol. 86, no. 4, pp. 311–342.

Coen, David and Thatcher, Mark (2008) "Network Governance and Multi-level Delegation: European Networks of Regulatory Agencies", *Journal of Public Policy*, vol. 28, no. 1, pp. 49–71.

Dehousse, Renaud (1997) "Regulation by Networks in the European Community: The Role of European Agencies", *Journal of European Public Policy*, vol. 4, no. 2, pp. 246–261.

Fowler, James H., Heany, Michael T., Nickerson, David W. et al. (2011) "Causality in Political Networks", *American Politics Research*, vol. 39, no. 2, pp. 437–480.

Gómez-Mera, Laura (2016) "Regime Complexity and Global Governance: The Case of Trafficking in Persons", *European Journal of International Relations*, vol. 22, no. 3, pp. 566–595.

Grandori, Anna and Soda, Giuseppe (1995) "Inter-firm Networks: Antecedents, Mechanisms and Forms", *Organization Studies*, vol. 16, no. 2, pp. 183–214.

Granovetter, Mark S. (1992) "Problems of Explanation in Economic Sociology", in: Nitin Nohria and Robert G. Eccles (eds.) *Networks and Organization: Structure, Form and Action*, Boston: Harvard Business School Press, pp. 25–56.

Gulati, Ranjay and Srivastava, Sameer B. (2014) "Bringing Agency Back into Network Research: Constrained Agency and Network Action", in: Daniel J. Brass, Giuseppe (JOE) Labianca, Ajay Mehra, Daniel S. Halgin and Stephen P. Borgatti (eds.) *Contemporary Perspectives on Organizational Social Networks, Research in the Sociology of Organizations*, vol. 40, Bingley: Emerald Group Publishing Limited, pp. 73–93.

Haas, Peter M. (1992) "Introduction: Epistemic Communities and International Policy Coordination", *International Organization*, vol. 46, no. 1, pp. 1–35.

Hafner-Burton, Emilie M., Kahler, Miles and Montgomery, Alexander H. (2009) "Network Analysis for International Relations", *International Organization*, vol. 63, pp. 559–592.

Heretier, Adrienne (2003) "Composite Democracy in Europe: The Role of Transparency and Access to Information", *Journal of European Public Policy*, vol. 10, pp. 814–833.

Hurrell, Andrew and Woods, Ngaire (1999) *Inequality, Globalization, and World Politics*, Oxford: Oxford University Press.

Jachtenfuchs, Markus (1997) "Democracy and Governance in the European Union", *European Integration Online Papers*, vol. 1, no. 2. http://www.eiop.or.at/eiop/texte/1997-002.htm.

Jensen, Thomas (2009) "The Democratic Deficit of the European Union", *Living Reviews in Democracy*, vol. 1, pp. 1–8.

Jordan, Andrew, Huitema, Dave, van Asselt, Harro et al. (2018) *Governing Climate Change. Policentricity in Action?*, Cambridge: Cambridge University Press.

Kadushin, Charles (2012) *Understanding Social Networks*, Oxford: Oxford University Press.

Keck, Margaret E. and Sikkink, Kathryn (1998) *Activists beyond Borders: Advocacy Networks in International Politics*, Ithaca: Cornell University Press.

Kelemen, Daniel R. and Tarrant, Andrew D. (2011) "The Political Foundations of the Eurocracy", *West European Politics*, vol. 34, no. 5, pp. 922–947.

Keohane, Robert O. and Nye, Joseph S. (1974) "Transgovernmental Relations and International Organizations", *World Politics*, vol. 27, no. 1, pp. 39–62.

Knoke, David (2012) *Political Networks: The Structural Perspective*, Cambridge: Press Syndicate of the University of Cambridge.

Kramer, Christian (2017) *Network Theory and Violent Conflicts: Studies in Afghanistan and Lebanon*, Cham: Palgrave Macmillan.

Krasner, Stephen D. (2005) "The Case for Shared Sovereignty", *Journal of Democracy*, vol. 16, no. 1, pp. 69–83.

Lechner, Silviya (2017) "Anarchy in International Relations", in: *Oxford Research Encyclopaedia of International Studies*. http://internationalstudies.oxfordre.com/view/10.1093/acrefore/9780190846626.001.0001/acrefore-9780190846626-e-79.

Maggetti, Martino and Gilardi, Fabrizio (2011) "The Policy-Making Structure of European Regulatory Networks and the Domestic Adoption of Standards", *Journal of European Public Policy*, vol. 18, no. 6, pp. 830–847.

Maggetti, Martino and Gilardi, Fabrizio (2014) "Network Governance and the Domestic Adoption of Soft Rules", *Journal of European Public Policy*, vol. 21, no. 9, pp. 1293–1310.

Maoz, Zeev (2010) *Networks of Nations: The Evolution, Structure, and Impact of International Networks, 1816–2001*, New York: Cambridge University Press.

Maoz, Zeev (2017) "Network Science and International Relations", in: *Oxford Research Encyclopedia of Politics*, Oxford: Oxford University Press. Retrieved 12 Feb. 2021, from https://oxfordre.com/politics/view/10.1093/acrefore/9780190228637.001.0001/acrefore-9780190228637-e-517.

Marsh, David and Smith, Martin (2000) "Understanding Policy Networks: Towards a Dialectical Approach", *Political Studies*, vol. 48, pp. 4–21.

Minhas, Shahryar, Hoff, Peter and Ward, Michael D. (2017) "Influence Networks in International Relations", Working Paper, Cornell University, https://arxiv.org/abs/1706.09072.

Moravcsik, Andrew (1993) "Preferences and Power in the European Community: A Liberal Intergovernmentalist Approach", *Journal of Common Market Studies*, vol. 31, no. 4, pp. 473–524.

Moravcsik, Andrew (1995) "Explaining International Human Rights Regimes: Liberal Theory and Western Europe", *European Journal of International Relations*, vol. 1, no. 2, pp. 157–189.

Morin, Jean-Frédéric, Louafi Sélim, Orsini Amandine and Oubenal, Mohamed (2017) "Boundary Organizations in Regime Complexes: A Social Network Profile of IPBES", *Journal of International Relations and Development*, vol. 20, no. 3, pp. 543–577.

Newig, Jens, Günther, Dirk and Pahl-Wostl, Claudia (2010) "Synapses in the Network: Learning in Governance Networks in the Context of Environmental Management", *Ecology and Society*, vol. 15, no. 4, pp. 1–16.

Oberthür, Sebastian and Stokke, Olav Schram (2011) *Managing Institutional Complexity: Regime Interplay and Global Environmental Change*, Cambridge, MA: MIT Press.

Orsini, Amandine (2013) "Multi-Forum Non-State Actors: Navigating the Regime Complexes for Forestry and Genetic Resources", *Global Environmental Politics*, vol. 13, no. 3, pp. 34–55.

Orsini, Amandine and Godet, Claire (2018) "Food Security and Biofuels Regulations: The Emulsifying Effect of International Regime Complexes", *Journal of Contemporary European Research*, vol. 14, no. 1, pp. 4–22.

Orsini, Amandine, Morin, Jean-Frédéric and Young, Oran (2013) "Regime Complexes: A Buzz, a Boom, or a Boost for Global Governance?", *Global Governance*, vol. 19, no. 1, pp. 27–39.

Papadopoulos, Yannis (2007) "Problems of Democratic Accountability in Network and Multilevel Governance", *European Law Journal*, vol. 13, no. 4, pp. 469–486.

Patty, John W. and Penn, Elizabeth M. (2017) "Uncertainty, Polarization, and Proposal Incentives under Quadratic Voting", *Public Choice*, vol. 172, no. 1–2, pp. 109–124.

Podolny, Joel M. and Page, Karen L. (1998) "Network Form of Organization", *Annual Review of Sociology*, vol. 24, pp. 57–76.

Postel-Vinay, Karoline (2014) *The G20: A New Geopolitical Order*, Basingstoke: Palgrave Macmillan.

Pouliot, Vincent (2013) "Methodology: Putting Practice Theory into Practice", in: Rebecca Adler-Nissen (ed.) *Bourdieu in International Relations: Rethinking Key Concepts in IR*, Abingdon: Routledge, pp. 45–58.

Powell, Walter W. (1990) "Neither Market nor Hierarchy: Network Forms of Organization", *Research in Organizational Behavior*, vol. 12, pp. 295–336.

Radicchi, Filippo, Castellano, Claudio, Cecconi, Federico et al. (2004) "Defining and Identifying Communities in Networks", *Proceedings of the National Academy of Sciences of the United States of America*, vol. 101, no. 9, pp. 2658–2663.

Raustiala, Kal and Victor, David G. (2004) "The Regime Complex for Plant Genetic Resources", *International Organization*, vol. 58, no. 2, pp. 277–309.

Seybolt, Taylor B. (2009) "Harmonizing the Humanitarian Aid Network: Adaptive Change in a Complex System", *International Studies Quarterly*, vol. 53, no. 4, pp. 1027–1050.

Skogstad, Grace (2003) "Legitimacy and/or Policy Effectiveness?: Network Governance and GMO Regulation in the European Union", *Journal of European Public Policy*, vol. 10, no. 3, pp. 321–338.

Slaughter, Anne-Marie (2004) *A New World Order*, Princeton, NJ: Princeton University Press.

Slaughter, Anne-Marie (2017) *The Chessboard and the Web Strategies of Connection in a Networked World*, New Haven, CT: Yale University Press.

Stevenson, William B. and Greenberg, Danna (2000) "Agency and Social Networks: Strategies of Action in a Social Structure of Position, Opposition, and Opportunity", *Administrative Science Quarterly*, vol. 45, no. 4, pp. 651–678.

Toope, Stephen (2000) "Emerging Patterns of Governance and International Law", in: Michael Byers (ed.) *The Rule of Law in International Politics*, Oxford: Oxford University Press, pp. 91–108.

Victor, Jennifer Nicoll, Montgomery, Alexander H. and Lubell, Mark (2017) *The Oxford Handbook of Political Networks*, Oxford: Oxford University Press.

Wang, Guang-Xu (2010) "A Theoretical Debate and Strategy to Link Structure and Agency in Policy Process Studies: A Network Perspective", *Journal of Politics and Law*, vol. 3, no. 2, pp. 101–109.

Wendt, Alexander E. (1987) "The Agent-Structure Problem in International Relations Theory", *International Organization*, vol. 41, no. 3, pp. 335–370.

White, Douglas R. and Harary, Frank (2001) "The Cohesiveness of Blocks in Social Networks: Node Connectivity and Conditional Density", *Sociological Methodology*, vol. 31, no. 1, pp. 305–359.

Wong, Wendy H. (2014) *Internal Affairs. How the Structure of NGOs Transforms Human Rights*, Ithaca: Cornell University Press.

Woods, Ngaire and Martinez-Diaz, Leonardo (2009) *Networks of Influence? Developing Countries in a Networked Global Order*, Oxford: Oxford University Press.

Zimmerman, Lisbeth. 2016. "Same Same or Different? Norm Diffusion Between Resistance, Compliance, and Localization in Post-conflict States", *International Studies Perspectives*, vol. 17, no. 1, pp. 98–115.

2
WORLD POLITICS AS A COMPLEX SYSTEM

Analyzing governance complexity with network approaches

Philipp Pattberg and Oscar Widerberg

Introduction

This chapter engages with the challenge of analyzing complexity in world politics, in particular, with appropriate methods to do so. Many issue areas in world politics have been described as increasingly institutionally complex, having moved from being primarily intergovernmental in nature to encompassing a broader range of actors and institutions beyond governments. The climate change governance arena is a case in point. While the United Nations Framework Convention on Climate Change (UNFCCC) and its 2015 Paris Agreement might arguably form the center of gravity, climate change is factually governed by a plethora of non-state institutions, involving actors ranging from municipalities to companies and non-governmental organizations (Pattberg and Stripple 2008; Chan et al. 2015) in addition to the multilateral negotiation process. The emerging governance system is becoming increasingly complex (Orsini et al. 2019). A key challenge, then, is how to best analyze and evaluate complex governance systems in world politics.

Insights from classical neoliberal regime theory, while useful for specific questions, seem less relevant for scrutinizing the structure and implications of complex governance. Much theorizing within this tradition is concerned with the emergence, performance, durability, and change of single institutions, rather than with the interactions among a multitude of governance approaches. We consequently suggest the utilization of network theory and methodologies to better understand complex global governance systems. We see three challenges emerging here: how to map and analyze the larger institutional structure; how to measure fragmentation and coherence; and how to identify important and central actors. Network theory can unravel patterns in complex governance systems that remain invisible through other means of analysis. For instance, as we will show in this chapter, institutions related to the European Union's FLEGT program are key players in the global forest regime complex due to their ability to connect public and private actors in the broader forest governance architecture.

This chapter proceeds by first, outlining the state of the art with regard to conceptualizations of governance complexity; second, by introducing the key ideas of complexity theory (as a theory of complex systems); and third, through exploring the added value of network theory and related methodologies for studying global governance complexity. Fourth, we illustrate our claim with the example of global forest governance before concluding with some lessons learned and next steps for research.

Conceptualizing governance complexity

In separate issue areas – ranging from climate change to finance, energy, cybersecurity, and health – authors have observed increasing institutional density, interactions, and resulting overlaps, unexpected and unintended consequences, as well as a proliferation of actors that possess agency in world politics (Walt and Buse 2000; Colgan et al. 2012; Henning 2019; Stevens 2017). A range of concepts has emerged in recent years that attempt to shed light on the deep transformation of world politics after the end of the Cold War. "Fragmegration" (Rosenau 1990), "new medievalism" (Friedrichs 2001), "assemblages" (DeLanda 2006; Sassen 2006), "bricolage" (Mittelman 2013), or "new anarchy" (Cerny and Pritchard 2017) try to make sense of the seeming complexity of world politics at the broad conceptual level. At the level of concrete institutional arrangements and governance instruments, scholars have noted "the presence of nested, partially overlapping, and parallel international regimes that are not hierarchically ordered" (Alter and Meunier 2009), referred to by others as "regime complexity" (Drezner 2009; Hafner-Burton et al. 2009; Orsini et al. 2013). As a consequence of increased institutional density and overlap, authors have observed the emergence of related "regime complexes" (Raustiala and Victor 2004; Keohane and Victor 2011), while other scholars have attempted to observe and measure the "fragmentation of global governance architectures" (Biermann et al. 2009) as an empirical property of complex governance systems. However, while complexity is frequently used as a qualitative description and metaphor, few authors have attempted to conceptualize and measure complexity, taking into account the perspective of complexity theory (for a fuller discussion of complexity theory and global governance, see Pattberg and Widerberg 2019). We, however, believe that complexity theory is a natural starting point for understanding the increased complexity of global governance. We will consequently outline some key tenets of complexity theory and how it links to network approaches in the next section.

Complexity theory and complex systems

Complexity theory is concerned with phenomena that arise from and are visible in complex systems. We can speak of complex systems – as opposed to simple systems – when systemic interactions among system components occur "whose outcomes are wholly unexpected and nearly impossible to predict" (Kavalski 2007, 437). An approximation is to say that the whole is greater than the sum of its parts. In other words, complex systems are complex because of the interactions of their components and not because of additive effects of all parts. A complex system approach consequently considers actions of agents (e.g. international and non-governmental organizations, companies, and cities) that produce macro-level phenomena by aggregation. Applied to the realm of global governance, it is therefore not sufficient to map all governance institutions in a given policy arena in order to deduce outcomes; in fact, interactions among constituent parts, including feedback loops and non-linearity, result in system-wide, so-called emergent properties. The practical implications are potentially far-reaching. If the interaction of the many policies, governance arrangements, institutions, and actors operating within an issue area (as possibly between various issue areas as well) produces unintended and unforeseeable effects, this might severely limit the ability of actors to engage in a rational design of broader governance systems or the subsequent orchestration of its parts (Abbott et al. 2015). Before addressing adequate methodologies for understanding complex systems, we briefly elaborate on two key qualities of those systems: non-linearity and emergent behavior.

In linear systems, when the value of a causal element changes, we can predict the change in the value of the dependent element. The changes in the latter are proportional to the changes in the former. Take, for example, the activity of baking a birthday cake. If we double the ingredients, we get roughly double the results, in this case a bigger cake. As Byrne and Callaghan (2013, 18) explain:

> Linearity is foundational to 'Newtonian' science by which we mean scientific accounts in which we can describe a current state in terms of values of parameters and have a covering law, a universal/nomothetic specification, which describes how the state will change if values in the parameters change.

Non-linear systems do not satisfy the superposition principle by which outputs are proportional to inputs. In other words, in non-linear systems, effects emerge that are disproportionate to the changes in the input and thereby might be qualified as "surprising" and hard to predict. What follows from non-linear dynamics is that often we can speak of *emergent properties* and phenomena that are qualitatively different from those of the individual units/agents that are aggregated (think of the difference between water molecules/water and brain cells/consciousness).

Emergent properties are defined as the "intricate intertwining or interconnectivity of elements within a system, and between a system and its environment" (Mitleton-Kelly 2000). A good example is a group of commuters competing for space on a road and causing a traffic jam. While the individual commuter is motivated by a simple goal, to get home as fast as possible, the aggregate phenomenon, a traffic jam, is hard to predict, evolve, and manage. It represents, in other words, an emergent phenomenon (see Johnson 2009 for an elaboration of the traffic jam example).

From the idea of non-linearity, it is only a small step to the concept of networks, as networks are an excellent embodiment of non-linearity. As Capra (1996, 82) noted: "The first and most obvious property of any network is its non-linearity—it goes in all directions. Thus, the relationships in a network pattern are non-linear relationships." In sum, the complexity of complex systems derives from the relationships among constituent parts, not from the parts themselves. As a result, methodologies are needed that are capable of mapping, visualizing, and analyzing interactions and changing relations rather than static properties. Consequently, relational ontologies (Emirbayer 1997) and related methodologies (Watts and Strogatz 1998) will feature prominently as an analytical tool in unraveling complex systems. We will now discuss network analysis as a way forward in studying global governance complexity.

The promise of network theory for unraveling complexity

Social network analysis (SNA) is the process of investigating social structures through the use of networks and graph theory. It characterizes networked structures in terms of nodes (individual actors, people, or things within the network) and the ties, edges, or links (relationships or interactions) that connect them.

While networks as a specific mode of organization (opposed to markets and hierarchies) have been recognized in global governance scholarship for some time (an example is Keck and Sikkink's concept of transnational activist networks, 1998), network analysis as a formal method of inquiry has been applied less frequently until quite recently. Kahler (2009, 2), for example, has argued that networks have become the "intellectual centerpiece of a new era" but criticizes that they have remained a "metaphor rather than an instrument of analysis". Improving our knowledge about networks in world politics could have far-reaching implications. Both Hafner-Burton and colleagues (2009) and Slaughter (2017) make a case that in a networked world, understanding the structural positions of actors and how they use them will be pivotal for analyzing power. It follows from this argument that power is not solely derived from individual attributes of nodes but rather from how and to whom they are connected. Hafner-Burton and colleagues (2009, 570) suggest that actors that are well connected have social power, meaning that they can more easily access resources from other nodes in the networks; network brokers have power by connecting marginalized nodes to the larger network; and, finally, connections determine an actor's potential for exiting the system. Hence, understanding where actors are situated in a network and how they are connected enables analysis of power structures along with more functional types of analysis.

Over the past decade, scholars have increasingly been using network analysis for understanding international relations beyond the metaphorical (e.g. Kim 2013). Here we suggest that network analysis can help unravel complexities in world politics at three levels: the system level, the cluster level, and the individual (institutional) level. The next sections will discuss each level in more detail, suggesting concrete approaches for measurement.

The system level

The increasing complexity of global governance is often discussed in terms of increasing institutional diversity, i.e., the proliferation of various types of institutions, beyond multilateral agreements between states (Zelli and van Asselt 2013). At the system level, this has, in turn, led to scholarly and policy discussions on the fragmentation of international governance and law, and the repercussions thereof (Brown Weiss 1993; Koskenniemi and Leino 2002; Oberthür and Gehring 2011). Key research questions have centered around various concepts related to coherency and fragmentation, and to what extent structural features of regime complexes influence the problem-solving capacity of the system. Biermann and colleagues argue that "fragmentation" is a value-neutral concept but that there are various degrees of synergy or conflict between different components of the system, for instance, through interaction of core-norms (Biermann et al. 2009). Increasing institutional complexity characterized by a growing number of institutions thus influences policy outcomes. However, few authors have managed to successfully measure the degree of fragmentation or coherence of regime complexes empirically, or compare various degrees of fragmentation of coherence across issue areas (Pattberg and Widerberg 2020). The lack of such research hinders the testing of hypotheses of the structure of regime complexes as an independent variable and problem-solving capacity as a dependent variable.

Network theory provides a few useful additional tools and metrics for measuring topological features of regime complexes at the system level. For instance, a key argument made by scholars working on global climate governance has been that the system is becoming increasingly polycentric, i.e., that there are multiple centers of authority that are more or less independent of each other (Jordan et al. 2015). To test that claim, one needs metrics to measure whether the regime complex is more or less coherent. Widerberg (2016), for instance, suggests that simple measures of centralization based on degree can be good first indicators for network structure in regime complexes. A high level of degree centralization in a regime complex suggests that power, authority, or any other type of connection is concentrated to one or a few important nodes with a relatively high number of connections, compared to all other nodes in the networks (Freeman 1979). Conversely, a low degree of centralization means that connections are more evenly distributed across nodes in the network.

The cluster level

Moving from the "macro", systems-level of regime complexes to the "meso" level entails studying clusters of institutions. Clustering could play an important role in global governance since they could plausibly form around distinct types of actors, activities, or what Dingwerth and Pattberg refer to as "organizational fields" (2009; see also DiMaggio and Powell 1983). An organizational field can be characterized by a group of actors and institutions that cluster around a specific function and "[include] communities of organizations with similar functions or roles insofar as these organizations are aware of each other, interact with each other and perceive each other as peers or 'like units' in some important sense" (Dingwerth and Pattberg 2009, 720). Fields should not be perceived as consciously or intentionally constructed but rather as self-organizing institutional constellations around a given issue that is embedded in a larger regime complex. A good example from the realm of climate governance is the organizational field consisting of institutions engaged in carbon accounting. Green (2013) identified 30 different voluntary public, private, and hybrid schemes that are in some way occupied with accounting and disclosing carbon emissions. These schemes devise standards and metrics for private and public actors to measure and manage their carbon emissions, often linked to various types of offsetting schemes. Most of the schemes are voluntary in the sense that they are not required by any law and actors that use the schemes do so on a voluntary basis. The schemes are, however, not separated from national and international regulations as most of them link to internationally recognized schemes such as the European Union's Emission Trading scheme, or the Clean Development Mechanism under the United Nations Framework Convention on Climate Change (UNFCCC). In this cluster (or field) of carbon management, there is competition and cooperation, where effectiveness must be considered at the meso-level. Looking at one individual institution (micro-level) tells us little about whether carbon accounting works at the cluster level, and conversely, looking at the regime complex as a whole (the macro-level) presents too many confounding variables. Consequently, for carbon accounting, the meso-level of the organizational field appears to be the appropriate level for analyzing regime complexes in terms of effectiveness, efficiency, and other impacts.

Identifying the various clusters in regime complexes using network analysis presents several avenues for the researcher. However, deciding on which measures and techniques to use clearly depends on the research question. Green (2013) provides a good example of using network analysis at the cluster level. By connecting carbon accounting schemes that recognize each other (for instance, the VER+ standard also recognizes the standards for the CDM), she is able to show how the field is dominated by a few international standards to which most other standards gravitate. It is a rare example of how network visualizations and simple metrics can be used to reveal new and highly relevant information, in this case, how a seemingly uncoordinated proliferation of private institutions use public institutions as "anchors" for their own activities, effectively questioning a narrative suggesting that private voluntary institutions somehow grow independently. Instead, private standards may be the result of previously implemented public standards. Another approach to better understanding organizational fields at the cluster level is to analyze whether the network has a tendency to divide into smaller clusters or whether links between nodes are more evenly spread. One such measure is to calculate the "clustering coefficient", which measures the degree to which nodes tend to form clusters in a network. Clusters are found when smaller groups of nodes tend to share a relatively high number of links compared to other groups in the network. The clustering coefficient is based on counting triplets in the network, i.e., whether a "friend of a friend is a friend", also called "transitivity" in network theory (Wasserman and Faust 1994).

The individual level

The emergence of regime complexes has resulted in a tendency among scholars of international relations to focus on the structural components of global governance. However, network analysis provides an excellent starting point and methodological toolbox for analyzing both structures and agents, in particular how these two interact. According to a network theory reading of international relations, the power and influence of an actor depends on its position in the structure rather than on some inherent qualities such as the amount of material resources, such as money or technology (Hafner-Burton et al. 2009). Pursuing more power thus requires identifying one's place in a network and how to most effectively use it. Consequently, strategic behavior in regime complexes suggests that actors should pursue new strategies, in essence increasing their "connectedness" to the "right" connections. Slaughter (2017) terms this "strategies of connection in a networked world", calling for new grand strategies for increasing "networked power". From this perspective, the EU, for instance, should think of problems arising from being either "too connected" (e.g. spread of diseases) or "not connected enough" (e.g. access to education or electricity) rather than in terms of relative capacities of various resources (e.g. money or technology) vis-à-vis other countries. Network analysis could support both analysts and decision makers in identifying important nodes for interventions. For instance, in 2002, the now famous study by Krebs of hijackers around the 9/11 terrorist attack showed the centrality of the terrorist Mohammed Atta using various measures of centrality from network analysis (Krebs 2002). Green (2013), mentioned in the previous section, also uses various conceptualizations of centrality to derive the most important institutions in carbon accounting, arguing that public standards such as the CDM and the ISO 14064-1 are the most central, and thereby relevant, standards in the network.

Centrality in a network can be interpreted in many different ways. For instance, as importance or prestige (having many connections), power and influence (being connected to important players), and brokerage (bridging various communities in the network). Depending on the research question, various centrality measures can be used to measure the structural position of an actor. *Degree* centrality, for instance, means the number of connections that a node has, i.e., suggesting something about the popularity of an actor. *Betweenness* and *closeness* centrality are measures for identifying what nodes could function as bridges across various communities in a network, and thereby claim a gate-keeping role of various flows of, for example, information and knowledge. Finally, *eigenvector* centrality provides an indication of what node is connected to more important other nodes, compared to other nodes in the network.

Modeling networks

Network analysis in the field of global governance has largely been confined to descriptive statistics and snap-shot data. For example, Widerberg (2016) discussing the macro-, meso-, and micro-structure of the climate regime complex and Kim (2013) describes the emergence of an international network of a multilateral environmental agreement. A more sophisticated analysis shows the interplay between natural and social systems using network analysis, for instance, that by Bodin and colleagues (2016), which conceptualizes the emergence of various network structures using network theory. However, to start testing various hypotheses on network emergence and various structures, more advanced statistics are needed.

Turning to inferential network analysis is a logical step in theory since it enables researchers to explore many of the assumptions and claims made about regime complexes in a more rigorous way. A range of tools has been developed over the past ten years for modeling political networks. Cranmer and colleagues (2017), for instance, mention three approaches: quadratic assignment procedure, exponential random graph models (ERGMs), and latent space network models, noting that they all outperform standard statistical methods that "usually require observational independence, or the assumption that actors do not influence each other's outcomes" (2017, 237).

A range of other models also deals with longitudinal data. Overall, such models have been tested on various environmental fields at the domestic and local level (see Lubell et al. 2012), such as discourse networks on climate policy (Ingold and

TABLE 2.1 Approaches towards modeling political networks based on Cranmer and colleagues, 2017; see *also Robins and colleagues* (2012)

Approach	Description	Example
Quadratic Assignment Procedure (QAP)	QAP is an extension of simple and multiple regression models for dyadic data that test whether two matrices are correlated (Krackhardt 1988)	Determining relationship between internet infrastructure and global air transport in cities (Choi et al. 2006)
Exponential Random Graph Models (ERGMs)	ERGMs predict presence or absence of ties between nodes relative to a random network, assuming that ties are formed stochastically based on their surrounding neighborhood.	Determining membership composition in international scientific assessments (Leifeld and Fisher 2017)
Latent Space Network models	Latent space models are Generalized Linear Models taking the distance between nodes in a network into account using an unobserved "social space" (Hoff et al. 2002)	Determining the relationship between trade networks and participation in transnational climate governance (Cao and Ward 2016)

Fischer 2014) but less prominently in global environmental governance. In fact, at the global level, in particular in relation to regime complexes, few examples can be found of moving toward using dynamic data and network modeling. This is somewhat surprising given the various potential benefits attributed to applying models to dynamic network data. Prominent exceptions include the work of Hollway and colleagues trying to model the emergence of a global regime complex for fisheries, in particular including regional fishery management organizations (Hollway and Koskinen 2016).

Modeling networks, however, presents an important challenge for analysts. Modeling networks at the level of regime complexes requires a substantial amount and quality of data which has been largely unavailable to researchers. Kim (2013) and Hollway and Koskinen's (2016) works use explicit referrals between various multilateral and bilateral environmental agreements. However, if regime complexes are characterized by a large number of non-state and sub-national actors and private and hybrid institutions, then how and what type of data should be collected to enable network modeling remains an important question.

Finally, network analysis also presents a number of pitfalls for the researcher. First, data-collection is generally quite labor intensive, in particular if one is looking for dynamic data for modeling purposes. There are few global datasets for researchers to use to study institutional complexity. Second, an important question concerns the meaning of networks. While the network analysis toolkit enables an immense amount of descriptive statistics, it is not always clear what the implications are of different network structures, cluster formations, or individual measures of centrality. Third, network analysis is highly sensitive to variations in system boundaries. A micro-perspective on a sub-field of a governance system may yield a completely different picture than a macro-perspective on the entire architecture. In this sense, features of institutional systems such as "complexity" and "fragmentation" can always be considered as being in the eyes of the beholder.

The forest governance domain: Loosely coupled or coherent system?

Some scholars have called forest governance a "non-regime" (Dimitrov 2003), referring to the lack of a global agreement similar to ones for climate change (the United Nations Framework Convention on Climate Change, the UNFCCC) or biodiversity (the Convention Biological Diversity, the CBD). However, despite the absence of a global agreement, forest governance – including various issues such as deforestation, afforestation, and sustainable forest management – is characterized by an increasingly dense landscape of international and transnational public, private, and hybrid institutions. Consequently, the system is marked by overlaps and institutional interaction, raising questions about potential conflicts or synergies in forest governance. Moreover, forest governance occurs at the intersection of biodiversity and climate change governance (Van Asselt 2011), coupling governance initiatives in climate change (see e.g. UN-REDD program) and biodiversity (e.g. the CBD). Large knowledge gaps remain regarding the question of how global forest governance institutions are distributed and arranged (Agrawal et al. 2008).

In two consecutive reports, the CONNECT-project (see Pattberg et al. 2014) mapped the emergence of a regime complex for forest governance (Dias Guerra et al. 2015; see also McDermott et al. 2010). A total of 84 institutions were identified, of which slightly more than 50% are public, 24% represent a mix of public and private actors, and nearly 20% comprise private and/or civil society actors. Interestingly, public actors (e.g. government agencies, cities, and regions) are part of 80% of the institutions, suggesting that the absence of a multilateral international agreement on forestry has not hindered states from cooperating on global forestry governance in other ways. Figure 2.1 depicts the overall global governance system for forests using the heuristic of a governance triangle.

To better understand the emerging regime complex of forest governance and to show the added value of network approaches, we will present a brief analysis of global forest governance along the three analytical levels and related network

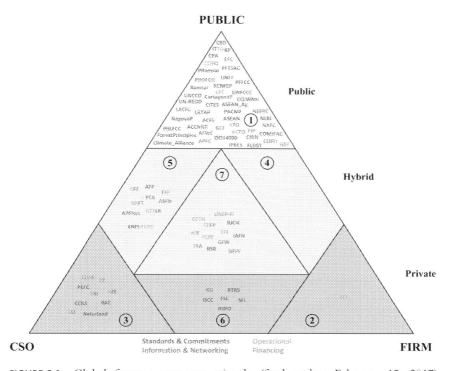

FIGURE 2.1 Global forest governance triangle (final update February 15, 2017). Modified from Abbott and Snidal (2009a, 2009b), Abbott (2012), and Keohane and Victor (2011).

approaches discussed above. The first level of analysis, as introduced above, is the system level. In this section we discuss the overall institutional structure and the level of degree centralization. At the system level we find 84 institutions connected via 6,239 members. Projecting the networks from a two-mode to a one-mode network, i.e., connecting institutions that share membership, allows for visual representation of the network (see Figure 2.2).

The figure shows a tightly knit network of institutions with a substantial amount of shared membership. The nodes are colored by type of members, with red nodes representing the "public" institutions, also the most common ones.[1] The degree distribution also suggests that the average node is quite well connected (average degree is 34), as shown in the histogram on the degree distribution shown below.

In fact, 25 institutions have a degree above 50, the vast majority of these being international public institutions such as the CBD, the United Nations Forum on Forests (UNFF), and the Global Environment Facility (GEF).

At the cluster level, we are interested in how institutions form smaller issue and functional clusters. The visual analysis of the network suggests that there are few clear clusters being formed in the forest regime complex. The clustering coefficient also confirms that there is a relatively high level of transitivity in the network. Rather than forming distinct organizational fields, most institutions in global forest governance are loosely coupled and interacting sufficiently to prevent the emergence of specialized clusters.

Finally, at the individual level, network analysis can help to identify important actors/institutions, e.g. by measuring centrality. In the forest governance domain, we observe that multi-stakeholder initiatives such as the 'Tropical Forest Alliance 2020' and the 'Congo Basin Forest Partnership' score very high in terms of degree centrality, meaning that they connect to most of the other institutions via shared membership. This is perhaps not surprising since they are more likely to connect various public and private institutions. However, analyzing the betweenness centrality we find that other institutions, such as the Round Table on Responsible Soy and the European Neighborhood and Partnership Instrument East Countries Forest Law Enforcement and Governance II Program, are better at tying various institutions together.

Conclusions

This chapter engaged with the challenge of analyzing complexity in global governance and suggested applying a network approach to studying regime complexes, fragmented governance architectures and increased interactions across policy domains. Starting from complexity theory, we understand the totality of world politics as a "system of complex systems" that should be analyzed, taking non-linearity and emergent properties into account. To be more specific: analysis of individual institutional components of global governance arenas is insufficient for understanding system-wide behavior and outcomes. For systems in which performance is influenced by interactions rather than

World politics as a complex system **45**

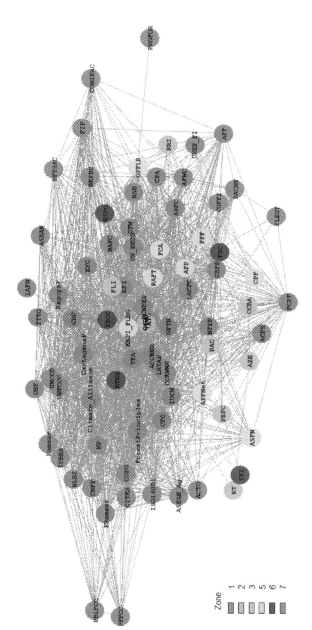

FIGURE 2.2 Visual representation of the network by nodes.

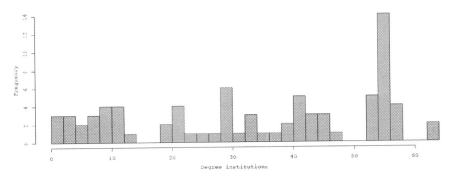

FIGURE 2.3 Degree distribution in the forestry regime complex.

static properties of units, network analysis might provide additional instruments for mapping, visualization, and analysis.

In more detail, we suggest in this chapter to apply network approaches at three analytical levels: the system level (i.e., the regime complex or governance architecture), the cluster level (functional or organizational fields within broader regime complexes, for example, carbon accounting as part of the climate change governance regime complex), and the individual level (institutions and organizations constituting the other two levels). Various measurements can be used to analyze the system and its components, including *betweenness*, *closeness*, and *eigenvector* centrality. However, a number of limitations are also apparent. First, moving from network descriptions to modeling presents a major challenge to the analyst in terms of data availability and quality. Furthermore, important questions around the actual interpretation of network data exist. While the network analysis toolkit enables impressive descriptive statistics, implications of network analysis results remain unclear. Finally, network analysis is highly sensitive to variations in system boundaries, i.e., decisions that are outside the data but involve value judgment and interpretation by the analyst.

After presenting various network approaches for studying complex global governance systems, this chapter has briefly illustrated its usefulness by discussing the global forest governance domain along the three suggested levels of analysis. We find that global forest governance is a tightly connected network with a substantial amount of shared membership, in particular among the public actors involved. As a next step, this type of overview allows the analyst to zoom in on specific relevant players, to analyze the nature of flows and connections in more detail, and to scrutinize the overall quality of interactions with a view toward improving governance arrangements.

In sum, the increasing complexity of global governance calls for conceptual and methodological innovation and renewal among analysts. In this chapter, we have argued that world politics constitutes a system of complex systems, and that in order to scrutinize it beyond static analysis, new approaches are necessary. We hope to have convinced the reader that network approaches should take center stage in our methodological toolkit for understanding world politics.

Note

1 Note that the network only shows connected nodes. A total of four nodes do not share any members with other institutions and have therefore been removed.

References

Abbott, K.W., 2012. The transnational regime complex for climate change. *Environment & Planning. Part C, Government & Policy* 30, 571–590.
Abbott, K.W., 2015. Orchestration. In P. Pattberg, F. Zelli (Eds.), *Encyclopedia of Global Environmental Governance and Politics*. Edward Elgar Publishing, Cheltenham, pp. 487–495.
Abbott, K.W., Snidal, D., 2009a. *The Governance Triangle: Regulatory Standards Institutions and the Shadow of the State. The Politics of Global Regulation*, eds. Walter Mattli and Ngaire Woods. Princeton University Press, Princeton.
Abbott, K.W., Snidal, D., 2009b. Strengthening international regulation through transnational new governance: Overcoming the orchestration deficit. *Vanderbilt Journal of Transnational Law* 42, 501–578.
Abbott, K.W., Genschel, P., Snidal, D., Zangl, B., 2015. *International Organizations as Orchestrators*. Cambridge University Press, Cambridge.
Agrawal, A., Chhatre, A., Hardin, R., 2008. Changing governance of the world's forests. *Science* 320, 1460–1462. https://doi.org/10.1126/science.1155369
Alter, K.J., Meunier, S., 2009. The politics of international regime complexity. *Perspectives on Politics* 7, 13–24.
Biermann, F., Pattberg, P., van Asselt, H., Zelli, F., 2009. The fragmentation of global governance architectures: A framework for analysis. *Global Environmental Politics* 9, 14–40. https://doi.org/10.1162/glep.2009.9.4.14
Bodin, Ö., Robins, G., McAllister, R.R.J., Guerrero, A.M., Crona, B., Tengö, M., Lubell, M., 2016. Theorizing benefits and constraints in collaborative environmental governance: A transdisciplinary social-ecological network approach for empirical investigations. *Ecology and Society* 21(1), 40.
Brown Weiss, E., 1993. International environmental law: Contemporary issues and the emergence of a new world order. *Georgetown Law Journal* 81, 675–710.
Byrne, D., Callaghan, G., 2013. *Complexity Theory and the Social Sciences: The State of the art*. Routledge, Oxon.
Cao, X., Ward, H., 2016. Transnational climate governance networks and domestic regulatory action. *International Interactions*, 1–27. https://doi.org/10.1080/03050629.2016.1220162
Capra, F., 1996. *The Web of Life: A New Scientific Understanding of Living Systems*. Anchor Books. New York.
Cerny, P.G., Prichard, A., 2017. The new anarchy: Globalisation and fragmentation in world politics. *Journal of International Political Theory* 13(3), 378–394. https://doi.org/10.1177/1755088217713765
Chan, S., van Asselt, H., Hale, T.N., Abbott, K.W., Beisheim, M., Hoffmann, M., Guy, B., Höhne, N., Hsu, A., Pattberg, P., et al., 2015. Reinvigorating international climate policy: A comprehensive framework for effective nonstate action. *Global Policy* 6, 466–473.
Choi, J.H., Barnett, G.A., Chon, B.-S., 2006. Comparing world city networks: A network analysis of Internet backbone and air transport intercity linkages. *Global Networks* 6, 81–99. https://doi.org/10.1111/j.1471-0374.2006.00134.x
Colgan, J.D., Keohane, R., van de Graaf, T., 2012. Punctuated equilibrium in the energy regime complex. *Review of International Organizations* 7(2), 117–143.

Cranmer, S.J., Leifeld, P., McClurg, S.D., Rolfe, M., 2017. Navigating the range of statistical tools for inferential network analysis. *American Journal of Political Science* 61, 237–251. https://doi.org/10.1111/ajps.12263

DeLanda, M., 2006. *A New Philosophy of Society: Assemblage Theory and Social Complexity*. London and New York: Continuum Books.

Dias Guerra, F., Isailovic, M., Widerberg, O., Pattberg, P., 2015. *Mapping the Institutional Architecture of Global Forest Governance* (Technical Paper No. R15- 04). Institute for Environmental Studies (IVM), Amsterdam, the Netherlands.

DiMaggio, P.J., Powell, W.W., 1983. The iron cage revisited - institutional isomorphism and collective rationality in organizational fields. *American Sociological Review* 48, 147–160.

Dimitrov, R.S., 2003. Knowledge, power, and interests in environmental regime formation. *International Studies Quarterly* 47, 123–150. https://doi.org/10.1111/1468-2478.4701006

Dingwerth, K., Pattberg, P., 2009. World politics and organizational fields: The case of transnational sustainability governance. *European Journal of International Relations* 15, 707–743.

Drezner, D.W., 2009. The power and peril of international regime complexity. *Perspectives on Politics* 7(1), 65–70. https://doi.org/10.1017/S1537592709090100

Emirbayer, M., 1997. Manifesto for a relational sociology. *American Journal of Sociology* 103, 281–317. https://doi.org/10.1086/231209

Freeman, L.C., 1979. Centrality in social networks conceptual clarification. *Social Networks* 1, 215–239.

Friedrichs, J., 2001. The meaning of new medievalism. *European Journal of International Relations* 7(4), 475–501. https://doi.org/10.1177/1354066101007004004

Green, J.F., 2013. Order out of Chaos: Public and private rules for managing carbon. *Global Environmental Politics* 13, 1–25.

Hafner-Burton, E.M., Kahler, M., Montgomery, A.H., 2009. Network analysis for international relations. *International Organization* 63, 559–592.

Henning, R.C., 2019. Regime complexity and the institutions of crisis and development finance. *Development and Change* 50(1), 24–45.

Hoff, P.D., Raftery, A.E., Handcock, M.S., 2002. Latent space approaches to social network analysis. *Journal of the American Statistical Association* 97, 1090–1098. https://doi.org/10.1198/016214502388618906

Hollway, J., Koskinen, J., 2016. Multilevel embeddedness: The case of the global fisheries governance complex. *Social Networks* 44, 281–294.

Ingold, K., Fischer, M., 2014. Drivers of collaboration to mitigate climate change: An illustration of Swiss climate policy over 15 years. *Global Environmental Change* 24, 88–98.

Johnson, N., 2009. *Simply Complexity. A Clear Guide to Complexity Theory*. OneWorld Book, London.

Jordan, A.J., Huitema, D., Hildén, M., van Asselt, H., Rayner, T.J., Schoenefeld, J.J., Tosun, J., Forster, J., Boasson, E.L., 2015. Emergence of polycentric climate governance and its future prospects. *Nature Climate Change* 977–982. https://doi.org/10.1038/nclimate2725

Kahler, M. (Ed.), 2009. *Networked Politics: Agency, Power, and Governance*. Cornell University Press, Ithaca.

Kavalski, E., 2007. The fifth debate and the emergence of complex international relations theory: Notes on the application of complexity theory to the study of international life. *Cambridge Review of International Affairs* 20, 435–454.

Keck, M.E., Sikkink, K., 1998. *Activists Beyond Borders: Advocacy Networks in International Politics*. Cambridge University Press, Cambridge.

Keohane, R.O., Victor, D.G., 2011. The regime complex for climate change. *Perspectives on Politics* 9, 7–23.

Kim, R.E., 2013. The emergent network structure of the multilateral environmental agreement system. *Global Environmental Change* 23, 980–991.

Koskenniemi, M., Leino, P., 2002. Fragmentation of international law? Postmodern anxieties. *Leiden Journal of International Law* 15, 553–579.

Krackhardt, D., 1988. Predicting with networks: Nonparametric multiple regression analysis of dyadic data. *Social Networks* 10, 359–381. https://doi.org/10.1016/0378-8733(88)90004-4

Krebs, V.E., 2002. Mapping networks of terrorist cells. *Connections* 24, 43–52.

Leifeld, P., Fisher, D.R., 2017. Membership nominations in international scientific assessments. *Nature Climate Change* 7, 730–735. https://doi.org/10.1038/nclimate3392

Lubell, M., Scholz, J., Berardo, R., Robins, G., 2012. Testing policy theory with statistical models of networks. *Policy Studies Journal* 40, 351–374. https://doi.org/10.1111/j.1541-0072.2012.00457.x

McDermott, C.L., Humphreys, D., Wildburger, C., Wood, P., 2010. Mapping the core actors and issues defining international forest governance. In J. Rayner, A. Buck, P. Katila (Eds.), *Embracing Complexity: Meeting the Challenges of International Forest Governance - A Global Assessment Report Prepared by the Global Forest Expert Panel on the International Forest Regime*. International Union of Forest Research Organizations, Tampere, pp. 19–36.

Mitleton-Kelly, E., 2000. *Complexity: Partial Support for BPR?* Springer.

Mittelman, J.H., 2013. Global *Bricolage*: Emerging market powers and polycentric governance. *Third World Quarterly* 34(1), 23–37. https://doi.org/10.1080/01436597.2013.75535

Oberthür, S., Gehring, T., 2011. Institutional Interaction: Ten Years of Scholarly Development, in: *Managing Institutional Complexity: Regime Interplay and Global Environmental Change*. MIT Press, Cambridge MA, pp. 25–58.

Orsini, A., Morin, J.-F., Young, O., 2013. Regime complexes: A buzz, a boom, or a boost for global governance? *Global Governance: A Review of Multilateralism and International Organizations* 19, 27–39. https://doi.org/10.5555/1075-2846-19.1.27

Orsini, A., Le Prestre, P., Haas, P.M., Brosig, M., Pattberg, P., Widerberg, O., Gomez-Mera, L., Morin, J.-F., Harrison, N.E., Geyer, R., Chandler, D., 2019. Complex systems and international governance. *International Studies Review*. https://doi.org/10.1093/isr/viz005

Pattberg, P., Stripple, J., 2008. Beyond the public and private divide: Remapping transnational climate governance in the 21st century. *International Environmental Agreements: Politics, Law and Economics* 8, 367–388.

Pattberg, P., Widerberg, O., 2019. Smart mixes and the challenge of complexity: The example of global climate governance. In J. van Erp, M. Faure, A. Nollkaemper, N. Philipsen (Eds.), *Smart Mixes in Relation to Transboundary Harm: Interactions between International, State, and Private Regulation*. Cambridge: Cambridge University Press, 49–68.

Pattberg, P.H., Widerberg, O.E., 2020. Global sustainability governance: Fragmented, orchestrated or polycentric? *Civitas Europa* 452(2), 373. https://doi.org/10.3917/civit.045.0373

Pattberg, P., Widerberg, O., Isailovic, M., Dias Guerra, F., 2014. *Mapping and Measuring Fragmentation in Global Governance Architectures: A Framework for Analysis* (No. Report R-14/34). IVM Institute for Environmental Studies, Amsterdam.

Raustiala, K., Victor, D.G., 2004. The regime complex for plant genetic resources. *International Organization* 52, 277–309.

Rosenau, J.N., 1990. *Turbulence in World Politics: A Theory of Change and Continuity*. Princeton University Press, Princeton.

Sassen, S., 2006. *Territory, Authority, Rights: From Medieval to Global Assemblages*. Cambridge University Press, Cambridge.

Slaughter, A.-M., 2017. *The Chessboard and the Web: Strategies of Connection in a Networked World*. Yale University Press, New Haven.

Stevens, T., 2017. Cyberweapons: An emerging global governance architecture. *Palgrave Communications* 3, 16102 doi: 10.1057/palcomms.2016.102.

van Asselt, H., 2011. Integrating biodiversity in the climate regime's forest rules: Options and tradeoffs in greening REDD design. *Review of European Community & International Environmental Law* 20, 139–149. https://doi.org/10.1111/j.1467-9388.2011.00704.x

Walt, G., Buse, K., 2001. Partnership and fragmentation in international health: Threat or opportunity? *Tropical Medicine and International Health* 5(7), 467–471.

Wasserman, S., Faust, K., 1994. *Social Network Analysis: Methods and Applications*. Cambridge University Press, Cambridge.

Watts, D.J., Strogatz, S.H., 1998. Collective dynamics of 'small-world' networks. *Nature* 393, 440–442.

Widerberg, O., 2016. Mapping institutional complexity in the Anthropocene: A network approach. In P. Pattberg, F. Zelli (Eds.), *Environmental Politics and Governance in the Anthropocene: Institutions and Legitimacy in a Complex World*. Routledge, London, pp. 81–102.

Zelli, F., van Asselt, H., 2013. Introduction: The institutional fragmentation of global environmental governance: Causes, consequences, and responses. *Global Environmental Politics* 13, 1–13.

3
CONTROLLING GOVERNANCE ISSUES IN PROFESSIONAL-ORGANIZATIONAL NETWORKS

Lasse Folke Henriksen and Leonard Seabrooke

Introduction

How do actors navigate complex governance systems? Complexity is many things: complex systems involve multidimensional interdependencies between elements; elements that behave differently and have dynamic characteristics; and elements that often interact in non-linear relatively unpredictable ways and across levels (see also Pattberg and Widerberg, this volume). Complexity, however, does not necessarily entail a lack of cohesion. In social systems, the competent molding of instrumental as well as norm-driven forms of behavior among individual and collective actors enable actors to adapt to complexity, to develop ways of dealing with it and even exploiting it. When it comes to regime complexes in transnational governance, this is certainly also true. Such regimes contain both public and private institutions that develop rules for the governance of particular issues. The European Union is one such environment where policy-making is articulated through interactions between various agencies and experts, as well as at multiple levels of governance and implementation. In this chapter, we conceptualize a "space for action within complex systems" in terms of multi-level networks involving professionals and organizations acting to control issues. Our focus is on the complex interactions between professionals and organizations, interactions that sometimes improve cohesion in the system and sometimes work against it.

In this chapter we focus on the role of professional networks; how the expert professionals working on complex governance issues traverse their own peer networks as well as the organizational networks formally and informally involved in governing issues. Professional networks increasingly provide the context of interaction for issue-specific work within and across governance institutions (Seabrooke and Henriksen 2017). Those setting the rules and standards for governance, promulgating them, and making sure they are implemented and evaluated increasingly consider themselves "professionals". This entails that work practices pertaining to all stages of the governance process move from being considered non-professional to undergoing some degree of professionalization. A field that is professional entails actors directing attention at each other as professional peers. This can evoke a sense of community and belonging around collective professional identities and mutual recognition around shared competencies and methodology. Think of the spread of economics as a global profession firmly embedded in international institutions (Fourcade 2006), the widespread sense of agreement around core methodological and theoretical principles in economics (Reay 2012), and the use of commonly agreed upon ways of forecasting macroeconomic dynamics (Henriksen 2013).

Professionalization in issue-specific governance fields, however, can also follow more messy trajectories where expertise based on complex institutional experience – having traversed institutional conflict-ridden ecologies marked by opposition of material interest and/or normative worldviews – becomes the driver of peer recognition (Henriksen and Seabrooke 2016; Seabrooke and Tsingou 2021). In this chapter we argue that what we call "issue professionals" have risen as a prominent type of actor within institutionally hybrid fields of governance. These are fields that entail intense interactions between institutionally diverse actors, such as firms, NGOs, states, and international organizations, at one or several stages of the governance process. "Issue professionals" are actors who are seen as "knowing well" within an issue-specific field of governance, and a source of recognition among their professional peers is often based on a combination of specialized technical expertise and complex institutional experience.

Hybrid fields of governance often involve a mixed set of actors from the private and public domain, as well as policy and regulatory institutions at various governance scales with overlapping or even conflicting mandates of agenda-setting, rule creating, and implementation. Hybridity can foster institutionally complicated environments for decision-making, but also offer the potential to include more stakeholders in finding common treatments to complex issues. Think of biofuel governance in a European Union (EU) context: here, agricultural policies blend in with environmental concerns across different commissions to create an EU-wide standardized market for biofuels (Laurent 2015). At the same time, ongoing processes of regulatory standard setting at the global level, notably via a number of multi-stakeholder initiatives (Henriksen 2015) and intensive inter-governmental collaboration in technical standard-setting bodies such as the International Organization for Standardization (ISO) and the International Organisation of Legal Metrology (IOLM) has led to a complex regime of rules and policies that blend into the ongoing multi-level governance dynamics in Europe (Ponte and Daugberg 2015). A complex in which a considerable amount of professional mobility can be observed and where a new form of issue-specific governance professionalism is emerging from a blend of occupational and organizational values anchored in relatively *depoliticized yet highly professionalized* principles of sustainability management (Henriksen and Seabrooke 2016).

To the extent that a policy consensus emerges around issues, and in extension also policy cohesion across otherwise compartmentalized public policy institutions, such an outcome can be due to parallel, overlapping dynamics (Mahoney 2007; Kemfert 2004). One dynamic which has so far not been studied sufficiently is the role of issue professionals traversing the complex professional-organizational networks that are active in inducing or blocking consensus and convergence. This is the focus of this chapter and it consists of four sections. The first section introduces the concept of issue professionals as an important ideal type actor. The second section introduces issue control as an outcome of two-level network dynamics. While our focus is on professional networks, our framework also includes organizational networks. The third section locates hybridity as a key feature of contemporary interactions and argues that the increasing prominence of issue professionals stems in part from their ability to exploit opportunities in hybrid bodies. In the fourth section we present six trajectories where issue professionals act in differential ways to produce issue control.

Issue professionals

Professionals are individuals with abstract higher-level learning and specific skill sets to address tasks. Doctors and lawyers come to mind when we are to characterize what is exceptional about professional work. We suggest that transnationally professionalism is often linked tighter to issues than to formal boundaries of professional groups. We suggest that "issue professionals" are a particular type of professional who is engaged in transnational organizing and particularly important in how issues are treated and governed transnationally. Transnationality, as noted above, is important for their capacity to not conform to defined jurisdictional roles common in a national context. Rather than located in specific associations, such as the American Medical Association or the like, these professionals combine knowledge and skills to enhance their attempts at control on a specific issue. Rather than relying on the conventional link between professionals and organizations in how issues are addressed (Noordegraaf 2011), issue professionals actively foster professional and organizational networks in their attempts at issue control.

Issue professionals are different from "issue entrepreneurs" (Carpenter 2007). As a category, the concept of "issue entrepreneurs" is used to provide an actor-based explanation of issue emergence. Issue professionals are not necessarily inventors of issues, but they are involved in generating, maintaining, and defending attempts at issue control. There is also greater flexibility in how issue professionals determine their tasks in treating issues. Tasks include the modalities of action for professionals in how they classify, reason, and take action on identified problems, or how they diagnose, infer, and treat their identified problems (Abbott 1988). Changes to tasks can occur through processes of professionalization, including demands for conducting work in particular ways, according to codes of ethics, as well as treating professionalism as a capacity to manage and organize tasks rather than the knowledge and training that inform their execution (Faulconbridge and Muzio 2008; Evetts 2013). Issue professionals have particular tasks, but they are customized for the issue of concern rather than belonging to, and being reinforced by, one particular expert discipline. On issues that are highly technical and narrow, professional tasks and the transnational issue control may go hand in hand. Transnational organizing on the SARS and bird flu crises provide an example, where medical experts aligned with international organizations (IOs) to diagnose and treat the problems. Here "classic" professional tasks were closely matched to how a transnational issue was treated. In the domestic context, professional coordination can be made more difficult through jurisdictional battles over tasks and who is permitted to work on what issues. Transnationality matters here in liberating issue professionals to use their career experience and different skills in a context where domestic jurisdictions are not relied upon, can potentially be ignored, or are secondary in how issues are treated.

This is not to say that there are not struggles over who can work on what issues, but that issue professionals are not constrained to the common domestic understanding of national professional jurisdictions. Issue professionals have a strong incentive to maintain their position within a network by excluding others who do not agree with their understanding of issues or threaten their resources. In some areas, such as financial reform, issue professionals behave according to prestige incentives and will be reluctant to introduce controversial ideas and topics in which they have little expertise, such as shadow banking, or political power, such as tax havens. Rather, they will control debates in a manner that confirms their affiliations and prestige networks (Tsingou 2010; Seabrooke and Tsingou 2014). Similarly, as is well known in Organization Studies, professionals can network to ensure that knowledge production is under their control rather than by bureaucracies formally running the organization (Brivot 2011; Kamoche et al. 2011).

Investigating how professionals engage with their own peer networks and organizational networks is useful in considering how transnational organizing happens. We see transnational issues as organized through a professional-organizational nexus that is fruitfully conceived as a two-level network. We develop this idea further in the following section.

The professional-organizational nexus as a two-level network

We argue that it is a professional-organizational nexus that is the key to explaining how complex multi-level policy interactions play out. Professionals in our framework draw on organizational and professional networks at the same time – building alliances where they can to control how issues are treated. While others prefer to describe professionals as operating in organizational fields, we stress that both professionals and organizations have agency in forming strategies – and that neither provides a passive space for the other to operate within (Seabrooke and Henriksen 2017).

Understanding the professional-organizational nexus as a two-level network permits us to look at relations between two different sets of actors when it comes to processes of issue control. Our two-level network consists, first, of professional networks that are inter-personal and build throughout careers and activities linked to issue-specific work. Professionals will extend their networks through common identification with other similarly trained professionals, though often not through formal professional associations, or by creating alliances with professionals with different but complementary sets of skills. Those who manage to exploit opportunities to enhance their influence on an issue are likely to maximize issue control beyond their intrinsic organizational capacities. Second, organizational networks exist where alliances between organizations or their subunits endure in ways that do not hinge on specific professionals. The two analytically distinct levels of our network model should not be conflated with a multi-level governance system. Yet, when applied to multi-level governance dynamics, e.g. in a European Union context, an additional distinction between governance scales can be introduced – with organizational ties spanning local and national governments, inter-governmental bodies, and transnational bureaucracies as well as private regulatory institutions.

In fact, in such as context, professional networks are likely to be at the core of where network cohesion is established – cohesion that enables policy coordination, the diffusion of norms, and the dissemination of standards and work practices (see, most recently, Hylde and Hopwood 2019). Policy cohesion in multi-level systems, from this perspective, can very well come from the social cohesion arising from concrete interactions and ties traversing diverse institutions and governance actors operating at different levels, network theorists tell us. Within the EU the coordination of domestic political agendas with regulatory and administrative networks has been an important topic (Maggett and Gilardi 2011; Mastenbroek and Martinsen 2018).

It is important to note that social cohesion is not a given when seen through a network theoretical lens. Networks are equally characterized by tensions and conflict – dynamics that are often then associated with fragmentation in the structure of the network. Ron Burt's (1992, 2004) work on structural holes is informative here because it forces us to think about the structural-relational configuration of interest conflict between organizational actors such as between nation-states or between nation-states and inter-governmental bodies. Essential to Burt's theory though is that from such conflict – i.e., regions in the social structure marked by scarce network connectivity – also emerges opportunities for organization, and perhaps more importantly, individual agents to play off the conflicting parties against each other and to push for solutions that benefit those intermediary agents. Complexity here is not fathomless. Network theory asks us what kinds of complexity are at play in what context, and how specific forms of complexity inform actors' strategies and outcomes.

Figure 3.1 depicts an illustration of a simple two-level network that is involved in organizing a particular transnational issue. Organizations are networked on the top of the illustration, pursuing their strategies. Below them are professionals developing their own strategies and tactics through networks. Within such two-level networks prominent professionals are often "multiple insiders" (Vedres and Stark 2010) through shared memberships and participation in events, organizations, committees, commissions, expert groups, etc., through which they build their issue-specific personal networks, but also get access to varied organizational contexts. These professionals will often inhabit similar "thought worlds" across different organizational contexts (Baunsgaard and Clegg 2013), occasionally alerting organizations to potential conflicts with their particular objectives. Accordingly, organizations also strategize about where to send staff to participate in these events, committees, etc., which give them advantages in terms of access to knowledge but also give professionals opportunities beyond their pre-defined work role. To understand how cohesion might emerge in complex multi-level systems, the overlapping structure of institutions and social groups is important to consider. Cohesion in governance and policy is rarely an equilibrium outcome of boundedly rational actors striking a compromise; ironing out differences. Rather competition, struggle, and tensions can continue to inform behavior and dynamics in complex adaptive systems. Network positions, occupied by actors with their own strategies and tactics, are important to identify. Doing so can tell us about what professionals can block change by fueling ongoing

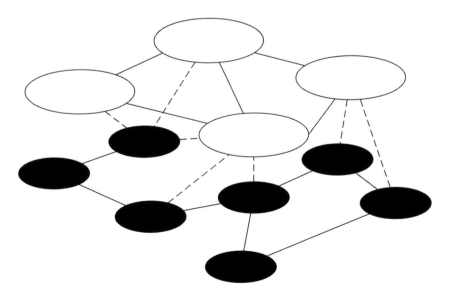

FIGURE 3.1 Professional-organizational two-level network. Source: Henriksen and Seabrooke 2016, 726.

conflicts, and who proposes the reform of old institutions, or the building of new ones.

Organizations also have a range of strategies in their attempts at issue control. One is to increase the technicality of the issue to fend off competitors without the necessary expertise or language (Büthe and Mattli 2011). If organizations control areas of expertise that are deemed legitimate as a solution to a given issue, or if professional and organizational logics overlap, this strategy may yield successful outcomes. But if expertise for the governance of a highly technical issue is not controlled by a particular organization, professionals may gain considerable discretion and develop strategies to control issues in a manner that differs from or opposes the organizations that seek to protect their control over an issue. Organizations may also pursue the strategy of politicizing or moralizing an issue, bringing principles and value to the fore to trump expert opinion. Also there may be issues that are beyond the formal mandate of public policy institutions and bureaucracies such as the EU Commission but which the Commission wishes to be informed about and potentially also inform unofficially. This requires their informal participation in, say, private or hybrid regulatory processes. This can be observed when Commission bureaucrats participate in multi-stakeholder bodies in non-binding policy conferences such as in the case of aviation biofuel standards (Henriksen and Ponte 2018). The opposite movement from private to public can be observed when think tanks, consultants, and lobbyists are invited into policy-making processes even when they have no direct mandate (Momani 2013, 2017).

Describing the professional-organizational nexus as a two-level network permits us to consider how professionals and organizations take positions on particular issues relative to their peers, as well as the character of the ties between those involved on the transnational issues. Our focus is not on networks as coherent actors unto themselves (cf. Kahler 2009) and more on professional and organizational interaction within networks. As such, professional and organizational networks must be studied through interaction on issues of concern, through the allocation and defense of professional tasks. We draw on network theory to assist us in doing so.

A key lesson from network analysts is that the formation of social alliances in attempts at achieving control cannot be fully understood by ever more subtle categories of groups and identities, but has to take seriously the concrete patterns of interaction in which individuals and organizations are embedded (Granovetter 1985, 1973). A network is a set of actors, or nodes, along with a set of specific relations that connect them. Relations in networks interconnect through shared points and thus form paths or pipes that indirectly link actors that would otherwise not be directly related. This conception enables a view of a network as a connected system, where local behaviors are linked to the system as a whole. Much network analysis is concerned with characterizing network structures and actor positions and relating structural properties and positions to group and actor outcomes. Network theory makes claims about the mechanisms and processes that interact with a network structure to allow certain actors in the network to act (Borgatti and Halgin 2011). In general, a network view of strategy pays attention to the flow of knowledge and resources between professionals and organizations and the strategic behavior emerging from their attempts to gain control over the ongoing distribution patterns within these flows.

Two-level networks also exhibit so-called "small world" network characteristics that have implications for the strategies of issue control that professionals and organizations may pursue. The idea of a small world comes from the experience that actors in a "big world" often experience being surprisingly close to each other (Watts 1999). For transnational organizing the professional networks have large geographical distances and the number of individuals and organizations doing work may be in the thousands. This multiplies the social distances across which organizing must be performed. Forging ties to central organizations can minimize these distances, creating what have been termed "global microstructures" (Knorr Cetina and Bruegger 2002). Such tie formation is often facilitated by pre-established inter-personal ties that establish trust about the motivations of counterparties. Small world characteristics come into place when the formation of a few ties decreases the average social distance between actors significantly. Even if these networks are clustered inside organizations or densely concentrated around organizational alliances or professional communities, a few connections across these clusters or alliances is likely to lead to the experience of the network as a small world. Through being central nodes in a network, professionals can use their skills and knowledge to shape the way organizations treat and organize issues (Kroeger 2011; Huang et al. 2016)

Understanding the character of ties between professionals is also important. We know that professionals build connections transnationally by spending otherwise valuable work time at seemingly inconsequential conferences or events that may actually be important in organizing how issues are treated (Lampel and Meyer 2008). This network activity can be experienced as superfluous, but exchanging business cards may actually be reason enough to contact a potential ally. Such "weak ties" may generate unique knowledge of activities that are at a greater social distance from an actor's immediate neighborhood (Granovetter 1973). This is not only useful for people who are searching for new challenges in their professional lives but also important in understanding why organizations value professionals who can demonstrate high job mobility.

Professionals of high job mobility that are not linked to any particular organization or organizational type can be seen as "weak but broad" in their embedding strategy across two-level networks. Their sources of knowledge as well as their reach for influence are likely to be more "robust" (Padgett and Ansell 1993; Bothner et al. 2010). When professionals occupy sparse network regions (Burt 2004) abundant with "structural holes" (Burt 1992), they are able to obtain new ideas about how to treat and control their issues. Structural holes are network locations where two nodes are disconnected, presenting an opportunity for a third node to bridge the gap and gain control of the flow of information between the otherwise disconnected nodes. In transnational arrangements, where network densities are often comparatively low, exploiting disconnections can be a successful strategy for organizations and professionals working to change perceptions on particular issues (Goddard 2009). While our aim here has not been to provide a thorough review of existing network theories, we wish to demonstrate that the structural properties of networks are important in understanding how agents can behave in two-level dynamics.

Hybrid two-level networks

Our general advice to students of networks and governance is to be wary about assuming the location and form of organizational action. Our analytical move has links to problematizations of organizational nominalism that has been voiced as part of the "relational turn" in sociology (Emirbayer 1997). Considering our two-level network framework enables us to render meaningful the hybridity of otherwise overwhelmingly complex patterns of interactions (see Figure 3.2), we suggest using explorative methods to make sense of hybrid interactions. Elsewhere we have advocated for the use of Social Network Analysis as a tool for locating important – or perhaps even unimportant – actors within governance fields. We have also demonstrated how sequence analysis of professional careers – identifying prominent career strings in a given field of governance – can be used to understand what skills and identities are valued among professionals and organizations in governance and what kinds of networks they engender (Henriksen and Seabrooke 2017). Below we present a hypothetical example of what an analysis combining the two methods might look like.

Let us say that this is a transnational hybrid network to govern standards on household chemicals. The legend in the top left of the figure provides the

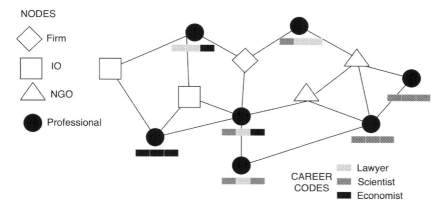

FIGURE 3.2 Issue professionals in a hybrid network. Source: Henriksen and Seabrooke 2017b, 296.

symbols for the nodes in the network, showing different organizational types (IOs, NGOs, firms) and professionals.

One can see in the diagram that some organizations are connected to each other and that professionals serve an important role in connecting some organizations that would otherwise not be connected. The professional in the center of the diagram is the most important in having significant ties to a firm, an NGO, and an IO, while these three organizations are not otherwise connected. Other brokers can be seen at the top of the diagram between a firm and an IO and, separately, between a firm and an NGO. Still, the broker in the middle is most important in controlling flows of knowledge within this network and in knowing at the field level where the issue is going. The legend at the bottom right of the diagram provides shades for career codes according to roles during a career as a lawyer, scientist, or economist. There are only three stages here for simplicity and could easily be different work roles and types of career experience rather than nominated by formal training. From our abstract example it can be seen that our central broker has a mixed career history and was a scientist, then a lawyer, then an economist. The two brokers at the top also have mixed careers, with a lawyer who became an economist, and a scientist who became a lawyer. They provide a contrast to those with steady careers as economists (on the left) or scientists (on the right) who are networked within their own professional community and organizational types, but not across types. From this hypothetical example we can speculate on who controls knowledge in this network and the drivers of transnational standard setting. We can note that mixed career histories may be important for "intrepid brokers" in having resources to make connections to different types of organizations on an issue (Burt 2010), as well as assessing how organizational characteristics matter in assisting or inhibiting such entrepreneurship (such as those listed in the previous section).

We may also wonder about the professional at the bottom of the diagram who has ties to other professionals but no formal ties to an organization, and if this person has power in this network. To find this out we would have to delve further using different methods, such as ethnographic interviews. We may also want to differentiate career roles and network locations from actual positions toward home chemical use, such as cost and efficiency questions, the legality of patents and use, and the risks and dangers of use on the inhabitants. This would require determining what is at stake for the different professionals and experts involved, as investigated using Bourdieusian "field" methods (Madsen 2018). A combination of ethnographic research and field methods could also establish positions on a subject as well as means of influence within the "advice networks" formed by those involved (Lazega 2001). Using a mix of methods we can distinguish not only professional and organizational characteristics but also different types of activities.

The above methods could be used to further clarify the distinction between what we call "issue professionals" and "issue entrepreneurs" and how they operate in two-level networks (Carpenter 2011; Seabrooke and Tsingou 2014, 402). We already have a range of clues to draw upon. Consider the composition and mandates of "Expert Committees" or "Taskforces". Organizations commonly use expert committees to provide external validation for internal reform. For example, the International Monetary Fund was formally advised by the amusingly named "Committee of Eminent Persons" – led by the late Andrew Crockett, former Director General of the Bank for International Settlements and President of JPMorgan Chase International – to reform its fundamental business model (Seabrooke and Nilsson 2015: 243). Such committees explicitly rely on what we call "issue professionals" – people with a long-term interest in maintaining control over an issue and who strategize to maintain their networks – in doing so, relying on career prestige and professional recognition as sources of legitimacy and authority.

Independent taskforces are more likely to be comprised of issue entrepreneurs who wish to push forward a cause independent of organizational mandates, and where experience can be drawn upon as a source of authority (Eyal 2013; Seabrooke and Tsingou 2015). The issue entrepreneur versus issue professional distinction also helps us distinguish how experts engage power. While the stress in the literature has been on how professionals, notably economists, are used by politicians (Lindvall 2009; Hirschman and Berman 2014; Henriksen 2013), the influence of experts is not only a function of how they are politically manipulated but also what they are willing to do. Using the methods outlined above we can distinguish different types of professionals in transnational governance, including whether they rely on occupational or organizational professional competencies (Faulconbridge and Muzio 2011). We can further distinguish organizational behavior that provides professionals with mandates and how professionals use different forms of organizing.

Trajectories of issue control

Professional strategies vary across cases, in how centralized and distributed they are, with some professional strategies aligning well with organizational strategies, while in other cases professionals actively work around organizations in their attempts at issue control, or view organizations as arenas for their activities. We hasten to add that organizational opportunities are determined by organizational strategies to dominate an issue.

Figure 3.3 depicts abstract conceptions of trajectories of issue control. The illustrations are abstract, depicting organizations as black circles and professionals as white circles, with the process of change indicated by the directed arrows. We draw examples from the contemporary literature on transnational governance to illustrate how they work.

The first identified trajectory of issue control is *decoupling*. Here the process starts from the interaction between a known organization and an established professional group. This professional group then fractures and decouples, and

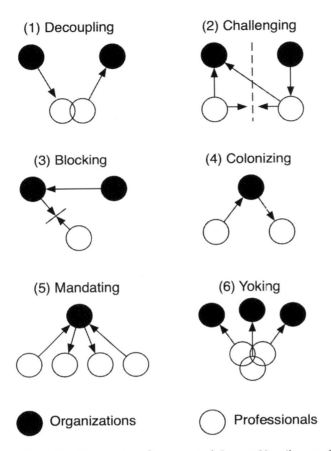

FIGURE 3.3 Trajectories of issue control. Source: Henriksen and Seabrooke 2017b, 288.

then seeks to influence an organization that is more responsive to its demands for issue control. A case can be found in Thistlethwaite and Paterson's (2016) investigation of environmental and social disclosure in accounting. From left to right we have accounting firms as organizations and the accountancy profession as an established group. Within this group are professionals who decouple from "purist" accountancy to foster the use of environmental and social reporting standards. To do so they engage in "epistemic arbitrage", playing off differences in knowledge between accountancy firms and NGOs (Seabrooke 2014). They then use this strategy to directly inform NGOs as organizations and their treatment of environmental and social reporting issues.

Challenging is our second trajectory of change. Here a parallel professional group and organization form to push and criticize established issue treatment. The parallel professional group is not decoupled in the sense of creating a new dimension of professional work. The friction between professionals in *challenging* is more about normative tensions and what is deemed appropriate knowledge for issue treatment. It is also about carving out organizational alliances that provide professionals with resources and a platform for critique. A case can be found in Eagleton-Pierce's (2018) study of how "critical technicians" challenge international trade policy and transnational standards. Eagleton-Pierce details how a parallel system exists that engages the WTO (the first organization) and its associated experts (the first professional group). With support from Oxfam (the second organization) a group of critical technicians (the second professional group) formed to actively contest trade experts and to inform the WTO on issue treatment.

Our third trajectory of change is *blocking*. Sending's (2015) studies of humanitarian professionals provide a clear case of this dynamic. Sending details how an international organization (the first organization) can come under pressure from donor states (the second organization) on humanitarian issues, especially for professional work in the field to be standardized, to make it more efficient and accountable to them. The international organization then seeks to place pressure on the issue professionals (the professional group of humanitarian workers) who resist and block change by appealing to a different standard of professional behavior. For them, "bearing witness" is more important than top-down efficiency measures. Cohesion within the professional group allows them to block change.

Colonizing is our fourth trajectory. This can be found in Boussebaa's (2015, 2017) work on core-periphery relationships in global professional service firms and their operations. Boussebaa describes how Western professionals (the first professional group) work through a global professional service firm (the organization in the diagram) in a unidirectional manner that imposes defined forms of issue treatment. These are replicated and enforced through knowledge management systems and the cultivation of internal professional hierarchies (see also Hasselbalch and Seabrooke 2018).

Our fifth and sixth trajectories speak to general phenomena. Fifth is *mandating*, where professional groups (on the far left and far right in the diagram) work to impose particular forms of issue treatment on other professionals (the center professional groups) via organizations. Examples of mandating can be found far and wide. A recent example is Littoz-Monet's (2017) work on how bureaucrats within UNESCO actively engaged external professionals to provide them with "epistemic authority" on bioethical standards, which then permitted them to impose a depoliticized view of the issue on other professionals.

Our final trajectory is *yoking*. Yoking is when a new professional group is created from boundary interactions between different established groups. Yoking can occur when established professional boundaries are delegitimized or when new boundaries are accentuated (Abbott 2001, 272–273). A good example can be found in Karlsrud and Mühlen-Schulte's (2017) study of semi-professional "mapsters", a group of professionals within the UN system of humanitarian affairs who brought in skills from IT and "big data" professionals (the lower professional groups) to advance a new mapping technology to identify humanitarian crises. Forming a cohesive network around the Standby Action Taskforce, they challenged established professional boundaries of humanitarian work and succeeded in placing themselves between various UN agencies (the top organizations), changing how the issue of humanitarian crisis is identified and treated.

We suggest that decoupling, challenging, blocking, colonizing, mandating, and yoking are trajectories of change that not only appear in this volume but are also more generalizable. All of these strategies speak to the concept of a two-level professional-organizational network. This conceptual device permits us to study relationships between professionals and organizations while isolating the characteristics of both. For research looking to study issue control in an EU context, multi-level games between EU institutions and the member states would have to be reflected in the analysis.

Matching professional and organizational characteristics

An important claim in our approach is that professional characteristics matter for how networks are composed and articulated, and that these networks shape how policy is written and problems understood in transnational governance. The same applies for policy within the European Union and in relation to European actors that seek to navigate and influence issues within and across a variety of complex regimes.

If there is a general trend toward transnational organizing, then we need theoretical tools to disaggregate what may appear to be an isomorphic process (Henriksen and Seabrooke 2016). We suggest that our two-level network is a useful conceptual device here. It helps us to isolate professional characteristics, as discussed above. It also assists us in specifying why organizational types should not necessarily follow through to particular forms of behavior because the organizational network is responding to changes in the professional network, and vice versa. This, however, does not entail that organizations including governments are not important units of analysis. But it does entail that we need to think about how they operate in a different manner. We suggest that organizational forms and logics can be differentiated by five characteristics that become increasingly important as competition within professional networks intensifies:

1. *Scope* – the scope of their mandate
2. *Autonomy* – the level of autonomy they have from their principals
3. *Resources* – how they acquire resources to fund their activities
4. *Staffing* – the openness of hiring of professionals
5. *Knowledge centralization* – the degree of knowledge centralization within the organization on the issue they seek to control.

Scope, autonomy, resources, hiring, and knowledge centralization differ strongly within the conventional categories of IOs, NGOs, and firms. Common assumptions about interest formation as a linear process originating from organizational form have to be relaxed as a result. Reflecting on how professionals use networks to navigate organizational logics tends to follow these characteristics more than the formal designation of the organization. If patterns of professional competition lead to a widening of the overall scope of an issue, organizations must respond to such change.

Our general point here is that matching professional and organizational characteristics permits us to disaggregate assumed organizational traits into smaller components that more feasibly engage with professionals who create action. Rather than reifying and idealizing organizational types as fixed properties, we argue that organizational characteristics provide opportunity structures that can be exploited by professionals as they adapt to their environment by fostering their own networks.

References

Abbott, A. (1988) *The System of Professions*, Chicago: University of Chicago Press.
Abbott, A. (2001) *Time Matters*, Chicago: University of Chicago Press.
Baunsgaard, V.V. and Clegg, S.R. (2013) "'Walls or Boxes': The Effects of Professional Identity, Power and Rationality on Strategies for Cross-Functional Integration," *Organization Studies* 34(9): 1299–1325.
Borgatti, S.P. and Halgin, D.S. (2011) "On Network Theory," *Organization Science* 22(5): 1168–1181.
Bothner, M., Smith, E.B. and White, H.C. (2010) "A Model of Robust Positions in Social Networks," *American Journal of Sociology* 116(3): 943–992.
Boussebaa, M. (2015) "Professional Service Firms, Globalisation and the New Imperialism," *Accounting, Auditing & Accountability Journal* 28(8): 1217–1233.
Boussebaa, M. (2017) "Global Professional Service Firms, Transnational Organizing and Core/Periphery Networks," in L. Seabrooke and L. Henriksen (eds.) *Professional Networks in Transnational Governance*, Cambridge: Cambridge University Press, 233–245.
Brivot, M. (2011) "Controls of Knowledge Production, Sharing and Use in Bureaucratized Professional Service Firms," *Organization Studies* 32(4): 489–508.
Burt, R.S. (1992) *Structural Holes*, Cambridge, MA: Harvard University Press.
Burt, R.S. (2004) "Structural Holes and Good Ideas," *American Journal of Sociology* 110(2): 349–399.
Burt, R.S. (2010) *Neighbor Networks: Competitive Advantage Local and Personal*, Oxford: Oxford University Press.
Büthe, T. and Mattli, W. (2011) *The New Global Rulers: The Privatization of Regulation in the World Economy*, Princeton: Princeton University Press.
Carpenter, R.C. (2007) "Setting the Advocacy Agenda: Theorizing Issue Emergence and Nonemergence in Transnational Advocacy Networks," *International Studies Quarterly* 51(1): 99–120.
Carpenter, R.C. (2011) "Vetting the Advocacy Agenda: Networks, Centrality and the Paradox of Weapons Norms," *International Organization* 65(1): 69–102.
Eagleton-Pierce, M. (2018) "Professionalizing Protest: Scientific Capital and Advocacy in Trade Politics," *International Political Sociology* 12(3): 233–255.
Emirbayer, M (1997) "Manifesto for a Relational Sociology," *American Journal of Sociology* 103(2): 281–317.

Evetts, J. (2013) Professionalism: Value and ideology. Current sociology, 61(5-6), 778–796.
Eyal, G. (2013) "The Origins of the Autism Epidemic," *American Journal of Sociology* 118(4): 863–907.
Faulconbridge, J. and Muzio, D. (2008) "Organizational Professionalism in Global Law Firms," *Work, Employment and Society* 22(1): 7–25.
Faulconbridge, J. and Muzio, D. (2011) "Professions in a Globalizing World: Towards a Transnational Sociology of the Professions," *International Sociology* 27(1): 136–152.
Fourcade, M. (2006) "The Construction of a Global Profession: The Transnationalization of Economics," *American Journal of Sociology* 112(1): 145–194.
Goddard, S.E. (2009) "Brokering Change: Networks and Entrepreneurs in International Politics," *International Theory* 1(2): 249–281.
Granovetter, M. (1973) "The Strength of Weak Ties," *American Journal of Sociology* 78(6): 1360–1380.
Granovetter, M. (1985) "Economic Action and Social Structure: The Problem of Embeddedness," *American Journal of Sociology* 91(3): 481–510.
Hasselbalch, J.A. and Seabrooke, L. (2018) "Professional Strategies in Transnational Projects," in M. Saks and D. Muzio (eds.) *Professions and Professional Service Firms: Private and Public Sector Enterprises in the Global Economy*, London: Routledge, chapter 4, pp. 46–64.
Henriksen, L.F. (2013) "Economic Models as Devices of Policy Change: Policy Paradigms, Paradigm Shift, and Performativity," *Regulation & Governance* 7(4): 481–495.
Henriksen, L.F. (2015) "The Global Network of Biofuel Sustainability Standards-Setters," *Environmental Politics* 24(1): 115–137.
Henriksen, L.F. and Ponte, S. (2018) "Public Orchestration, Social Networks, and Transnational Environmental Governance: Lessons from the Aviation Industry," *Regulation & Governance* 12(1): 23–45.
Henriksen, L.F. and Seabrooke, L. (2016) "Transnational Organizing: Issue Professionals in Environmental Sustainability Networks," *Organization* 23(5): 722–741.
Henriksen, L.F. and Seabrooke, L. (2017). 'Networks and Sequences in the Study of Professionals and Organizations', in L. Seabrooke and L.F. Henriksen (eds) Professional Networks in Transnational Governance, Cambridge: Cambridge University Press: 50–64
Henriksen, L.F. and Seabrooke, L. (2017a). "Networks and Sequences in the Study of Professionals and Organizations," in L. Seabrooke and L.F. Henriksen (eds.) *Professional Networks in Transnational Governance*, Cambridge: Cambridge University Press, 50–64.
Henriksen, L.F. and Seabrooke, L. (2017b). "Issue Professionals and Transnational Organizing," in L. Seabrooke and L.F. Henriksen (eds.) *Professional Networks in Transnational Governance*, Cambridge: Cambridge University Press, 286–299.
Hirschman, D. and Berman, E.P. (2014) "Do Economists Make Policies? On the Political Effects of Economics," *Socio-Economic Review* 12(4): 779–811.
Huang, Y., Yadong, L., Liu, Y. and Yang, Q. (2016) "An Investigation of Interpersonal Ties in Interorganizational Exchanges in Emerging Markets," *Journal of Management* 42(6): 1557–1587.
Hydle, K.M. and Hopwood, N. (2019) "Practices and Knowing in Transnational Knowledge-Intensive Service Provision," *Human Relations*, https://doi.org/10.1177/0018726718815555
Kahler, M. (ed.) (2009) *Networked Politics: Agents, Power, and Governance*, Ithaca, NY: Cornell University Press.

Kamoche, K., Pang, M. and Wong, A.L.Y. (2011) "Career Development and Knowledge Appropriation: A Genealogical Critique," *Organization Studies* 32(12): 1665–1679.

Karlsrud, J. and Mühlen-Schulte, A. (2017) Quasi-Professionals in the Organization of Transnational Crisis Mapping," in L. Seabrooke and L.F. Henriksen (eds) *Professional Networks in Transnational Governance*, Cambridge: Cambridge University Press, 50–64.

Kemfert, C. (2004) "Climate Coalitions and International Trade: Assessment of Cooperation Incentives by Issue Linkage," *Energy Policy* 32(4): 455–465.

Knorr Cetina, K. and Bruegger, Ú. (2002) "Global Microstructures: The Virtual Societies of Financial Markets," *American Journal of Sociology* 107(4): 905–950.

Kroeger, F. (2011) "Trusting Organizations: The Institutionalization of Trust in Interorganizational Relationships," *Organization* 19(6): 743–763.

Lampel, J. and Meyer, A.D. (2008) "Field-Configuring Events as Structuring Mechanisms: How Conferences, Ceremonies, and Trade Shows Constitute New Technologies, Industries, and Markets," *Journal of Management Studies* 45(6): 1025–1035.

Laurent, B. (2015) "The Politics of European Agencements: Constructing a Market of Sustainable Biofuels," *Environmental Politics* 24(1): 138–155.

Lazega, E. (2001) *Micropolitics of Knowledge: Communication and Indirect Control in Workgroups*, New York: Aldine de Gruyter.

Lindvall, J. (2009) "The Real but Limited Influence of Expert Ideas," *World Politics* 61(4): 703–730.

Littoz-Monnet, A. (2017) "Expert Knowledge as a Strategic Resource: International Bureaucrats and the Shaping of Bioethical Standards," *International Studies Quarterly* 61(3): 584–595.

Madsen, M.R. (2018) Reflexive sociology of international law: Pierre Bourdieu and the globalization of law. In Research Handbook on the Sociology of International Law. Edward Elgar Publishing.

Maggetti, M. and Gilardi, F. (2011) "The Policy-Making Structure of European Regulatory Networks and the Domestic Adoption of Standards," *Journal of European Public Policy* 18(6): 830–847.

Mahoney, C. (2007) "Networking vs. Allying: The Decision of Interest Groups to Join Coalitions in the US and the EU," *Journal of European Public Policy* 14(3): 366–383.

Mastenbroek, E. and Martinsen, D.S. (2018) "Filling the gap in the European Administrative Space: The Role of Administrative Networks in EU Implementation and Enforcement," *Journal of European Public Policy* 25(3): 422–435.

Momani, B. (2013) "Management Consultants and the United States' Public Sector," *Business and Politics* 15(3): 381–399.

Momani, B. (2017) "Professional Management Consultants in Transnational Governance," in L. Seabrooke and L.F. Henriksen (eds.) *Professional Networks in Transnational Governance*, Cambridge: Cambridge University Press, 245–265.

Noordegraaf, M. (2011) "Remaking Professionals? How Associations and Professional Education Connect Professionalism and Organizations," *Current Sociology* 59(4), 465–488.

Padgett, J.F. and Ansell, C. (1993) "Robust Action and the Rise of the Medici, 1400–1434," *American Journal of Sociology* 98(6): 1259–1319.

Ponte, S. and Daugbjerg, C. (2015) "Biofuel Sustainability and the Formation of Transnational Hybrid Governance," *Environmental Politics* 24(1): 96–114.

Reay, M. (2012) "The Flexible Unity of Economics," *American Journal of Sociology* 118(1): 45–87.

Seabrooke, L. (2014) "Epistemic Arbitrage: Transnational Professional Knowledge in Action," *Journal of Professions and Organization* 1(1): 49–64.

Seabrooke, L. and Henriksen, L.F. (eds.) (2017) *Professional Networks in Transnational Governance*, Cambridge: Cambridge University Press.

Seabrooke, L. and Nilsson, E.R. (2015) "Professional Skills in International Financial Surveillance: Assessing Change in IMF Policy Teams," *Governance: An International Journal of Policy, Administration, and Institutions* 28(2): 237–254.

Seabrooke, L. and Tsingou, E. (2021) "Revolving Doors in International Financial Governance," *Global Networks*, 21(2): 294–319.

Seabrooke, L. and Tsingou, E. (2014) "Distinctions, Affiliations, and Professional Knowledge in Financial Reform Expert Groups," *Journal of European Public Policy* 21(3): 389–407.

Seabrooke, L. and Tsingou, E. (2015) "Professional Emergence on Transnational Issues: Linked Ecologies on Demographic Change," *Journal of Professions and Organization* 2(1): 1–18.

Sending, O.J. (2015) *The Politics of Expertise: Competing for Authority in Global Governance*, Ann Arbor: University of Michigan Press.

Thistlethwaite, J. and Paterson, M. (2016) "Private Governance and Accounting for Sustainability Networks," *Environment and Planning C: Government and Policy* 34(7): 1197–1221.

Tsingou, E. (2010) "Transnational Governance Networks in the Regulation of Finance—The Making of Global Regulation and Supervision Standards in the Banking Industry," in M. Ougaard and A. Leander (eds.) *Theoretical Perspectives on Business and Global Governance: Bridging Theoretical Divides*. London: Routledge, 138–155.

Vedres, B. and Stark, D. (2010) "Structural Folds: Generative Disruption in Overlapping Groups," *American Journal of Sociology* 115(4): 1150–1190.

Watts, D.J. (1999) *Small Worlds*, Princeton: Princeton University Press.

PART 2
Case studies in global networks and European actors

4

RULING IN A COMPLEX WORLD

Private regulatory networks and the export of European data protection rules

Guillaume Beaumier

Introduction

In today's global economy, markets are built on regulations developed in multiple jurisdictions and by multiple actors. As states open up their national economies, notably through the negotiation of bilateral and multilateral trade agreements, their domestic regulatory systems also start to interact (Bach and Newman 2007; Farrell and Newman 2010). Private companies nowadays have to consider how various jurisdictions may regulate differently the same activities before starting to produce many types of goods and services. States, however, no longer have a "monopoly position in the production of public goods" (Grande and Pauly 2005: 288). Both actors "above" and "below" the state now contribute to regulating various spheres of the economy (Abbott and Snidal 2009). International organizations, like the World Trade Organization (WTO) or Organization of Economic Co-operation and Development (OECD), regularly promulgate rules on issues ranging from taxation to intellectual property. Similarly, non-governmental organizations (NGOs) and business associations do not sit idly by while public actors decide how to regulate them. On the contrary, they increasingly take the role of rule-makers instead of rule-takers (Avant, Finnemore and Sell 2010; Cutler et al. 1999; Green 2013; Haufler 2001).

Taken together, all these initiatives create a complex international regulatory environment, which can be quite costly to comply with. In some cases, it might even make some economic activities entirely worthless. Both states and private actors thus have an interest in agreeing on a set of harmonized rules. Yet, the distributive effects of doing so will not be equally shared among all actors (Krasner 1991; Bach and Newman 2007). The ones who will succeed in projecting their rules onto others obviously stand to gain the most. Economically speaking, they would benefit from having access to wider markets with zero adaptation costs. More importantly, though, they would also be able to set the rules according to their normative preferences, which can trump any simple cost-benefit analysis. The European Union (EU) wants, for example, to have its food standards adopted globally not only for economic gains but also because it sees them as being normatively superior to those that exist in the United States (US).

In line with the puzzle of this book, a fundamental question is how can an actor, like the EU, succeed in having its rules adopted in such a complex system? Over the past decade, this simple question was at the heart of an important literature in international political economy (i.e., Bach and Newman 2007; Drezner 2007; Posner 2009; Farrell and Newman 2010; Young 2015). As the EU's role in shaping global market regulation grew over time, many authors similarly became interested in explaining the capacity of Europe to project its rules globally (Bradford 2012; Damro 2012; Lavenex 2014; Newman and Posner 2015). Together, these authors have developed an increasingly comprehensive framework of analysis to explain under which circumstances the EU (or another great power) can persuade other jurisdictions to adopt its rules. One common lacuna, though, is that they all give a rather limited role to private actors. Most of the time, they are either plainly disregarded or mentioned peripherally. As one exception, Newman and Posner specifically recognize that transnational actors and forums "often enjoy considerable rule-making authority" (2015: 1324). Yet they are analyzed as one element of the international institutional environment and thus no substantive explanation is given of how private actors influence which rules are applied globally. They are, moreover, portrayed as if they acted in isolation from each other, which actually hides how they can contribute to the diffusion of rules globally.

This chapter seeks to fill these gaps by highlighting the role played by *private regulatory networks* in exporting European data privacy rules to the United States (US) in the years following the adoption of the Safe Harbor Agreement (1998–2003). More precisely, it is argued that through their interactions with American private actors, European private actors helped diffuse EU data protection rules across the Atlantic. This supports a functional extension explanation, which emphasizes the "flexible and functionally specific" nature of global governance systems (Lavenex 2014: 888). At the same time, this does not mean that the EU did not play a central role in this process. On the contrary, I show that the EU actually influenced the shape of these private regulatory networks, notably by funding their activities, which in turn affected the capacity of the EU to export its rules on data privacy. As discussed by Godet and Orsini (Chapter 1), the network approach here helps to "round the angles" between the state-centric and world society's conceptualizations of the international system. In effect, this chapter shows that while the EU has the capacity to purposively influence the regulation of global issues like other classical foreign policy actors, it is embedded in both transgovernmental and transnational networks which can both limit and reinforce its actions. This means that the external regulatory influence or power of the EU also depends on the relationship between sectoral bureaucracies or, in the case of this chapter, private actors.

This chapter is divided into three sections to articulate this broad argument. The first reviews the literature on regulatory interdependence and the externalization of European policies in an increasingly complex international environment. It highlights the insufficient role that has been given to private regulatory networks and maintains that they should be included in order to better grasp how the EU or another jurisdiction can export its regulations. It then introduces the concept of private regulatory networks and discusses how a network approach can contribute to explaining how some actors have more or less regulatory influence. The second introduces the issue of data protection and explains how the American and European approaches diverge. It also emphasizes the essential role played by private actors in regulating the digital economy in both jurisdictions. The third finally shows how private regulatory networks, including both European and American private associations, have helped the EU export its rules to the US.

Rule-setting in a complex interdependent world

Just like goods and services, regulations frequently cross borders. Without necessarily always knowing it, citizens and companies all around the world often end up applying regulations that were developed outside of their main jurisdiction of activity. The most obvious situation in which this happens is perhaps when national laws have an extraterritorial scope of application. Many citizens recently became acquainted with this legal concept when the new General Data Protection Regulation (GDPR) entered into force. In effect, the GDPR now requires any private companies dealing with the personal data of Europeans to follow European rules, regardless of its place of activity. This is also the case with a number of countries applying their criminal law in an extraterritorial fashion. France, for example, can prosecute its citizens for crimes they have committed outside of its territory.

This extraterritorial application of national or regional laws is, however, not the only way that regulations can cross borders or influence foreign jurisdictions. In recent years, the interaction between domestic regulatory systems has often been more subtle and difficult to conceive. Foreign laws have notably been a source of inspiration or catalyst for the adoption of new regulations in some countries (Gilardi 2012). In some cases, private companies may also simply decide to abide by foreign rules for simplicity and to avoid duplication of costs. More than 20 years ago, David Vogel was already observing this phenomenon inside the US as many companies decided to follow the more stringent environmental rules developed in California, leading to a "trading up" phenomenon (1995). Nowadays, many believe the EU takes the role of California on the global stage (Vogel 2012; Young 2015).

In this context, conceiving domestic regulatory systems as closed systems, as certain research currently does, has many shortcomings (Fioretos 2011). While it can be a useful simplification, it obscures many ways through which states, and more generally our societies, interact with each other. As alluded to, it notably hides how one jurisdiction might indirectly end up applying the rules developed in another jurisdiction. To remedy this situation, it is relevant to adopt a "new interdependence approach" as suggested by Farrell and Newman (2014). In their seminal work, Keohane and Nye (1977) famously held that states were not necessarily independent from each other. As opposed to the predominant realist view of their time, they held that states were actually linked by multiple channels of contact involving multiple actors on a wide range of issues. Over the years, the literature adopting their initial insight became increasingly intertwined with institutionalism, which progressively came to see the concept of interdependence as an exogenous variable. As such, most studies ended up not considering how interests and institutions vary according to transnational interactions (Farrell and Newman 2014).

The new interdependence approach seeks to do the exact opposite. It aims to put back transnational interactions at the heart of the study of international politics and explain how they shape domestic institutions and their ability to affect global outcomes. In line with the puzzle of this book, a key question is again, how can an actor, like the EU, purposively influence the regulation of global issues? This question appears all the more relevant as the number of actors involved in global governance has exponentially grown over the years (Abbott and Snidal 2009). Next to states, there is now a plethora of private actors and international organizations, which contribute to regulating many areas of global production. This can notably be seen with the proliferation of the International Standards Organisation (ISO) norms with which most people interact every day. In such a complex regulatory environment, it is not obvious how one actor can impose its preferences. Yet, the EU influence in global regulation is increasingly recognized (Bradford 2012; Damro 2012; Lavenex and Schimmelfennig 2009; Newman and Posner 2015; Vogel 2012; Young 2015). Together, these authors identified a number of mechanisms behind the export of European rules, which Lavenex quite well divided into two types of external relations: (I) traditional foreign policy; and (II) functionalist extension (2014: 888).

The first type of external relation actually reflects "classical foreign policy analyses" (Lavenex 2014: 889), which puts forward a state-centric perspective of international relations. In the context of the EU, it presupposes that it has the same type of agency that traditional states are assumed to have. In other words, it is broadly viewed as a unitary entity whose interests are represented on the global scene by its government (i.e., the European Commission). Based on this type of external relation, the EU succeeds in exporting its rules when it both possesses sufficient material resources and the capacity to mobilize them strategically (Lavenex 2014: 889). Here, the EU finds itself in a hierarchical relationship where it can notably use political conditionality or legal authority to export its rules.

While having the most powerful effect on neighboring states wishing to formally join the EU, conditionality can also function with foreign states which only want to gain access to its internal market. Using the case of data protection in the transatlantic area, Bach and Newman (2007) argued that the EU was able to export its rules because of the strength of its internal market and the regulatory capacity it had built following the adoption of its Data Protection Directive (DPD) in 1995. One defining feature of the DPD was the creation of an institution – the Article 29 Working Party – which was tasked with advising European policymakers working on issues related to data protection and, perhaps more importantly, making adequacy decisions on third-country legislation (Bach and Newman 2007: 835). The capacity to make adverse adequacy decisions was significant because it meant that it could prohibit the transfer of Europeans' personal data to third countries. Practically speaking, it gave the EU the capacity to close its internal market to private companies wishing to do business online in Europe from countries with insufficient data protection rules. This effectively pushed countries, like Canada, to adopt privacy laws approximating European requirements (Bach and Newman 2007: 833).

This classical type of external relation can, however, only explain so much. Not all countries following the adoption of the DPD decided to modify their laws to sensibly reflect European rules. The US is obviously the most important case to come to mind as it never adopted a comprehensive privacy law, even though it was probably the country which stood to lose the most from an adverse EU adequacy decision. As the US was and still is the home of most of the largest global digital companies, it was more exposed to the potential negative consequences of being excluded from the European digital market. It thus had a great incentive to find a way to keep it open for its companies. In the end, it did so through the negotiation of the Safe Harbor agreement. The latter is a set of negotiated principles between the US and the EU, which US private companies had to voluntarily abide by if they wanted to collect and use personal data from Europeans. While they partly represent the European rules found in its DPD, the principles found in the Safe Harbor were not entirely similar. Yet, some still argued that American companies adopted rules only found in the DPD at the time. (Bamberger and Mulligan 2015). This export of European rules reflect the second type of external relation identified by Lavenex: the functionalist extension (2014).

As opposed to classical foreign policy analyses, a functionalist extension explanation does not focus on the EU direct capacity to impose its rules. It rather puts the emphasis on the capacity of the EU to indirectly project its rules via socio-economic interactions (Lavenex 2014). In this case, Lavenex identifies three different structures of interaction: community, network, and market (2014: 889). As of now, the market-type of interaction has been the most widely discussed mechanism in the context of the export of European data protection rules. It argues that a jurisdiction with a significant market and pushing for stricter rules will support a "trading-up" (Vogel 1995). In short, the idea is that as private companies prefer to follow one set of rules to reduce their compliance costs, they will decide to align themselves on the most stringent rules put forward by the largest economies. While both the EU and the US could set the rules according to this explanation, the EU has in recent years been particularly successful, so much so that many contributions talked about the "Brussels' effect"[1] to describe this phenomenon (Bradford 2012).

The main weakness of the market explanation is that it greatly overlooks all temporal considerations and simplifies the interactions between public and private actors. With regard to the issue of data protection, it does not explain when American private actors actually decided to apply European rules. Bradford, for example, maintains that US corporations have adopted "privacy policies that satisfy the EU requirements" following the adoption of the DPD (2012: 18). She does not explain, however, why few private companies actually joined the Safe Harbor agreement in the years following its negotiation (Farrell 2003: 286), even though all the scope conditions that she identified were present. Moreover, the market explanation mostly portrays private actors as acting in isolation from each other and according to a simple cost minimization logic.

It is here considered that a focus on network-type interactions can help solve these issues. As part of the functionalist extension explanation, Lavenex explains that the EU can also project its rules through "transgovernmental co-operation among regulators", which favors learning and socialization processes (Lavenex 2014: 890). Here, learning refers to a rational (i.e., Bayesian) process, while socialization follows the logic of appropriateness (Checkel 2005). Both can occur through formal and informal meetings between European and foreign officials. In the case of data protection, the International Conference of Data Protection and Commissioners (ICDPPC), which brings together data protection agencies of countries around the world, is notably a forum where both American and European regulators meet and exchange views on their respective data policies. According to Schwartz, a legal expert on transatlantic data privacy issues, these types of "harmonizing networks" are precisely what drive the future of data governance (2017: 174). In contrast to the market explanation, it emphasizes the gradual process through which rules can be exported following the creation of interconnections between regulators in different jurisdictions. However, one element that is missing from both Lavenex's and Schwartz's conceptualizations of their networks is that regulators do not need to only be governmental agencies. Green (2013) forcefully argued that private actors could show signs of "entrepreneurial authority", meaning that they can propose rules in the absence of delegation. Moreover, Braithwaite and Drahos convincingly showed that the globalization of regulation in a number of issue areas was the result of complex processes involving both public and private actors linked through complex "webs of regulatory influences" (2000: 31). In this book, Godet and Orsini (Chapter 1) actually point out that in addition to transgovernmental networks, international relation scholars have, over the years, looked at various types of networks involving non-state actors. Epistemic communities and transnational advocacy networks are two prominent examples.

In this chapter, I argue that private regulatory networks are another important type of network, which can notably help provide a better understanding of how the EU was able to export its data protection rules to the US. Private regulatory networks are understood as a mode of organization through which private actors who make rules to be adopted by other actors create lasting relationships with each other. As further explained below, two private associations will be considered to be linked with each other when they have worked together to develop a self-regulatory program. As discussed in both Godet and Orsini (Chapter 1) and Pattberg and Widerberg's (Chapter 2) chapters, these relations are assumed to allow the transfer of information and best practices. The structure of the network will, moreover, determine which actors get socialized or learn from whom.

At this stage, it is already important to reiterate that it is not the point of this chapter to show that private regulatory networks have been the sole factor at play. On the contrary, as the third section will explain, the export of European data rules has been successful because the EU was actually actively involved. As such, it highlights that the "classical foreign policy" and "functionalist extension" explanations in Lavenex's framework are not necessarily in opposition. In other words, the hierarchical and network mode of organization discussed in Godet and Orsini (Chapter 1) and Pattberg and Widerberg's (Chapter 2) chapters can actually be complementary. As discussed at greater length below, the adoption of the DPD and the Safe Harbor agreement created the impetus for American private associations to develop self-regulatory programs. The EU, moreover, influenced the shape of the private regulatory network, which led some American private associations to adopt European-type rules in their self-regulatory programs. Before going further in this reflection, the next section will introduce at greater length the case of data protection in the transatlantic area.

The transatlantic regulation of data protection and the role of private actors

Over the past 20 years, the Internet has dramatically altered the world economic landscape. Following its privatization in the mid-1990s, major businesses like Amazon and eBay broke new ground by using it for commercial purposes (Rothchild 2016: 2). Since then, consumers and producers throughout the world have been quick to join the electronic marketplace, so much so that e-commerce now seems ubiquitous. The rise in popularity of e-commerce is obviously due to the many new economic opportunities that it offers to both consumers and producers. The latter can now interact with each other more easily than ever, even when they are in two distant areas. Moreover, e-commerce supports the "servicification" or "dematerialization" of the economy, a process by which more and more goods are consumed as services. Perhaps more important, though, it allows private companies to collect and store the personal data of consumers to an extent inconceivable only a few years ago.

The potential of a data-driven economy has been widely praised. In 2011, a report by the McKinsey Global Institute notably maintained that Big Data[2] analytics was bringing us to "the cusp of a tremendous wave of innovation, productivity, and growth" (Manyika et al. 2011: 2). For example, according to their work, the annual value of Big Data analytics for Europe's public sector could amount to €250 billion. Five years later, a second report went even further and held that this predicted value was too conservative (Nicolaus et al. 2016).

In the contemporary context, the benefits of the use of data analytics have yet to fully materialize. While it remains to be seen to what extent it will really revolutionize our economies, perils have quickly appeared. The risks of privacy violations and uncompetitive practices have notably been pointed out by many experts (Ciocchetti 2007; Pasquale 2015; Stucke and Grunes 2016; Spencer 2016). In this context, many countries around the world reflected on the question of how to regulate the collection and use of personal data as early as the mid-1990s.[3] The US and the EU, as the two leading economies, were at the forefront of this discussion, promoting two different approaches.

The regulatory divergence between European and American approaches to data protection can be divided into three. First, at the most abstract level, both regulatory models have simply "different visions of data privacy" (Schwartz and Peifer 2017: 121). Even though both are based on a liberal paradigm, whereby privacy rights are conferred to an individual, they actually differ in their basic conceptions of these individuals. In Europe, individuals are seen as data subjects with a fundamental right to data protection. Meanwhile, in the US, individuals are seen as consumers who need to be protected from market abuses. Far from being a simple theoretical difference, these different views of the individual lead to different legal treatment of personal data. Most notably, the European regulatory system foresees that personal data should only be collected and processed with a valid legal basis. This requirement is reversed in the US where private companies can collect and process personal data as they see fit unless prohibited by law (Schwartz and Peifer 2017: 132).

Second, the EU and US approaches also differ in terms of their substantive rules to protect personal data. At the time of writing (March 2019), no comprehensive data privacy law exists in the US. They instead rely on a number of sectoral laws, notably dealing with children, health, and financial data, and on self-regulation by private companies. In the case of self-regulation, the Federal Trade Commission (FTC) did put forward a guideline in 1998 to help set a basic standard, but they remained voluntary. When compared to the European DPD or the recent GDPR, US regulations thus still lack many substantive protections (Schwartz and Peifer 2017: 137). In 2018, the state of California adopted privacy rules giving similar rights to the GDPR to its citizens. There are now talks in the US of adopting a federal privacy law to ensure a consistent level of protection across all federal states. It remains to be seen if or when that will happen considering that previous attempts at establishing a federal privacy law repeatedly failed.

Third, the EU and US also diverge in their view of the role of private regulations. While Europe is actually not against private actors' initiatives,[4] it does not believe they should lead. More precisely, private regulations are mostly seen as tools to help European regulators to implement their policies. In effect, the development of private regulations approximating European rules was seen as a way to ensure a uniform application of data protection rules all across Europe by the European Commission when it adopted its DPD in 1995. In contrast, since the publication by the White House of the Framework for Global Electronic Commerce in 1997, the US has maintained that states should not hamper innovations in the digital realm by adopting restrictive rules. Instead, it should rely on the capacity of private actors to self-regulate by adopting codes of conduct or guidelines. This, however, does not mean that the US government is entirely absent. In fact, it is generally recognized that it can more easily impose sanctions than the EU. The FTC, for example, sued a number of private companies for not complying with their own privacy policies. In light of this, Newman and Bach maintained that the US favored a legalistic approach to private regulation and the EU a coordinated approach (2004: 397).

These differences clashed when the EU adopted its DPD in 1995 and created an entity – the Article 29 Working Party[5] – which could impede the transfer of personal data from Europeans to third countries with insufficient data protection rules. As it became clear that the US would not be recognized as a third country with sufficient protection, both economies wished to find a solution to avoid economic losses. As previously mentioned, this came in the form of the Safe Harbor agreement, which established a set of principles that private companies could voluntarily decide to abide by and that could be enforced by a mix of public and private actions.

All of this activity in both the EU and the US spurred the development of private codes of conduct dealing with the issue of data protection. These codes of conduct are sets of rules that private associations encourage their members to apply in order to safely collect and use personal data online. As illustrated in Figure 4.1, the cumulative number of these codes promoted in the transatlantic area significantly increased at the beginning of the 2000s and following the negotiation of the Safe Harbor agreement.[6] As of 2019, there are now just a little bit less than 30 associations which actively promote rules on data protection in the US and the EU.[7]

Combined with the international actions taken by both the EU and the US, these private initiatives have since contributed to the creation of the global regime governing the digital economy (Ibáñez 2008). In effect, their decisions to self-regulate with regard to the collection and use of personal data affects the ways it is done on a daily basis. In the US, they clearly have a lot of room to do it as the

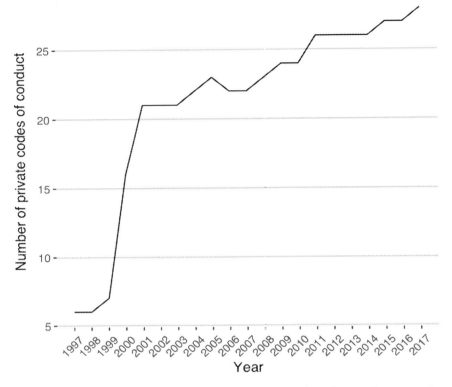

FIGURE 4.1 Cumulative number of active private codes of conduct on data protection in the Transatlantic area (Source: Author's data).

federal government wants to see them behind the wheel, but even in Europe they can play an important role. Private associations are most notably not impeded from building upon the rules put forward by public actors. Data controllers from the private sector actually often do more than what is requested from them by public authorities (Bamberger and Mulligan 2015). As it is quite burdensome to change public regulations, there is actually a case to make that private actors can more easily adapt their rules to fit the fast-paced reality of technological change. Aware of this fact, the Article 29 Working Party, an EU body created by the European DPD, actually worked with private actors to ensure that they would respect the spirit of the Directive.

In such a complex regulatory environment, networks can help exchange information and, concomitantly, facilitate the transfer of rules from one actor to another. The next section will more precisely highlight how the creation of private regulatory networks helped the EU export its rules in the years following the negotiation of the Safe Harbor agreement. It will also show how the EU was also able to purposively influence the role of private regulatory networks.

Private regulatory networks in action: European data protection approach travels across the Atlantic

From 1997 to 2003, 21 private codes of conduct were developed in the transatlantic area.[8] Among them, we find codes developed by private associations like TRUSTe (now TrustArc) and the Council of Better Business Bureau (BBB) in the US; the Federation of European Direct and Interactive Marketing (FEDMA) and Eurocommerce in the EU; and the Global Business Dialogue on e-Commerce (GBDe) and the International Chamber of Commerce (ICC) in transnational forums involving both European and American companies. While all cover the issue of data privacy, they all diverge with regard to the requirements that they set for private companies. In effect, some contain an extensive list of rules, whereas others entail almost no obligations for private companies.

Importantly, these 21 codes of conduct were not static over time. Between 1997 and 2003, most of them were actually revised multiple times by the private associations supporting them. To analyze their evolution and check the influence of European rules in the US, this last section builds on an extensive coding of almost all these codes. In the end, 72 different rules were identified based on both previous research (i.e., Cavoukian and Crompton 2002) and an inductive analysis. These 72 rules are divided into 14 sub-categories, which range from transparency to data use limitations.[9] To give an example, the first norm is described as follows:

01.01 Privacy statement

- Include the obligation for data controllers to publish a privacy notice or statement on their website
- Include any mention that a data controller should broadly inform or describe its privacy practices to data subjects

All private codes of conduct previously identified were then checked to see which of the 72 rules they included. The first observation that comes out of this exercise is that there was a clear trend toward the adoption of more and more comprehensive private codes, both in the US and the EU. From codes which had sometimes even less than ten rules, we moved toward an environment where most codes included at least 20 rules. This significant shift actually mirrors the boom in the number of private codes at the end of the 1990s (see Figure 4.1) and is obviously no stranger to the negotiation of the Safe Harbor agreement, which was putting a lot of pressure on private actors to self-regulate.

This rise in both the number of codes of conduct and of rules per codes, notably in the US, certainly plays well with the theory of the "Brussels' effect" (Bradford 2012). Again, it helds that the combination of the European market size with its regulatory capacity made it compelling for private actors to adopt privacy rules in the US, even though no federal laws required them to do so. The international negotiation of the Safe Harbor agreement can then either be seen as a catalyst or a way to institutionalize this mechanism of rule export.

Yet, as powerful as this explanation looks to be, it does not capture everything. For one, it does not explain the variation in the level of integration of European rules in private codes of conduct. Even though all private codes of conduct moved toward more comprehensive codes of conduct, not all adopted the same rules. Most notably for this research, some American private associations went further than others in incorporating European rules found in the DPD. In fact, some went as far as using concepts from the European human rights' vision of data privacy in their codes as it will be shown below. A second lacuna of the "Brussels' effect" explanation is that it does not explain the time effect. As previously mentioned, it mostly holds that after the EU adopted its rules for privacy, foreign private actors, including American ones, were under increasing pressure to adjust their activities to European standards. Why it took longer for some actors to do so is a question that is completely disregarded. This second source of variance, however, seems worth looking at as it might shed light on a different mechanism through which regulations cross borders.

Both the variation in content and adoption time of private codes of conduct actually appear to be explained by looking at private regulatory networks. In fact, next to the adoption of private codes of conduct, it is noteworthy that private associations in both the EU and the US also exchanged best practices and even worked to jointly develop rules for data privacy. A group of private actors under the leadership of both consumer and business groups notably worked on the development of a European-wide trustmark. While primarily targeting EU actors, it included important transnational associations like the GBDe and the ICC, which represent American private companies. Moreover, the BBB, FEDMA, and Eurochambres also agreed to work to merge their codes of conduct. These initiatives contributed to establishing private regulatory networks, as depicted in Figure 4.2.

Figure 4.2 more precisely depicts the evolution of the interactions between private associations active across the US and the EU. The nodes represent the private associations which were promoting a code of conduct on data protection in 1997 and 2002. European associations are moreover depicted with a circle, while non-European associations are in square. A link was established between two nodes when two organizations had official and sustained interaction. This was considered to be the case when it was mentioned on the website of one of the organizations that it was collaborating with the other or when two organizations collaborated on a specific project (i.e., development of a code of conduct) together. As we can see, two years after the EU had adopted its DPD there were very few organizations that had direct interactions. The only two transatlantic links (i.e., FEDMA – DMA & IBA Europe – IAB) were, moreover, between sister organizations. This can be explained by the fact that self-regulation in this area was relatively new. Five years later, the picture was completely different. There were still many associations that did not have interactions with their

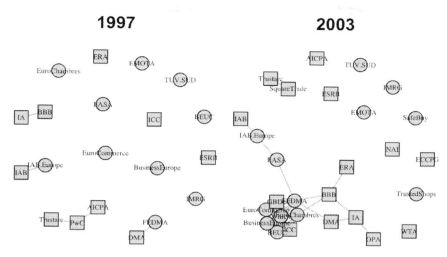

FIGURE 4.2 Evolution of transatlantic private regulatory networks on data protection 1997–2003 (Source: Author's data).

counterparts, but there was also a cluster of organizations that had appeared, which included both American and European private actors.

As discussed in the first section, networks can help rules move across borders by fostering learning and socialization (Lavenex 2014). It is notoriously difficult to differentiate the various diffusion mechanisms (Meseguer 2005), and in this case, know if private actors learn or were socialized. This chapter deliberately does not try to do so. It is, however, possible to observe that network interactions do have an impact on the diffusion of rules. It stands out that the ICC, GBDe, and BBB, three private associations representing American interests, all became closer to the European model of privacy protection after interacting with European private associations.

In the case of the ICC, it is not purely an American association. It actually represents private companies in more than 100 countries. This, however, also means that it does not represent only European interests. As it represents such a diverse set of private companies, we could have expected that its code of conduct for privacy was going to be more "American" as it is more flexible and less constraining. Nevertheless, it is striking that it went as far as adopting the European narrative on rights associated with data protection. In its code on advertising and marketing online of 2001 it clearly made mention of data subject's rights, something that is still not accepted by all active codes of conduct in the US, which continue to approach it as a consumer protection issue. In addition, the 2001 ICC code includes some substantive rules that were not present in codes developed by other American associations (i.e., Trustee and Webtrust). This includes rules requiring that companies should not keep personal data for longer than necessary and that they should obtain consent before sharing personal data with third parties. These are rules that clearly reflect the European DPD and were promoted by European private associations with which the ICC interacted while working on the European trustmark.

In comparison to the ICC, the BBB is an American association. Since 1912, this organization has worked to develop trust in the American and Canadian markets. It does so by building industry self-regulation like the BBB online code of conduct that it developed for data protection in 2000. In this code, the BBB did not go as far as the ICC in its adoption of the European approach. It did not, for example, adopt the European rights' narrative alluded to above. However, it interestingly still borrowed the term "data subjects" to speak of the users at the source of the data collected. This might not seem so important, but this language is actually purely European. Other American codes of conduct or the FTC guidelines talk of consumers when dealing with data privacy issues. Again, this might not change a lot "on the ground", but it shows that the BBB was influenced or, at least, aware of what was going on in Europe. It is thus also not surprising to see that it adopted substantive European rules found in the DPD, like the need to obtain the consent of an individual before sharing their personal data with other companies.

Finally, the GBDe was a transnational actor that was active, as with the ICC, from the end of 1999 to 2012. It was actually one of the first industry-led initiatives specifically aimed at developing rules for e-commerce. It rallied together CEOs of many leading companies on e-commerce. As such, it cannot be said that it is intrinsically an American actor. However, as many of the largest e-commerce companies were, and actually still are, American, one might assume that its approach would mostly reflect the American approach. In effect, its code clearly uses the language traditionally found in the US. The division of its code adopted in 2000 also closely follows the FTC guidelines. At the same time, it includes rules on data retention and data sharing similar to those found in the European DPD. We can thus, once again, observe and infer that its rules became closer to the European ones after having interacted with European private associations.

As previously hinted, these results should, however, not be interpreted as meaning that private regulatory networks were devoid of public influence. It is obviously impossible to deny that the adoption of the DPD and the negotiation of the Safe Harbor agreement clearly pushed private actors in both the EU and the US to adopt private codes of conduct. It, moreover, appears that the transatlantic private regulatory network depicted in Figure 4.2 was significantly shaped by the EU. In effect, the EU repeatedly used its regulatory capacity to force private actors to work together. For example, the group of private actors which worked on a European-wide trustmark did so as part of the Action plan "eEurope 2005" developed by the European Commission (EC 2011). Meanwhile, while FEDMA was partnering with the BBB to merge their rules, it was also working with the Article 29 Working Party to have the first private code of conduct approved by the EU.

This actually shows that various structures of interaction can simultaneously be at play in the transfer of rules across borders. In effect, it clearly appears that the EU used its hierarchical position to force private associations to work together. At the same time, the EU was not in a situation where it could control which organizations would be part of this network and what information would be shared. These were actually left to the internal dynamics of the private regulatory network being developed in this case. As such, the export of European data rules was both the result of "classical foreign policy" and "functionalist extension", which are the two types of external relations that were precisely identified by Lavenex (2014).

Conclusion

This chapter made the argument that private regulatory networks play an important role in the governance of the digital economy. More specifically, it maintained that they actually helped the EU export its rules to the US. In doing so, it built on the concepts of market power in Europe (Damro 2012) or the "Brussels' effect" (Bradford 2012). Following the recognition that EU market size certainly pushed private associations in the US to adopt codes of conduct to self-regulate, it argued that private regulatory networks could help in understanding how and when European data protection rules were adopted by private actors in the US. This brought to the forefront the reality that the EU is part of a complex regulatory system, which is not only made of public but also of private regulations.

In addition to giving a greater role to private actors, focusing on private regulatory networks also allows us to understand why not all private actors act alike. Or, in this case, why do they not all adopt the same rules and at the same time? As explained, this variance in terms of content and adoption time can partly be explained by the links that private actors share with each other. Through their interactions, private actors effectively share their respective practices, learn from each other and get socialized to follow a specific set of rules. Depending on whom they work with, private actors will tend to adopt a different set of rules. In this case, the ICC, BBB, and GBDe all started to adopt an approach more similar to the one put forward in Europe after having interacted with European private associations.

In line with other chapters in this book, this chapter shows that the EU can benefit from various types of networks to purposively influence the regulation of global issues, like data protection. Rather than having to solely rely on its hierarchical or market position, it can notably benefit from the multiple interactions that European private actors entertain with their counterparts in other countries to project its rules in other jurisdictions. In the present case, the EU couldn't succeed in making the US adopt its vision of data protection, but it was still able to indirectly push American private actors toward its regulatory model. Interestingly, this does not mean that public actors have no part to play. As indicated in the last section, the European Commission played a crucial role in pushing private actors to self-regulate and the creation of the transatlantic private regulatory network working on the issue of data protection. In doing so, it helped European actors to be relatively more important than their American counterparts. As seen in Figure 4.2, European actors clearly ended up being at the heart of this network. Again, this shows that both types of external relations identified by Lavenex (i.e., classical foreign policy and functionalist extension) can be at play at the same time. It similarly illustrates that a network approach can help bridge the divide between the "state-centric and world society" views of the international system (Godet and Orsini, Chapter 1). In effect, it was argued in this chapter that the EU has the legal authority to act as a traditional international actor, but it is also embedded in global networks that can limit or increase its influence.

With the adoption of the GDPR by the EU in 2018 and an increasing interest to regulate the digital economy in the US, it will be interesting going forward to see how this will affect the role of private actors and private regulatory networks. One result of the GDPR was clearly to further increase the regulatory capacity of the EU. The clear extraterritorial application of the GDPR now makes it increasingly difficult for American private actors to ignore European rules. Additionally, the significant increase in fines that the European Commission could potentially apply following any type of privacy violations will put more pressure on private actors to follow the letter of the GDPR. In that context, it could be assumed that private regulatory networks will play a less important role in the future as foreign digital companies processing European data will be directly asked to adopt EU data protection rules. At the same time, many grey zones remain with regard to how the GDPR should be applied. Private regulatory networks, in this context, remain crucial in facilitating a consistent implementation of the GDPR across jurisdictions.

Notes

1 Interestingly, this market explanation was initially developed by Vogel, who dubbed it the "California effect". In his case, he highlighted that the state of California was able to influence regulations in other American states.
2 Big Data is generally defined in terms of four Vs: Volume, Velocity, Variety, and Veracity. Some have recently added Value to this list of characteristics.
3 Debates on the protection of personal data were actually not new in the mid-1990s. Following the invention of the computer, many European countries actually adopted their first regulation on data protection in the 1970s (Newman 2008). The use of the Internet for commercial purposes, however, created a new impetus to discuss data protection regulations.
4 The DPD and the GDPR contain an article promoting the adoption of codes of conduct by private actors.
5 The Article 29 Working Party has now been replaced by the European Data Protection Board in the GDPR.
6 These codes were all identified following an exhaustive review of literature (e.g. Nannariello 2001; Farrell 2003; EC 2011).
7 This number actually only includes private codes applied in all the US, Europe, or both. Private codes developed only for one European country or one American federal state were not included.

8 All codes of conduct were found online on the respective website of each private associations. The Internet archive and, most notably, its Wayback Machine tool was used to access codes of conduct, which had been taken down by a private association following the adoption of a revised version.
9 The full list of 14 sub-categories is found in Annex 1.

References

Abbott, Kenneth W. and Duncan Snidal. 2009. "The Governance Triangle: Regulatory Standards Institutions and the Shadow of the State." In *The Politics of Global Regulation*, ed. Walter Mattli and Ngaire Woods. Princeton, NJ: Princeton University Press, pp. 44–88.

Avant, Deborah D., Martha Finnemore and Susan Sell. 2010. *Who Governs the Globe?* Cambridge: Cambridge University Press.

Bach, David and Abraham L. Newman. 2007. "The European Regulatory State and Global Public Policy: Micro-Institutions, Macro-Influence." *Journal of European Public Policy* 14(6): 827–846.

Bamberger, Kenneth A. and Deirdre K. Mulligan. 2015. *Privacy on the Ground: Driving Corporate Behavior in the United States and Europe*. Cambridge, MA: MIT Press.

Bradford, Anu. 2012. "The Brussels Effect." *Northwestern University Law Review* 107(1): 1–68.

Braithwaite, John and Peter Drahos. 2000. *Global Business Regulation*. Cambridge: Cambridge University Press.

Cavoukian, Ann and Malcolm Crompton. 2002. *Web Seals: A Review of Online Privacy Programs*. Ontario: Information and Privacy Commissioner.

Checkel, Jeffrey T. 2005. "International Institutions and Socialization in Europe: Introduction and Framework." *International Organization* 59(4): 801–826.

Ciocchetti, Corey A. 2007. "E-Commerce and Information Privacy: Privacy Policies as Personal Information Protectors." *American Business Law Journal* 44(1): 55–126.

Cutler, Claire A., Virginia Haufler and Tony Porter. 1999. *Private Authority and International Affairs*. Albany: State University of New York Press.

Damro, Chad. 2012. "Market Power Europe." *Journal of European Public Policy* 19(5): 682–699.

Drezner, Daniel W. 2007. *All Politics Is Global – Explaining International Regulatory Regimes*. Princeton, NJ: Princeton University Press.

EC. 2011. *EU Online Trustmarks – Building Digital Confidence in Europe*. Publications Office of the European Union. https://ec.europa.eu/digital-single-market/en/news/eu-online-trustmarks-building-digital-confidence-europe-smart-20110022.

Farrell, Henry. 2003. "Constructing the International Foundations of E-Commerce – The EU-US Safe Harbor Arrangement." *International Organization* 57(2): 277–306.

Farrell, Henry and Abraham Newman. 2010. "Making Global Markets: Historical Institutionalism in International Political Economy." *Review of International Political Economy* 17(4): 609–638.

Farrell, Henry and Abraham Newman. 2014. "Domestic Institutions beyond the Nation-State: Charting the New Interdependence Approach." *World Politics* 66(2): 331–363.

Fioretos, Orfeo. 2011. *Creative Reconstructions: Multilateralism and European Varieties of Capitalism after 1950*. Ithaca: Cornell University Press.

Gilardi, Fabrizio. 2012. "Transnational Diffusion: Norms, Ideas, and Policies." In *Handbook of International Relations*, ed. Walter Carlsnaes, Thomas Risse and Beth Simmons. Thousand Oaks: SAGE Publications, pp. 453–477.

Grande, Edgar and Louis W. Pauly. 2005. *Complex Sovereignty: Reconstituting Political Authority in the Twenty-First Century*. Toronto, ON: Toronto University Press.
Green, Jessica F. 2013. *Rethinking Private Authority: Agents and Entrepreneurs in Environmental Governance*. Princeton, NJ: Princeton University Press.
Haufler, Virginia. 2001. *A Public Role for the Private Sector: Industry Self-Regulation in a Global Economy*. Washington, DC: Brookings Institution Press.
Ibáñez, Josep. 2008. "Who Governs the Internet? The Emerging Regime of e-Commerce." In *Transnational Private Governance and its Limits*, ed. Jean-Christophe Graz and Andreas Nölke. Abingdon: Routledge. chapter 10, pp. 142–155.
Keohane, Robert O. and Joseph S. Nye. 1977. *Power and Interdependence*. Boston: Little Brown.
Krasner, Stephen D. 1991. "Global Communications and National Power: Life on the Pareto Frontier." *World Politics* 43(3): 336–366.
Lavenex, Sandra. 2014. "The Power of Functionalist Extension: How EU Rules Travel." *Journal of European Public Policy* 21(6): 885–903.
Lavenex, Sandra and Frank Schimmelfennig. 2009. "EU Rules beyond EU Borders: Theorizing External Governance in European Politics." *Journal of European Public Policy* 16(6): 791–812.
Manyika, James, James Chui, Brad Brown, Jacques Bughin, Richard Dobbs, Charles Roxburgh and Angela Hung Byers. 2011. *Big Data: The Next Frontier for Innovation, Competition, and Productivity*. McKinsey Global Institute.
Meseguer, Covadonga. 2005. "Policy Learning, Policy Diffusion, and the Making of a New Order." *Annals of the American Academy of Political and Social Science* 598(1): 67–82.
Nannariello, Guido. 2001. *E-commerce and Consumer Protection: A Survey of Codes of Practice and Certification Processes*. Brussels, Belgium: European Commission, Joint Research Centre.
Newman, Abraham. 2008. *Protectors of Privacy: Regulating Personal Data in the Global Economy*. Ithaca, NY: Cornell University Press.
Newman, Abraham and David Bach. 2004. "Self-Regulatory Trajectories in the Shadow of Public Power: Resolving Digital Dilemmas in Europe and the United States." *Governance* 17(3): 387–413.
Newman, Abraham and Elliot Posner. 2015. "Putting the EU in its Place: Policy Strategies and the Global Regulatory Context." *Journal of European Public Policy* 22(9): 1316–1335.
Nicolaus, Henke, Jacques Bughin, Michael Chui, James Manyika, Tamim Saleh, Bill Wiesman and Guru Sethupathy. 2016. *The Age of Analytics: Competing in a Data-Driven World*. McKinsey Global Institute.
Pasquale, Frank. 2015. *The Black Box Society: The Secret Algorithms That Control Money and Information*. Cambridge, MA: Harvard University Press.
Posner, Elliot. 2009. "Making Rules for Global Finance: Transatlantic Regulatory Cooperation at the Turn of the Millennium." *International Organization* 63(4): 665–699.
Rothchild, John A. 2016. *Research Handbook on Electronic Commerce Law*. Cheltenham: Edward Elgar.
Schwartz, Paul M. and Karl-Nikolaus Peifer. 2017. "Transatlantic Data Privacy Law." *Georgetown Law Journal* 106: 115–179.
Spencer, Shaun B. 2016. "Predictive Analytics, Consumer Privacy, and E-commerce Regulation." In *Research Handbook on Electronic Commerce Law*, ed. John A. Rothchild. Cheltenham: Edward Elgar, pp. 492–518.

Stucke, Maurice E. and Allen P. Grunes. 2016. *Big Data and Competition Policy*. Oxford: Oxford University Press.
Vogel, David. 1995. *Trading up: Consumer and Environmental Protection in a Global Economy*. Cambridge, MA: Harvard University Press.
Vogel, David. 2012. *The Politics of Precaution: Regulating Health, Safety, and Environmental Risks in Europe and the United States*. Princeton, NJ: Princeton University Press.
Young, Alasdair R. 2015. "The European Union as a Global Regulator? Context and Comparison." *Journal of European Public Policy* 22(9): 1233–1252.

Annex I – 14 Categories of data protection rules

1. Transparency
2. Consent
3. Collection limitations
4. Use limitations
5. Disclosure
6. Quality
7. Individual participation
8. Sensitive data
9. Children data
10. Data security
11. Data retention
12. Data breach
13. Enforcement
14. Education

5

NAVIGATING AN EMERGING KNOWLEDGE STRUCTURE

Where does the EU stand on sustainable finance?

Andreas Dimmelmeier

Introduction

In its closing report after a mandate of four years, the United Nations Environment Programme's Inquiry into a sustainable financial system (UNEP Inquiry) found that policy and regulatory efforts aimed at connecting the financial system with sustainability had doubled since 2013 and now amount to 300 measures in 54 jurisdictions (Zadek and Robins 2018: 25). One of these measures is the European Commission's (EC) creation of a high-level expert group (HLEG) that delivered its final report on how to align the Capital Markets Union (CMU) with sustainability demands – expressed in terms of the Paris Agreement (for more context see Dupont, this volume) and the Sustainable Development Goals (SDGs) – in February 2018. Less than two months later, the Commission published an ambitious action plan on sustainable finance. On a tight two-year timeline, the plan entails potentially far-reaching measures such as updating the guidelines on fiduciary duty for institutional investors, a taxonomy on sustainability in finance, an EU green bond label, an overhaul of the Markets in Financial Instruments Directive (Mifid II) regarding a requirement to assess clients' sustainability preferences, and a possible incorporation of sustainability-related risks into capital requirements (EC 2018).

These proposals make the EU a leading actor on sustainable finance, albeit by far not the only one. Already in 2016, the Chinese regulatory commission adopted a 35-point guideline on green credit. France, meanwhile, issued a law in 2015 that requires institutional investors to come up with a portfolio management strategy consistent with the Paris Agreement. Moreover, ministries, task forces, and central banks from different countries, including the UK, Switzerland, Morocco, the Netherlands, and Italy have already launched the preparation and implementation of comprehensive action plans on sustainable finance (cf. Zadek and Robins 2018; UNEP Inquiry/World Bank 2017). On the international level, transnational fora like the Financial Stability Board's Task Force on Climate Related Financial Disclosures (FSB-TCFD) and the G20's Green Finance Study group aim to provide a coordinating function.

In light of this heightened international activity on sustainable finance, the question arises as to where the activities of the EU can be located. I will approach this question using a constructivist approach and focus on the knowledge and ideas that EU-sponsored research has produced. A constructivist research design is a sensible choice to answer the question of the EU's position, insofar as international political economy (IPE) scholarship has shown that during fast transitions in economic governance, ideational factors play a prominent role. The importance of ideas arises from the observation that in phases of great uncertainty, ideas are able to provide involved parties with roadmaps on a given issue and help them to clarify their stake in it (e.g. Hall 1993; Blyth 2002; Widmaier et al. 2007; Widmaier 2016). The relatively complicated and technical (or obscure) nature of finance and its regulation further increases the relevance of ideas (e.g. Baker 2013; Baker 2015; see also de Goede 2005). In the case of sustainable finance, the heightened activity in terms of expertise production has arguably led to the emergence of an important issue (cf. Carpenter 2007). However, the growing salience of sustainable finance has meant that a field of activity that was formerly confined to niche actors and strategies is now in the process of either challenging or being assimilated by mainstream finance (cf. Dörry and Schulz 2018).

To measure the presence of such different lines of thinking, I will break down the ideational positioning of the EU on sustainable finance into two dimensions. The first details with whom the EU collaborates on sustainable finance. By looking at the historical context of the actors with whom the EU partners in its knowledge production, it is possible to identify where it stands in the debate. Secondly, I will look at the concepts that are found in EU-sponsored knowledge. In addition to the descriptive results of either dimension, social network analysis allows me to make statements about the structure that emerges at the meso-level (see Chapter 2) through the combination of the different EU-sponsored initiatives. By looking at this structure, assessments about the "location" of the EU in relation to other public, private, and civil society actors that are engaged on sustainable finance can be made.

The remainder of this article contains four sections. First, the historical context of sustainable finance is briefly described. Second, the theoretical background for understanding sustainable finance from a network perspective is outlined. Moreover, the seven EU-sponsored studies which form the data underlying the analysis are introduced. The third section contains the results of the assessments of the two dimensions, i.e., the actors that are proximate to the EU's knowledge through collaboration or citation and the concepts that unify different texts sponsored by the EU. The findings suggest that the EU's efforts on sustainable finance are very cohesive and are closely related to the dominant actors of the transnational expert community on sustainable finance. The last section summarizes the findings and points out possible omissions and shortcomings of the knowledge produced by the EU so far. Finally, the limitations of an approach based on network analysis are discussed and future avenues for research that can provide a more comprehensive analysis are suggested.

The historical context of sustainable finance

Albeit not necessarily known under the name of sustainable finance, some of its features have been around for several decades. On the one hand, the increasing preoccupation of activist investors with Environmental, Social, and Governance (ESG) issues in the 1990s (cf. MacLeod and Park 2011) led to the creation of sustainability indicators and the emergence of specialized consultancies. Since then, these consultancies, alongside think tanks and private sustainability accounting standards, have continued to develop a definition of sustainability from an investor perspective (cf. Thistlethwaite and Paterson 2016). The engagement of investors with sustainability has often been separated into different phases. A common narrative is that in the first stage, ethical investors like the pension funds of religious institutions focused on the exclusion of sectors and activities that were inconsistent with their values (e.g. the tobacco and armament industries or highly polluting activities). In a second stage, a broader set of investors started to look at sustainability issues from a risk perspective. This is mostly associated with environmental risks and climate-related risks, in particular, as investors explored the effects that physical damages from unmitigated climate change or alternatively the devaluation of carbon-intensive assets – so-called "stranded assets" – due to rapid policy changes (e.g., via a sudden and high carbon price) would have on their portfolios. More recently, this kind of thinking has moved from an exclusive focus on risk to also emphasizing a possible upside of the transition to a low carbon economy, which could arise from the investment in sectors and technologies that are expected to benefit in the process. The last stage that has been described is a wholesale transition, where investors pursue the holistic optimization of overall *common good value*. This stands in contrast to the second phase, in which financial value remains the target metric that is then subjected to sustainability risks and opportunities. The last phase has, however, been adopted only by a negligible part of the investment community as of today (cf. Robins and McDaniels 2016; Schoenmaker 2017).

A second and different source of sustainable finance arose from financial instruments designed to provide funding for projects with a sustainability dimension. Such instruments increasingly proliferated after the Clean Development Mechanism made it possible to quantify, sell, and buy abstract environmental value in the form of carbon credits. The projects funded with these instruments were mostly located in developing countries, where supposedly greater climate mitigation gains could be achieved at a lower cost. The implementation and monitoring of these projects, however, required the creation of complex auditing and certification schemes, since the comparability of different methods for greenhouse gas abatement, let alone the comparability of different gases, had to be ensured and fraudulent activity had to be curbed (cf. Newell and Paterson 2010). Since this project funding from financial instruments often went to the same regions or even the same projects as more traditional forms of funding like official development aid, an overlap between people and organizations concerned with either of those two issues emerged.[1] Another financial instrument that serves a similar purpose is the so-called "green bond", which was pioneered by the World Bank and the European Investment Bank in 2008. The money raised through such bonds can only be used for "green activities" like, for example, financing of renewable energy or retrofitting of buildings to increase energy efficiency. Green bonds are issued and audited in line with standards such as the Green Bond Principles from the International Capital Markets Association or the certification scheme from the Climate Bonds Initiative. The market in certified green bonds grew exponentially over the past decade from $2 billion dollars in 2008 to $389 billion of outstanding bonds in 2018. National and multilateral development banks have been major issuers of this financial instrument (Filkova et al. 2018).

Lastly, on a more systemic level, several International Organizations (IOs) have populated the issue of sustainable finance. As early as 1993, UNEP started to engage with the banking and insurance industry to enroll them for funding the transition toward sustainable development. This led to the creation of the UNEP Finance Initiative (UNEP FI) in 2003, which later initiated various spin-offs like the Principles for Sustainable Insurance (2012). In 2014, UNEP launched its Inquiry into a sustainable financial system, doubling down its efforts on sustainable finance. Furthermore, in 2016 the OECD established a Centre on green finance and investment, which has a similar purpose. Finally, in 2015 the G20 created a green finance study group, which works together with UNEP, at the initiative of the Chinese presidency. While it is not possible to consider the contributions of these initiatives at length, it can be said that their general focus is on taking stock and bringing together existing actors as well as on developing systemic, macroeconomic assessments, and delivering policy recommendations for states and regulators.

If one surveys these various traditions and the people and organizations present therein over time, it is possible to reconstruct how sustainable finance emerged as an issue and what its constituent dimensions are. However, rather than being a simple addition, this is a more dynamic process, in which new communities and novel forms of knowledge are developed. As sustainable finance gained traction and became more "real" and recognizable by outsiders, people, and organizations who identify with sustainable finance and were frequently present in the discussions surrounding the issue started to appear. One might conceptualize this as the emergence of *issue professionals* belonging to a transnational expert community. This conception is similar but with a broader scope to that examined in the context of carbon pricing (Paterson et al. 2017; see also Henriksen and Seabrooke 2016; Henriksen and Seabrooke, this volume).

Studying the EU as an actor in sustainable finance: Theory and method

To study the interactions of these different communities and the position of the EU within them, I turn to the concept of emergence as a more general framework and to the work on regime complexes, in particular (see also Pattberg and Widerberg, this volume). Emergence is a concept from complexity theory that holds that a structure at the *meso-level* is constructed by the uncoordinated but related activities of actors at the *micro-level*. The result of this is a system that is neither functional nor organic as would have been the case if it had been planned by a central authority. However, the system is neither entirely dysfunctional nor "chaotic", since the actors adapt over time as a result of the feedback they receive from the system. This process of adaptation results in a movement toward a more or less stable position (cf. Miller and Page 2007; Arthur 2013). When applying these theoretical insights on complex adaptive systems to knowledge on sustainable finance, emergence could be understood as the creation of a common knowledge structure through the interaction of different expert communities, whose research is sponsored through different parts of the European institutions. More specifically, concerning regime complexes, Morin et al. (2016) argue that successful regime management consists in brokering between the different regimes focusing on different issue areas. Each of these different regimes exhibits a distinctive history, a privileged form of knowledge and consensual norms and principles. The purpose of the "boundary organization", i.e., a "regime manager", is then to represent the various issue areas to create "credible, legitimate and salient knowledge" (Morin et al. 2016: 26). This inclusive process of knowledge creation ensures that biased assessments, which could possibly lead to adverse consequences, are avoided. In addition to that, greater representation makes the knowledge more legitimate with stakeholders, and thus recommendations can be implemented more easily.

In the case of sustainable finance, the historical roots outlined above can arguably be conceived of as distinct issue areas. With regard to the management, there is, however, no formal boundary organization that is entrusted with managing the regime. Instead, the issue or the regime in itself is still "under construction" with input coming from various communities that were revisited above. Nevertheless, an assessment of the representation of different forms of knowledge coming from such heterogeneous sources can still be carried out in a fashion that is similar to the assessment of more formalized regime complexes. Instead of focusing on a formal organization as the unit of analysis, one can look at the knowledge production itself, thus choosing a more inductive strategy. Applied to the EU, this means asking what kind of research the European institutions commissioned and with which parts of the expert community on sustainable finance they engaged.

To operationalize and visualize the emerging knowledge structure that was referred to in the previous paragraph and to determine the position of the EU interventions *in relation* to a number of communities, a method that is able to display relational phenomena is required. Social Network Analysis (SNA) has, over the past decades, been successfully mobilized to describe the dynamic interaction of systems in the natural and social sciences (cf. Strogratz 2001). Concerning the production of knowledge and expertise, scientometric networks most often detailing (co-)citation have been constructed from readily available online databases for many academic fields, including IPE (e.g. Seabrooke and Young 2017). Since the preoccupation of this chapter is, however, not with the scientific knowledge of an existing discipline but with policy relevant expertise in an emerging field, I rely on an original dataset that was created exclusively for the purpose of exploring sustainable finance.

The data underlying the analysis consists of linkages between 1,776 authors and 616 documents on sustainable finance over the period from 1998 until 2017.[2] The documents are, amongst others, scientific reports, policy recommendations, consultation notes, literature reviews, strategy documents, declarations, and speeches. Documents were collected from the websites of 145 organizations active on sustainable finance in its various dimensions. The 145 organizations had been identified previously by sampling 236 organizations engaged with the issue using the reputational and relational method of boundary specification (cf. Knoke 1993: 30). If the affiliation networks are collapsed, authors are linked by co-publication (as in Morin et al. 2016: 15) and documents by co-authorship in non-directed, weighted graphs, respectively. In addition to that, a network detailing the intra-citation of the sampled documents was created using string search algorithms. This network consists of 398 documents and 831 citations amongst them.

To assess the role of the EU in the network, the dataset was checked for documents that were published, commissioned, or otherwise supported by the European institutions. At the beginning of this check, publications that received funding in the form of research grants, notably the EU LIFE grants and the DOLFINS project of the Horizon 2020 funding, were excluded. This exclusion was made because, even though there might be no strict boundary, these grants can be considered to be part of the research and innovation funding provided by the EU and not political interventions into the expert discourse. Moreover, since the analysis in this chapter is a first approximation to an emerging topic rather than a comprehensive assessment of a well-established object of study, a smaller sample is a pragmatic choice insofar as it allows for more granular engagement with the data, which is required for the more inductive strategy that was chosen.

The exclusion of these grant-funded texts leaves nine documents commissioned directly by EU institutions. Four of these nine documents were contracted by a Directorate General (DG) of the EC, one was published by the European Systemic Risk Board (ESRB), two were commissioned by the European Investment Bank (EIB), one was written by the Commission's internal think tank, the European Political Strategy Centre (EPSC), and lastly the interim report from the HLEG report was the outcome of an expert consultation initiated by DG FISMA. Table 5.1 provides an overview of eight of the nine documents described above. The text from the EPSC had to be excluded, because author details are not provided, and it does not show up in the citation network.

To enable a closer look on the region of the network, through which the actors connected to the EU are navigating, a network of the immediate neighborhood of the texts presented above was created. This was achieved by creating so-called "ego-graphs" for each of the texts presented above in both the co-publication network and the citation network. An ego-graph is a subgraph in which the neighborhood of one specified node (i.e., text in this exercise) is depicted. Hence, the graph consists of the targeted node (ego) and all the nodes that it is connected to (alter). The links in the ego-graph are the connections of "ego" to the "alters" as well as the connections amongst the alters (cf. Borgatti et al. 2013: 276ff). Subsequently, these networks were added into a single graph for both the co-publication and the citation network. That means that both graphs feature the presented texts as well as texts immediately connected to them as nodes. A link is defined by two texts having one or more common authors in the co-publication network and as a citation from one text to another in the citation network.[6] The analytical value of such a representation is twofold. Firstly, the cohesiveness or fragmentation of the research supported by the EU institutions can be assessed. Secondly, the extent to which EU-sponsored experts are contributing to the work of other actors (represented in the co-publication network) as well as the extent to which EU commissioned texts cite and are cited can provide measures on the relevance of EU interventions in the transnational debate on sustainable finance.

Lastly, a qualitative assessment of the content of the selected texts is provided. Many of the documents listed in Table 5.1 are very long and contain detailed literature reviews, presentation of data, case studies, and surveys. For reasons of comparability and space constraints, the description will, however, only focus on the overall outline as well as on the problems and policy recommendations identified in each publication. Bringing together this information with the results from the network analysis allows for an approximation of how EU-sponsored knowledge related to transnational expert networks in sustainable finance and how the EU fares in managing the complexity of said networks.

Analysis and results

Starting with the co-publication network, a first insight is that the graph is very cohesive as a comparatively high fraction of the nodes (94%) are linked together inside the largest component.[7] This shows that experts contracted by the EU are very well connected through EU-sponsored research. As the connections among these experts through non-EU-sponsored research are taken into account as well by this measure, the high cohesiveness also shows that the EU reinforces already existing connections between experts that have been established previously through other collaborations.[8] Furthermore, by looking at the degree distribution,

TABLE 5.1 Overview of selected documents commissioned directly by the EU institutions. Chronological ordering (month of publication considered, when published in the same year)

Title (short title)[3]	Commissioned by	Written by	Number of authors	Year of publication
The costs of climate change adaptation in Europe: A review (*Costs of adaptation*)	European Investment Bank (EIB)	German Institute for Economic research (DIW)	1	2012
Financing meaningful mitigation actions (*Financing mitigation*)	DG CLIMA	Trinomics, Ricardo AEA	7	2014
Shifting private finance toward climate friendly investments (*Shifting private finance*)	DG CLIMA	Trinomics, Climate Bonds Initiative, 2 degrees investing initiative, Climate Policy Initiative, Carbon Disclosure Project, Frankfurt School of Management/UNEP center, Climatekos, Get2c, cdc climat[4]	15	2015
Too late, too sudden	European Systemic Risk Board (ESRB)	ESRB Advisory scientific committee	7	2016
Study on the potential of green bond finance for resource efficient investments (*Study on green bonds*)	DG ENV	Adelphi, COWI Denmark, EUNOMIA, Energy Pro	10	2016
Financing a sustainable European economy (*HLEG interim report*)	DG FISMA[5]	High level expert group on sustainable finance	29	2017
Limited visibility: The current state of corporate disclosure on long-term risks (*Limited visibility*)	European Investment Bank (EIB)	2 degrees investing initiative	3	2017
Defining 'green' in the context of green finance (*Defining green*)	DG ENV	Adelphi, COWI Denmark, EUNOMIA	5	2017

i.e., the number of connections that any node has (cf. Godet and Orisini, this volume), the third parties are closest in their "use" of experts to the EU institutions can be determined. Table 5.2 presents the top ten documents by this measure and their publishers. Leaving the two EU commissioned texts at the top of the hierarchy aside, the remaining eight documents were (co-)published by five actors.

Of these five actors, both the 2 degrees investing initiative and the Institute for climate economics (I4CE) are French think tanks that focus on the assessment of current practices regarding climate change within the financial sector and (especially in the case of 2 degrees) on the development of methodologies that integrate climate-related factors into mainstream risk assessment tools. UNEP FI and UNEP Inquiry, on the other hand, are part of the UN system and act mostly as hubs and research providers for a variety of public and private sector

TABLE 5.2 TOP 10 texts of co-publication network by degree

Name (publisher)	Co-publication Degree	Citation In-degree	Out-degree	Sum (total degree)
Financing a sustainable European economy (**DG FISMA**)	79	7	16	23
Shifting private finance toward climate friendly investments (**DG CLIMA**)	66	5	9	14
Building a sustainable financial system in the EU (**UNEP Inquiry, 2 degrees investing initiative**)	61	5	10	15
Equity markets, benchmarks and the transition to a low carbon economy (**2 degrees investing initiative**)	60	–	–	–
Transition to a low carbon society (**2 degrees investing initiative**)	54	–	–	–
France's financial (eco)system (**Institute for climate economics, UNEP Inquiry**)	49	1	4	5
Climate strategies and metrics (**UNEP Inquiry**)	36	1	0	1
Bonds and climate change 2012 (**Climate Bonds Initiative**)	35	–	–	–
Bonds and climate change 2013 (**Climate Bonds Initiative**)	35	–	–	–
Carbon asset risk: discussion framework (**UNEP Financial Initiative**)	35	–	–	–

stakeholders. Lastly, the Climate Bonds Initiative (CBI) is a single-issue non-profit organization dedicated to the definition of criteria, quality oversight, tracking, and promotion of bonds, whose proceeds are used for activities that are aligned with a transition toward a below 2 degrees world economy. Relating these observations to the historical communities introduced in the first section, it can be noted that representative organizations of all three communities are present in the top ten list. The tools developed by the 2 degrees investing initiative are mostly aimed at the investor community, whereas the CBI has strong links with the community of development banks. Lastly, the two UNEP initiatives belong to the IO cluster, which displays a more systemic focus.

In the citation network, most documents (68%) are also linked to each other inside of one component.[9] Outside of this component lie the "Financing mitigation report", and a component of nine publications, which are linked to the "Too late, too sudden" paper. In Table 5.3, the top ten texts are ranked according to

TABLE 5.3 Top 10 documents by overall citations

Name (publisher)	Citation Sum (total degree)	In-degree	Out-degree	Co-publication Degree
Financing a sustainable European economy **(DG FISMA)**	23	7	16	79
Defining green in the context of green finance **(DG ENV)**	14	0	14	6
Shifting private finance toward climate friendly investments **(DG CLIMA)**	14	5	9	66
The financial system we need: From momentum to transformation **(UNEP Inquiry)**	12	3	9	28
Too late, too sudden **(ESRB)**	10	7	3	1
G20 green finance synthesis report 2016 **(G20 green finance study group)**	9	7	2	–
Definitions and concepts **(UNEP Inquiry)**	8	8	0	–
How stock exchanges can grow green finance **(Sustainable Stock Exchanges initiative)**	7	0	7	–
European SRI study 2016 **(Eurosif)**	6	0	6	28
Study on the potential of green bond finance **(DG ENV)**	4	1	3	1

the total number of ingoing and outgoing citations. Again, the HLEG interim report ranks at the top of the table. While it could be expected that the report has a high number of outgoing citations, which presumably reflect a mapping of the field, it is somewhat surprising that the text is ranked (together with two others) second in terms of being cited. This is because all these citations must have occurred in the six months between its publication and the end of the sampling period in December 2017. The "Defining green" study, meanwhile, has the most outgoing citations in the network. Lastly, the "Study on the potential of green bonds" node has one outgoing and one incoming link.

Turning to the non-EU commissioned texts that are widely being cited or widely cite the EU-sponsored texts and their immediate neighborhood, one encounters some of the actors already discussed in the co-publication network. UNEP Inquiry features again in the list of important actors. In addition to that, a report from the G20 green finance study group is widely cited. A new appearance is the latest issue of the European SRI (Sustainable and Responsible Investment) study, published bi-annually by Eurosif, the European umbrella association for national sustainable investment trade associations. Lastly, a text from the Sustainable Stock Exchanges initiative, which also operates within the UN system and is supported by the UNEP FI, is among the most citing documents. In this assessment only two of the three communities referred to previously are present. The IO cluster is represented by UNEP and the G20, whereas the investment community is this time directly involved through Eurosif. The community consisting of institutions that are active on development finance and the creation of new financial instruments for environmental priorities are, however, absent.

The preceding two sections have elaborated on the relations between EU-sponsored research in terms of personal overlap and citations. It remains, however, an open question, whether the relative coherence of these network structures translates into a common ground in terms of content. While the amount of written material[10] means that a comprehensive analysis of the texts sampled above is beyond the scope of this chapter, it is possible to compare them according to some common features. Features that can be found in each of the publications are the identification of one or more problems or barriers as well as a list of policy recommendations. In addition to these two categories, some context was added to each text's description by presenting the general outline of the publication at the beginning. Again, the EIB text on the "Cost of adaptation" was excluded because it did not feature in the network analysis and thus cannot be used to assess the relations between network measures and content. The remaining seven texts are subsequently presented in chronological order.

The "Financing effective mitigation" text published by DG CLIMA in 2014 is mostly concerned with understanding how climate finance is carried out in different locations and identifying the instruments in debt and equity finance that are used to fund climate-related projects. In order to map best practices, case studies on different sectors in four emerging economies were conducted. The case studies identify country-specific barriers linked to institutions and behavior as possible hindrances for climate finance (Holdaway et al. 2015: 6–7).

"Shifting private finance" was published by DG CLIMA in 2015 and seeks to identify tools that European policymakers can use to shift finance away from high carbon to low carbon and climate resilient activities (Moselner et al. 2015: 1). In terms of the sources of funding, the emphasis rests on institutional investors, whereas the suggested policy instruments are related to the CMU and the European Fund for Strategic Investments (ESFI) (Moselner et al. 2015: 3–7). Throughout the text a differentiation between short-term and long-term problems and policy recommendations is undertaken. The short-term problems are the deficient volume of green assets, which decreases the liquidity of the market, a worse risk/return profile of such assets due to risk factors related, amongst others, to technological and political uncertainty as well as a lack of experience on the part of investors. Moreover, the small size of many low carbon projects is problematic, because it leads to higher transaction costs. Political remedies to these short-term problems are market-making activities by public banks such as the EIB, which can help to educate other financial institutions and signal the viability of new, sustainable assets. In addition to that, credit enhancement mechanisms in which public institutions absorb some risk as well as publicly supported risk insurance schemes can make the risk/return profile of such assets more attractive. Lastly, putting a number of small projects together, i.e., green securitization, can bring down transaction costs and the standardization of accounting and disclosure related to the documentation of such instruments can decrease investors' confusion. As one of the long-term problems, the short-time horizons of financial markets are identified. Furthermore, lack of clarity on whether climate-related risks are material – that is, whether they are considered important enough for investors to take them into account in decision making – leads to inaction. To remedy these systemic problems, the development of new risk models as well as the reform of investors' mandates and stewardship codes is advocated. Also, accounting and disclosure of financial institutions could be updated (Moselner et al. 2015: III–IV, 15, 42–47, 55, 60, 79ff). Discussing these issues, the text makes repeated references to the EU's ("normative") convening and standard-setting power in an international context (Moselner et al. 2015: 51, 66).

The 2016 ESRB "Too late, too sudden" paper is concerned with the question of how climate change and the transition toward a low carbon economy could impact financial stability in the EU. Three possible transmission channels are identified. One consists of a macroeconomic shock that comes about due to a sudden increase in energy prices once countries carry out sudden and drastic actions to stay within their carbon budget. The second mechanism features an abrupt revaluation of fossil fuel–related financial assets causing losses and possibly a financial crisis. The third scenario identifies increased losses due to climate change's impact on the number of natural catastrophes as a transmission mechanism (Gros et al. 2016: 10ff). It is argued here that the disruptions of the three scenarios could be avoided in a benign transition or a "soft landing", in which climate action is taken immediately and carbon related capital gets phased out in an orderly way. However, problems such as the time inconsistency of reduction pledges and the mispricing of long-term risks by financial markets make a "hard landing" a likely outcome (Gros et al. 2016: 5–6). To both steer toward a soft landing and shore up the resilience of Europe's financial system, a variety of measures such as additional capital buffers, the issuance of carbon risk bonds, enhanced capital requirements and exposure limits for high carbon assets, and the development of carbon stress test methodologies is suggested (Gros et al. 2016: 16–18).

The 2016 "Study on the potential of green bond finance" from DG ENV seeks to identify bottlenecks related to green bonds and to formulate possible policy interventions to scale up green bond finance. Firstly, the relevant actors to the issuance and trade of green bonds are identified (Cochu et al. 2016: 8). Then five problem fields are presented. These consist of the lack of bonds and project pipelines for new bonds, the non-existence of project aggregation, the lack of common definitions and frameworks, deficient information and market knowledge, and the lack of a clear risk profile of green bonds (Cochu et al. 2016: 9). Suggested interventions are raising awareness for green bonds, a joint coordination mechanism between actors involved with green bonds, the establishment of a project list that could serve as a pipeline for new bonds, a mandatory disclosure of "green indicators" for all issued bonds, a standard for the European green bond market, and the issuance of sovereign green bonds by member state governments (Cochu et al. 2016: 10ff).

The interim report of the HLEG, that is, the "Financing a sustainable European economy" text, tries to help in the development of an overarching EU strategy on sustainable finance, which then would be integrated into EU financial policy (EC 2017: 5). The HLEG identifies the lack of externality pricing as a problem, because it (falsely) leads investors to think that sustainability-related risks are not material. Furthermore, the short-termism of financial markets disconnects finance from the real economy. This could make finance a part of the problem if the real economy is transitioning toward sustainability. Also, the lack of disclosure on sustainability indicators from companies as well as the lack of information regarding retail savers' preferences on this topic is problematic. Finally, regulation treating liquid assets in more favorable terms than long-term illiquid ones contributes to the culture of short-termism (EC 2017: 15–16). Suggested solutions include the development of an EU classification scheme for assets, an EU label for green bonds and Socially Responsible Investment (SRI) funds, the issuance of a single set of principles on fiduciary duty,[11] the strengthening of corporate disclosures, sustainability tests for new EU financial policy, a European sustainable infrastructure match-making facility, more involvement of the European Supervisory Authorities, and updated accounting guidance from Eurostat. Further suggestions that are to be considered in the future are, amongst others, the fostering of sustainability indices and favorable or unfavorable treatments of assets in terms of capital requirements according to their green/brown classification (EC 2017: 54–63). Furthermore, albeit that it is not listed in the section on policy recommendations, the report also advocates for the introduction of climate change–related stress testing from supervisory authorities.

As opposed to the comprehensive focus of the HLEG report, the "Limited visibility" study, published by 2 degrees in 2017 is targeted at one specific issue only. The study deals with the problem that companies only forecast and disclose their financial plans for a limited timeframe and thereby face the danger of missing out on risks that materialize in a more distant future (Dupré et al. 2017: 1). Proposed measures for regulators are the clarification of the investment horizon and the target audience for disclosure, the setting of minimum levels of precision in risk descriptions, and the application of equal access to asset-level data.

Finally, the "Defining green" text is concerned with providing an overview of the different definitions used in the practice of green finance. In addition to that, the research provides suggestions for a typology that can inform the classification efforts of the HLEG (Kahlenborn et al. 2017: VII). Rather than identifying problems, the text points to several trade-offs in the construction of typologies, categories, and indicators for green and sustainable finance (the former being a subset of the latter). Some of these trade-offs are between narrow and broad definitions, low and high detail indicators, and binary or incremental categories (Kahlenborn et al. 2017: 25ff). On the side of recommendations, the text suggests the development of a conceptual definition of green finance, a general typology, an EU-specific typology, a green rating mechanism, and process criteria for green investment (Kahlenborn et al. 2017: 40–51).

Table 5.4 lists all problems and policy suggestions from the discussion above that appear in at least two of the seven texts. From this information another network can be constructed, in which documents are linked by their use of common concepts. This approach is similar to so-called "discourse networks"

TABLE 5.4 Problems and policy recommendations with more than two mentions

Problem/ recommendation	Texts
Short termism	Limited visibility, HLEG report, Shifting private finance,
Differential capital requirements (i.e., brown penalizing, green supporting)	Shifting private finance, HLEG report, Too late, too sudden
Standardization and taxonomy development	Study on the potential of green bonds, HLEG report, Defining green
Green rating methodology	HLEG report, Defining green
Stewardship codes and investor governance reform	Shifting private finance, HLEG report
(Carbon) stress tests	Too late, too sudden, HLEG report, Limited visibility

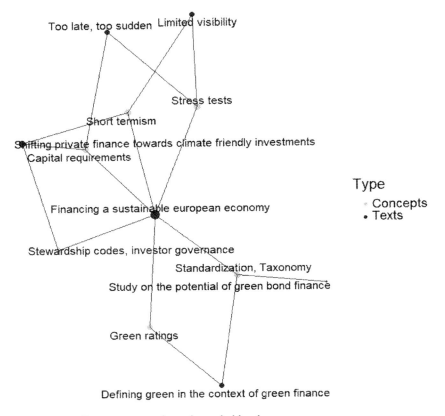

FIGURE 5.1   Concept network: nodes scaled by degree.

that have been used in political science to analyze changing discourses and the actors pushing for a certain way of understanding an issue (e.g. Ingold and Leifeld 2014).

Figure 5.1 presents such a discourse network for the texts in Table 5.4. The HLEG interim report occupies the center of the graph. Furthermore, the "Defining green" and the "Study on green bonds" texts that were already found to be connected in the co-publication network are also directly related in this graph. On the other side of the HLEG report, the remaining texts are clustered.

Bringing the findings from the three networks together

Considering the three indicators of co-publication, citation, and common content of EU-sponsored research on sustainable finance, certain preliminary observations can be made. First of all, a certain path dependency of DG ENV and DG CLIMA can be identified. Both texts sponsored by DG CLIMA have personal overlap in the co-publication network, as well as conceptual overlap evidenced in the discourse network. The two publications commissioned by DG CLIMA, on the other hand, display only a personal overlap, which, however, also extends to the HLEG report and one EIB sponsored publication. Secondly, the centrality of the HLEG interim report across all three indicators is worth noting. This can be explained by the fact that the group members were very active and well-connected experts (co-publication), that they undertook an extensive literature review (citation outgoing, common discourse), and that it was perceived as an important event by the expert community very soon after its conception (citation ingoing). Another possible explanation for the rapid uptake of EU-sponsored texts (i.e., the HLEG report and the ESRB paper) in the expert community could be attributed to the prominence of the institutions commissioning them. An implication concerning the navigation of complex networks that arises from such an interpretation is that the EU might not primarily play a role in innovating new analysis and perspectives. Instead, it might have a greater role in promoting and empowering certain actors as well as the use and development of concepts and methods that are already present in the debates on sustainable finance.

Moving from the discussion of single texts to the structure of the entire networks, it has been noted that there is a relatively high degree of cohesiveness both in the co-publication and the citation network. From a regime complexes background, cohesiveness is a relevant measure for the navigation of networks, insofar as very low levels of cohesiveness suggest fragmentation and a lack of coordination, while very high levels of cohesiveness are fraught with the dangers of *groupthink* and the stifling of innovation. Finally, rather than interpreting the cohesion as an instance of the EU's successful management of an emerging issue, this could also be an outcome of issue professionals acting between the two levels of their own networks and the more formal research cooperation sponsored by the EU (cf. Henriksen and Seabrooke, this volume).

As shown in the three dimensions, the EU interventions are overall relatively far away from the fragmentation extreme. As to the problem of too much cohesiveness, it is difficult to establish a universal benchmark. However, going back to the issue of promoting certain ideas vis-à-vis others, it is possible to make a preliminary assessment of the ideational diversity based on the observations on the use of common ideas in Table 5.4 and Figure 5.1. The problems and solutions identified there can be differentiated broadly into those that can be identified and solved within the current set-up of the financial system and those that are more systemic (cf. Meadows 1999 for a continuum of the systemic nature of changes on which such a classification is based). Tinkering with capital requirements as well as the development of standardizations and green ratings could be considered as part of the former category, insofar as they can be conceptualized as add-ons to or amendments of current practices. Meanwhile, short-termism is a more structural problem and reform of stewardship codes could be a radical measure as it pertains to the altering of the aims and *raison d'être* of investors. The introduction of stress tests, meanwhile, belongs to the emerging agenda of macroprudential regulation, which has been described in the IPE literature as an emerging paradigm that challenges the incumbent neoliberal governance in financial supervision (Baker 2013, 2015).

While this assessment reveals that the EU-sponsored research is not tilted exclusively toward *status quo* fixes or revolutionary changes, it should be maintained that it nevertheless excludes some radical measures that are perhaps a little further removed from the thinking of financial practitioners and regulators. For instance, the use of monetary policy and, in particular, Quantitative Easing for the purpose of leveraging funding for sustainable projects, which has been advocated both by academics (Campiglio 2016) and NGOs (Van Lerven and Ryan-Collins 2017) does not feature prominently within the body of EU commissioned research. In addition to that, neither outright prohibitions on certain assets like those linked to coal as favored by *Divestment* campaigners nor mandatory loan ratios that commercial banks have to allocate to sustainable or green assets, as, for example, practiced in China (cf. Zadek and Robins 2018), are a major concern in the texts. Perhaps most importantly, the texts appear to display a "climate bias". This means that while other issues of environmental and social dimensions of sustainability such as biodiversity loss, land degradation, or inequality are acknowledged, both analysis and recommendations focus predominantly on climate-related issues. The high level of aggregation used for this part of the analysis means that it is possible that the mentioned issues were indeed carefully discussed in the research and then not put into the analyzed sections. If it is, however, the case that the finding on such exclusions is accurate, then the EU, in line with the theory of boundary organizations, might be well advised to broaden its network of collaborators and the set of concepts and approaches it engages with. This is because, by doing so it can avoid negative consequences arising from the failure to engage with relevant knowledge from other sources.

Conclusion

This chapter has provided an outline of some of the main events in the field of sustainable finance. It has been suggested that this field is increasingly populated by a transnational community of experts and organizations. Subsequently, the question on what the EU institutions' position in this field is has been addressed by locating EU-sponsored research in the transnational debate on sustainable finance. This was done by mapping the positions of publications by EU institutions in (1) an expert co-publication network, (2) a citation network, and (3) a discourse network. The findings of this analysis suggest that the institutions are generally well integrated into the transnational debate and that the EU's efforts on sustainable finance are rather cohesive. Further research will be needed to determine the extent to which this cohesiveness is the result of the EU successfully taking a role in an emerging knowledge structure. One alternative explanation would be that the EU interventions are more an instrument that is played by issue professionals in and outside of the European institutions.

Leaving the question of the potential causes aside, it was also noted that according to the theory of complex regimes, too much cohesiveness is a risky strategy and that some broadening of the base of actors with which the EU engages could be beneficial. Lastly, it was suggested that the strength of well-recognized actors like the EU might lie less in innovating in terms of analysis and policy but in empowering already existing actors and approaches.

When considering these findings, it has to be noted that the networks considered above are an analytical tool rather than a representation of the reality as it is. This is because they base their conclusions on the assumption that the defined links (i.e., co-publication, citation, and conceptual overlap) are meaningful. Hence, they are different from networks, which correspond to a network in the real world, as it would be the case with a network of material entities like a river network or an electrical grid, or a network based on well-established and readily quantifiable social facts, such as an ownership network between companies or a network of debt relationships amongst banks (see Vitali et al. 2011 and Battiston et al. 2017 for examples of such "real" social networks). Consequently, the findings presented above can only hint at the emergence of a meso-level structure like a system of shared knowledge in the area of sustainable finance. To validate such a claim, ultimately, complementary sources such as interview data and comprehensive text analysis are necessary. This is because, while the network data can suggest that "something" is emerging, only these other sources can imbue this "something" with meaning, that is, they can both answer the questions of what is emerging and why it is emerging.

Notes

1 E.g. see evolution of Climate Funds Update (https://climatefundsupdate.org/) or the Climate Policy Initiative (https://climatepolicyinitiative.org/).
2 This data is itself a subset of a dataset that has a broader definition of authorship and links 5,207 individuals to 643 texts for the same period.
3 The short title will be used in the remainder of the chapter.
4 Cdc climat became the institute for climate economics in 2016 after a merger with climate research department of the Agence francaise de development.
5 In cooperation with DG CLIMA, DG ENV, DG ECFIN, DG ENER, and DG JUST.
6 In the case of two texts sharing multiple authors, a link with a weight equal to the number of co-authors is recorded, though this weighting will not feature in the analysis.
7 A component is a group of nodes which are all connected to each other (cf. Borgatti et al. 2013: 26).
8 An alternative interpretation would be that the EU's research establishes the base for future research collaborations. An answer to which of these interpretation is correct can only be given by looking at longitudinal data, which would be out of scope for this chapter.
9 Again, only seven out of the eight documents could be analyzed, since the *Cost of adaptation* text is neither cited nor does it cite other documents from the sample.
10 The seven texts considered in the analysis total 701 pages including references and appendices.
11 Fiduciary duty is broadly speaking a legal concept that specifies a set of principles that a person or entity that manages other people's money has to respect.

References

Arthur, W.B. (2014). "Complexity Economics: A Different Framework for Economic Thought," in The Economy and Complexity, Oxford University Press, 2014.

Baker, A. (2013). The New Political Economy of the Macroprudential Ideational Shift. *New Political Economy*, 18(1), 112–139. https://doi.org/10.1080/13563467.2012.662952

Baker, A. (2015). Varieties of Economic Crisis, Varieties of Ideational Change: How and Why Financial Regulation and Macroeconomic Policy Differ. *New Political Economy*, 20(3), 342–366.

Battiston, Stefano, et al. (2017). A Climate Stress-Test of the Financial System. *Nature Climate Change*, 7(4), 283–288.

Blyth, M. (2002). *Great Transformations: Economic Ideas and Institutional Change in the Twentieth Century*. Cambridge: Cambridge University Press.

Borgatti, S. P., Everett, M. G., & Johnson, J. C. (2013). *Analyzing Social Networks*. London: Sage Publications.

Campiglio, E. (2016). Beyond Carbon Pricing: The Role of Banking and Monetary Policy in Financing the Transition to a Low-Carbon Economy. *Ecological Economics*, 121, 220–230.

Carpenter, R.C. (2007). Setting the Advocacy Agenda: Theorizing Issue Emergence and Nonemergence in Transnational Advocacy Networks. *International Studies Quarterly*, 51(1), 99–120.

Cochu, A. et al. (2016). *Study on the Potential of Green Bond Finance for Resource-Efficient Investments*. Adelphi, COWI Energy Pro and Eunomia for European Commission.

De Goede, M. (2005). *Virtue, Fortune, and Faith: A Geneaology of Finance*. London: University of Minnesota Press.

Dörry, S., & Schulz, C. (2018). Green Financing, Interrupted. Potential Directions for Sustainable Finance in Luxembourg. *Local Environment*, 23(7), 717–733.

Dupré, S. et al. (2017). Limited Visibility: The Current State of Corporate Disclosure on Long-term Risks. 2 degrees investing initiative. Tragedy of the Horizon Research Report. September 2017.

European Commission. (2017). *Financing a Sustainable European Economy*. Interim Report of the High-Level Expert Group on Sustainable Finance. 170713-sustainable-finance-report_en.pdf.

European Commission (2018). COM (2018) 97 final: Action Plan: Financing Sustainable Growth

Filkova, M., et al. (2018). *Bonds and Climate Change. The State of the Market 2018*. CBI, Climate Bonds Initiative.

Gros et al. (2016) Too Late, Too Sudden: Transition to a Low-Carbon Economy and Systemic Risk. *ESRB* 22, 1–21.

Hall, P.A. (1993). Policy Paradigms, Social Learning, and the State: The Case of Economic Policymaking in Britain. *Comparative Politics*, 25(3), 275–296.

Henriksen, L.F., & Seabrooke, L. (2016). Transnational Organizing: Issue Professionals in Environmental Sustainability Networks. *Organization*, 23(5), 722–741.

Holdaway, E. et al. (2015). *Financing Meaningful Mitigation Actions: Part of the Scaling up Climate Finance in 2014 and beyond Project*. Ricardo-AEA, Triple E Consulting and Climatekos for European Commission DG CLIMA.

Ingold, K., & Leifeld, P. (2014). Structural and Institutional Determinants of Influence Reputation: A Comparison of Collaborative and Adversarial Policy Networks in Decision Making and Implementation. *Journal of Public Administration Research and Theory*, 26(1), 1–18.

Kahlenborn, W., et al. (2017). *Defining "Green" in the Context of Green Finance Final Report*. Adelphi, Eunomia and COWI for European Commission DG Environment.

Knoke, D. (1993). Networks of Elite Structure and Decision Making. *Sociological Methods & Research, 22*(1), 23–45.

MacLeod, M., & Park, J. (2011). Financial Activism and Global Climate Change: The Rise of Investor-Driven Governance Networks. *Global Environmental Politics,* 11(2), 54–74.

Meadows, D. (1999). *Leverage Points: Places to Intervene in a System*. Accessed May 24th 2017, http://donellameadows.org/archives/leverage-points-places-to-intervene-in-a-system.

Miller, J.H., & Page, S.E. (2007). *Complex Adaptive Systems*. Princeton, NJ: Princeton University Press.

Morin, J.-F., Louafi, S., Orsini, A., & Oubenal, M. (2016). Boundary Organizations in Regime Complexes: A Social Network Profile of IPBES. *Journal of International Relations and Development.* 20(3), 543–577.

Moslener, U., et al. (2015). Shifting Private Finance Towards Climate-Friendly Investments: Policy Options for Mobilising Institutional Investors' Capital for Climate-Friendly Investment. *DG CLIMA.*

Newell, P., & Paterson, M. (2010). *Climate Capitalism: Global Warming and the Transformation of the Global Economy*. Cambridge: Cambridge University Press.

Paterson, M., Hoffmann, M., Betsill, M., & Bernstein, S. (2017). Professions and Policy Dynamics in the Transnational Carbon Emissions Trading Network. In L. Seabrooke & L.F. Henriksen (Eds.), *Professional Networks in Transnational Governance* (pp. 182–202). Cambridge: Cambridge University Press.

Seabrooke, L., & Young, K.L. (2017). The Networks and Niches of International Political Economy. *Review of International Political Economy*, 24(2), 288-331.

Schoenmaker, P.D. (2017). *Investing for the Common Good: A Sustainable Finance Framework.* Brussels: BRUEGEL.

Strogatz, S.H. (2001). Exploring Complex Networks. *Nature*, 410(6825), 268–276.

Thistlethwaite, J., & Paterson, M. (2016). Private Governance and Accounting for Sustainability Networks. *Environment and Planning C: Government and Policy,* 34(7), 1197–1221.

Robins, N. & McDaniels, J. (2016). *The United Kingdom: Local Hub, Global Dynamics.* UNEP Inquiry.

Zadek, S. & Robins, N. (2018). *Making Waves: Aligning the Financial System with Sustainable Development*. UNEP Inquiry.

UNEP Inquiry/ World Bank (2017). *Roadmap for a Sustainable Financial System*.

Van Lerven, F. & J. Ryan Collins (2017). *Central Banking and the Transition to a Low Carbon Economy*. London: New Economics Foundation.

Vitali, S., Glattfelder, J.B., & Battiston, S. (2011). The Network of Global Corporate Control. *PLoS ONE, 6*(10), e25995

Widmaier, W.W. (2016). *Economic Ideas in Political Time: The Rise and Fall of Economic Orders from the Progressive Era to the Global Financial Crisis*. Cambridge: Cambridge University Press.

Widmaier, W.W., Blyth, M., & Seabrooke, L. (2007). Exogenous Shocks or Endogenous Constructions? The Meanings of Wars and Crises. *International Studies Quarterly,* 51(4), 747–759.

6
THE RISE OF THE EU IN INTERNATIONAL TAX POLICY

Rasmus Corlin Christensen

Introduction

Two decades ago, Claudio Radaelli (1997) observed that the EU was "not a major player in the attempt to govern the globalisation of taxation, forced to play the role of passive spectator" (p. 181). In contrast, Radaelli concluded that the status of the OECD, an informal "think tank" producing non-binding guidelines and recommendations, "goes beyond that of a 'talk-shop': its position is influential" (p. 177). Today, however, the EU has evolved into a vibrant arena for some of the most prominent international tax policy discussions, and a key challenger to the OECD's status as the historical organizational focal point of international tax policy.[1] In the context of the global financial crisis, EU tax networks have moved from an underdeveloped, narrow expert context to a highly heterogeneous, contested, politicized, and unstable setting, with a broad public, political, and interest group involvement. This has been accompanied by an unprecedented volatility of policy debate, spurring unexpected and expansive political initiatives, often in direct competition with the established "OECD consensus". As correctly predicted by Radaelli, "[l]eft to technocratic debates on the efficiency of the European tax systems, EU direct tax policy would never have gone further than minimal measures" (1999, 766).

This chapter explores the evolution of networks in and around EU tax policy, contrasting with the OECD, and discusses how this evolution has manifested itself in diverging policy discussions and outcomes in the two arenas. In particular, the chapter zooms in on the professional and organizational interactions within EU tax policy networks as a dimension of the EU's rise to prominence in international tax policy. Specifically, the chapter explores one recent contentious area of EU and international tax policy discussion, namely corporate tax transparency and the notion of country-by-country reporting (CBCR).[2] CBCR was an idea promoted by a coalition of issue professionals within civil society in the wake of the financial crisis, seeking to require multinational companies (MNCs) to disclose unprecedented information about their tax practices and economic activity on a country-by-country basis, as a way to ensure that multinationals would "pay their fair share" and help in the rebuilding of national fiscal systems hurt by the financial crisis. The idea was initially rejected by the OECD, but activists then found sympathetic allies in a rapidly changing EU tax community, resulting in new EU regulations requiring a minimalist CBCR from specific sectors, in a direct challenge to the OECD. The OECD community then took ownership of discussions about further expansion of CBCR regulations, but as soon as the OECD had finalized its (non-binding) recommendations, European tax policy networks advanced new binding EU regulations that were far more expansive than the OECD proposals, once again directly challenging the historical dominance of the OECD in international tax policy.

While focused on EU tax policy, the specific themes of this chapter bear crucially upon the broader topics of this edited volume, namely issue professionals (Chapter 3) and global regime complexity, coherence, and effectiveness (Chapter 2). Most prominently, the interactions of issue professionals and the rise of EU networks in international tax policy are illustrative of the significant and fundamental changes to the international tax regime in the post-crisis years (Christensen and Hearson 2019). The past decade has seen an explosion of media attention, issue salience, and broad public interest, which has contributed to broadening the type and number of actors involved in international tax policy discussions, as well as the dynamics of relations and interactions amongst these actors. The EU policy system has proved highly adaptive in adjusting to these macro changes and exploiting them to advance specific policy goals, and more broadly to challenge for higher status in the international tax policy hierarchy. The new, wider constituency of EU and international tax policy has contributed to an emerging fragmentation of the historically stable consensus around the OECD, and opened space for previously marginalized actors, ideas, and policy proposals.

The chapter proceeds as follows. Section one outlines the professional-organizational scenery of international tax policy, and its historical evolution, emphasizing the dominance of the OECD. Section two discusses the role of the European Union in international tax policy, including the basis of its competencies and the recent transformations of EU tax networks in the post-crisis context. Section three then offers an examination of the policy case, including the changing interactions of professionals and organizations in the EU tax policy context, in comparison with the OECD, and specifically an analysis of these changes in the case of corporate tax transparency and country-by-country reporting (CBCR).

The professional-organizational scenery of international tax policy

The increasing interrelation of world trade in the 20th century exposed a need for states to address the challenges of international taxation. Given that taxation was historically a pre-eminently national concern, tax policy began to contrast with international commerce, as different states would claim the rights to tax the same income or the same corporation. In particular, in light of consecutive large-scale conflicts in the early 20th century (the First and Second World Wars specifically), the need to raise revenue exacerbated inter-state conflict over international taxation, highlighting the problem of double taxation, leading to the earliest, systematic international cooperation on international tax policy (Scheve and Stasavage 2016; Jogarajan 2018).

In the context of increasing attention to the issue of international taxation, the League of Nations commenced a program of developing coordination amongst government experts in the 1920s, culminating in a set of model treaties for countries to sign bilaterally, setting out the exclusive rights of each nation-state to tax defined incomes (Jogarajan 2018). These treaties, and the ideas they enshrined about the division of the rights to tax multinational income, were initially developed by a small, cooperative community of tax experts, but would become the global standards over the next century as the number of countries involved in this international coordination and subscribing to the core treaty ideas expanded rapidly. Today, more than 3,000 bilateral tax treaties exist between countries, based significantly on the core ideas developed in the 1920s and 1930s under the auspices of the League, forming the crux of the infrastructure of the international tax governance system.

However, the leadership of international tax policy did not stay long with the League of Nations, as the organization collapsed in the wake of World War II. The OECD would go on to establish itself as *the* premier forum for international tax policy for the 20th century and beyond. While the OECD lacks a legitimate claim to be a truly global organization, such as the United Nations, its particular way of working has made it highly successful in tax policy. Specifically, the OECD's technical-bureaucratic nature is paramount – and the community's unparalleled ability to problem-solve based on consensus amongst technical expert tax professionals (Sharman 2006; Woodward 2009; Eccleston 2013). Over decades, the OECD professional community developed a shared culture and specific understandings of knowledge and appropriateness. The "thickness" of the community became stronger: "As similarly situated national officials with highly congruent professional training, those involved with the OECD activities tend to manifest a similar mindset" (Sharman 2012, 24). This "similar mindset" included broad normative adherence to a dominant issue definition, namely the avoidance of double taxation of cross-border economic activity (Genschel and Rixen 2015), and to expertise consensus-based policy discussions, for the deliberate evasion of "political" interference (Sharman 2012).

Moreover, the reach of the OECD tax networks was far broader and more effective, facilitating and using expert networks spanning the globe. The OECD acts as a "key node" in international tax cooperation matters, and as Woodward notes, "OECD bodies bind the brightest folk working in a given policy area together into transgovernmental networks of knowledge-based experts" (Woodward 2009, 53). Finally, the OECD had far more resources to pursue the development of international tax networks and outputs than any other international organization, a huge secretariat of 2,500 bureaucrats and convening more than 40,000 experts annually across policy areas (Salzman 2005; Woodward 2009, 50; Sharman 2012, 23). These dynamics helped build trust amongst expert policy-makers. These features have helped the organization avoid politicized conflict, bolster government buy-in, and build coherence in the policy-making community. This has also lent credence and authority to the OECD's *soft law* products – recommendations, guidelines, and treaty models – that, despite having no binding force, have been effective and popular policy outputs (Vega 2012).

This techno-bureaucratic identity of policy-making at the OECD has proved successful in establishing the OECD as the dominant international tax policy forum. However, political support from powerful states has also been central. The support of the United States, world's leading economy and military power, throughout the latter half of the 20th century, was particularly important. When the US did not support specific tax projects of the OECD, the result could easily be failure, such as when the Bush administration pulled out of the "Harmful Tax Competition" project in the late-1990s (Sharman 2006). In the early-2000s, however, the organization received further political boosts through its backing by the G7 and, importantly, the G20 (Christians 2010). Arguably, however, the power of the OECD has also subdued progressive reform in international tax policy (Eccleston and Woodward 2014; Morriss and Moberg 2012). This extends to the organizational landscape of international taxation, where the OECD and its constituency has actively resisted attempts to "forum shift" and move key contemporary policy discussions away from the OECD auspices and over to, for instance, the United Nations (Edwards 2017; Eurodad 2016).

The United Nations, in turn, remains an obvious alternative to the OECD, as a globally institutionalized setting where matters of economic policy, including taxation, are continually discussed. Moreover, it has a truly global scope, as opposed to the OECD, which has been criticized for being a "rich country's club" (Chonghaile 2016). However, while various UN bodies have been involved in tax policy discussions historically, it never really emerged as a serious option. First, while attempts were made to "pick up the slack" from the League of Nations through the UN Fiscal Commission, they failed "in the political atmosphere of the Cold War and decolonization" (Picciotto 1992, 48) and due to a "failure to gather institutional momentum" (Hearson 2018). Instead, discussions moved to the OECD. Second, when UN bodies made active attempts to influence particular policy discussions, such as on corporate tax transparency in the 1970s, their lack of support from a broad coalition, and active resistance by business interests and the OECD community, worked to subdue any traction (Ylönen 2015; Cobham et al. 2018). By the same token, other relevant global governance institutions, such as the IMF and the World Bank, were historically confined to specific areas of international tax policy, most notably advice and conditionality on domestic tax reforms and administrative assistance, and capacity-building for tax bureaucracies.

The EU in international tax policy and the crisis context

Where is the EU in this picture? In contrast to the OECD's dominance in international tax policy, the EU has arguably played a minor role in international tax affairs historically. The conventional view is that the EU has no or little power or influence in tax policy, given the deliberate constraints enshrined by member states in the EU's legal basis, due to concerns with national fiscal sovereignty. The Rome Treaty required unanimity in the Council, as opposed to (qualified) majority voting of other policy areas, for harmonization of direct tax policy, providing all member states with effective veto power on tax proposals. This principle has notably constrained the EU, both in terms of intra-EU and extra-EU tax policy. Intra-EU, while closer European integration in the late 20th century fostered continued discussions of the (lack of) coherence in member states' tax policies and its consequences (e.g. Commission of the European Communities 1992), the EU's formal competencies in tax policy remained largely constrained, although it is now more contested (Barbière 2017). Instead, with tax policy increasingly on the agenda, EU institutions have sought to use the authority available to them in other ways to shape member states' tax policies (Genschel and Jachtenfuchs 2011). Extra-EU wise, combined with the strong issue control of the OECD professional-organizational community, the sovereignty focus of EU member states in tax policy has restrained coherent EU action at the international level, favoring less strict cooperation of national policies (see Skjærseth 1994).

Most illustrative of the historical EU tax policy setting is perhaps the "embryonic epistemic community" of EU tax expert professionals, identified by Radaelli as the network core. Aligned around shared policy understandings, and mobilized by the European Commission, this network consisted mainly of professionals from the Commission and selected business interests, seeking to enhance EU direct tax reforms (Radaelli 1997, 95–100). The active participation of a more heterogeneous group of actors, such as the European Parliament, critical politicians, civil society professionals, and broader business coalitions, was conspicuously absent. The crux of EU tax policy-making and reform progress, then, was a small group of professionals with mutual understandings (Puchala 2013). Radaelli concludes on the broader outreach of the epistemic community that its failure "can be explained in terms of a missing link between academic knowledge and the business community's priorities" (Radaelli 1997, 99). In that sense, the preeminent trait of the professional networks in EU tax policy was similar to that of the OECD – a narrow, expert-based consensus model – but importantly with a level of expertise and political support that fell far short of the OECD's. Attempts to change this situation, such as the late 1990s' "politicization" strategy of the Commission described by Radaelli ultimately fell short of propelling EU tax networks to prominence. The result was political stability around a homogenous technical community, yet notable insignificance, both in terms of EU politics more broadly and specifically international tax policy, in sharp contrast to the OECD.

In the decade that has transpired since the 2007 global financial crisis, however, the picture has changed radically. Actors in and around the EU tax networks are now key players in international tax policy and have become established as key challengers to the OECD. How has it happened? Arguably, this rise of the EU in international tax policy must be viewed in the context of successive crises faced by the European Union and networks in its vicinity, reconfiguring the salience of the policy issue itself and the broader social context of tax networks and issue control. This includes the ongoing Eurozone but perhaps most significantly the global financial crisis and the long recovery that has followed. The latter crisis put unprecedented pressure on the fiscal and tax regimes of nation-states, with many EU member states hit particularly hard, highlighting the importance of sustainable national and international tax rules, and thus affording unprecedented political focus to international tax policy as a lever to address causes and effects of the crisis itself. Moreover, a string of large-scale "tax haven leaks", covered by massive media campaigns such as LuxLeaks in 2014, Panama Papers in 2016, and Paradise Papers in 2017, has contributed to an explosion of public interest in international taxation, and, accordingly, political action (Oei and Ring 2018; Dallyn 2016; Berg and Davidson 2017). More broadly, the empirical landscape of international tax regulation has been fundamentally reshaped in the crisis context, with a broadened constituency and more contested authority at the global level (Christensen and Hearson 2019).

In this context, networks in and around the EU, as sites for international tax policy discussion, cooperation, and competition, have now evolved into a vibrant milieu, with some of the most dynamic constellations and interactions of stakeholders, and some of the most significant policy discussions, actively contesting issue control of international tax policy. This transformation has been marked by a vastly broadened scope and heterogenization of EU tax policy networks. In particular, actors from the European Parliament (EP), the European Commission, and the wider issue ecology (businesses, the general public, and, notably, civil society) have helped broaden the constituency and become far more engaged players in EU tax policy discussions. In contrast, the technical-bureaucratic culture of the OECD, and its limited interactions with the broader community of stakeholders, meant the organization was not well positioned to accommodate or manage expansive politicization in international tax policy (Sharman 2006; Ougaard 2011).

To start with the EP, its evolving role in EU and international tax affairs is undeniably linked to the more general process of empowerment of the EP (Hix and Høyland 2013). However, in tax specifically, the Parliament – in the 1990s so marginal an institution that it featured only intermittently in EU tax politics studies – has jumped aggressively on the post-crisis agenda, proactively pursuing policy solutions in the wake of successive tax haven leaks by setting up successive investigative committees ("TAXE" and "TAX2" after LuxLeaks, "PANA" after the Panama Papers, and "TAXE3" after the Paradise Papers). Moreover, the Parliament has "grilled" those involved in the scandals, including Commission President Jean-Claude Juncker. In formal policy procedures, the EP has been equally active. For instance, in the case of CBCR (discussed in more detail below), the EP has adopted a number of reports and recommendations that underscore its commitment to public CBCR since the global financial crisis, specifically contesting resistance from individual member states in the Council of Ministers. In this regard, the EP has also been highly inventive. As a civil society activist noted, "the EP was just trying to stuff CBCR in *everything* – a new directive, the amended Shareholders' Directive, etc." (personal interview).

The newfound involvement and activism of the EP in EU and international tax affairs is linked to the newfound involvement and activism of *civil society advocates* in EU and international tax affairs. While civil society activism had been a significant feature of radical reforms in a host of global policy areas throughout the 20th century and beyond, NGOs had remained notably absent from international tax policy discussions, even as the international community turned to discuss issues of "tax competition" and "tax havens" more systematically in the 1990s (Sharman 2006). Even the OECD's chief tax policy-maker, Jeffrey Owens, lamented this absence at the time (Owens 2002). However, the 21st century has witnessed far more civil society interest in and purposeful action on international tax matters. Arguably, the starting point was marked by the 2003 founding of the Tax Justice Network (TJN), a focused activist organization that has been highly influential in EU and international tax affairs (Tax Justice Network 2016; Seabrooke and Wigan 2016; Dallyn 2016; Baden and Wigan 2017). While wielding relatively few material resources, the small close-knit group of experts-turned-activists in TJN contributed to a broader wave of activism on international tax policy, working with and pushing other NGOs on to the agenda (Forstater and Christensen 2017; Seabrooke and Wigan 2013).

Importantly, civil society activists have also built ties to policy-makers in formal EU institutions, including the EP and the Commission, focusing lobbying efforts on the EU context after a history of failures to influence private regulators and the OECD (Baden and Wigan 2017; Christensen 2021). While EU agencies broadly seek policy input from such stakeholders in order to obtain relevant information and meet procedural expectations, there is also often an explicit agenda for legislative control (Arras and Braun 2017). In the area of tax policy, such linkage to civil society activists has been applied to counterbalance member state authority, as discussed further below. The overall increase of civil society attention to international tax policy has been noticeable: "Without [civil society campaigners], a bunch of powerful international organisations – the G8 and the G20, the OECD, the IMF, the European Union – would not be committed, as they currently are, to design and implement some rather progressive reforms to international corporate tax" (Moore 2014).

In addition to the rise of the EP and civil society activism, the European Commission has become a more proactive force in politicizing tax policy and raising the profile of tax policy proposals. Specifically, the Commission has taken advantage of newfound public attention to EU tax policy to push its own long-standing harmonization projects and strengthen the profile of popular new ideas (e.g. Lips 2019; Roland 2019). In the wake of recent large-scale tax haven leaks, the Commission has launched a radical effort to harmonize member states' corporate tax policies (European Commission 2016b) and to require more transparency of multinational corporations (discussed below). All of this, the Commission argues, is in the name of addressing the problems exposed by tax haven leaks and renewed political attention, thus discursively tying its political proposals directly to salient, politicized issues, and challenging established policy ideas (Christensen and Seabrooke 2020). Stakeholders have taken note, too. As one technical expert observer said, critically, of the Commission's actions: "This is simply about power, and about more money for Brussels" (Thompson 2018).

The upshot of this transformation of the EU policy tax setting is that it has moved from an embryonic and insignificant network to a highly heterogeneous, contested, politicized, and unstable context, with a broad public, political, and interest group involvement. While the Council of Ministers and individual member states formally maintain exclusive veto power in the area of direct tax policy, they now have notable proactive competition from the Commission, the Parliament, and the broader issue ecology. The range of voices is now far more diverse than it has historically been in the EU. Moreover, the influx of attention has brought with it greatly increased resource spend on and salience of tax policy processes in and around EU networks, allowing them to more effectively participate in international tax discussions and challenge the long-standing dominance of the OECD. To examine these dynamics in more detail, the specific case of country-by-country reporting (CBCR) is explored below, emphasizing how changing professional-organizational interactions in EU tax policy networks have played out in a highly salient, contested policy case.

The case of country-by-country reporting (CBCR)

The idea of country-by-country reporting (CBCR) for multinational corporations on taxation, essentially nationally segmented disclosure of tax-related information, had initially been intermittently discussed in the 1960s and 1970s at the United Nations (Ylönen 2015). However, it only really found traction after it was adopted as a key global policy ask by the Tax Justice Network (Tax Justice Network 2005), and other NGOs, in its modern format developed by

TJN co-founder Richard Murphy (Murphy 2003). Over half a decade, a significant civil society coalition emerged to advance various versions of CBCR onto the political agendas of a range of governments and international organizations, including the United States, the EU, G7, G20, and the OECD (Lesage and Kacar 2013; Wojcik 2012; Baden and Wigan 2017).

In a first significant moment in 2010, the issue of CBCR was brought onto the agenda of the OECD. Both the OECD's Task Force on Tax and Development and its Global Forum on Development were considering it. However, only a year later, both fora had dropped the idea. The Task Force had concluded that there was "not clear unanimity on whether this [tax transparency] should go as far as country by country reporting" (OECD 2011), while the Global Forum's interest simply faded (Lesage and Kacar 2013, 274). At the same time in the European Union, the European Commission launched a consultation "to gather stakeholders' views on financial reporting on a country-by-country basis by multinational companies", which was eventually used to create momentum for new EU directives to require public CBCR disclosure for extractive and financial companies, agreed in 2013. This was despite the fact that the Council had expressly urged the EU member states to consider CBCR in the context of the OECD.[3]

A few years later, and *deja vu*: the EU was again quick to pip the OECD on CBCR. In 2013, the OECD considered CBCR once again. Following the advances in the EU (and in the US), as well as sustained civil society pressure and newfound support from the G8 and G20, the OECD picked up the topic in the context of its comprehensive Base Erosion and Profit Shifting (BEPS) project to reform the international tax system. This time, discussions led to new recommendations for national implementations of a CBCR standard, published in September 2014, which exceeded the coverage of the prior EU directives by requiring CBCR for large companies in all sectors, but limited disclosure to tax authorities rather than the public and with the primary aim of "providing adequate information conduct transfer pricing risk assessments".

Once more, however, the European Union was quick to advance further than the OECD. Activists and other critics had continued to express criticisms about the specific content of OECD CBCR standard, specifically concerns about (lack of) public access to the information and imposed limitations on the scope of information to be disclosed. And thus, less than two years after the new OECD standard was released, in April 2016, following another public consultation, the European Commission proposed a new directive to require public CBCR for *all* sectors, emphasizing the need for maximalist public CBCR to "tackle corporate tax avoidance", a move explicitly rejected by the OECD policy-makers in 2014. The new directive proposal renewed momentum for the CBCR agenda, accommodating concerns about public access, while also causing a new concern about limitations on the information required to be reported (ActionAid et al. 2016). These debates on the public CBCR directive provide an interesting window into the broader changes of EU actors in international tax policy.

One significant area of conflict around the public CBCR directive has been its formal legal basis in the EU law-making system (European Parliamentary Research Service 2017). The Commission formally proposed the directive as an *accounting* measure, requiring only QMV (qualified majority voting) by member states and providing the Parliament with joint authority. In contrast, had it been classified as a *tax* measure, the directive would only pass with unanimity in the Council, a far more difficult proposition given the internal distributional implications highlighted by increased corporate tax transparency (Dover 2016; European Commission 2016a). No doubt the Commission's choice was made with an eye for an easier path to implementation. And it has received formal support for its position by the Parliament, as well as critical NGOs, while the Council and individual member states have asserted that the public CBCR proposal is a tax measure and, if it is not considered as such, would infringe directly upon national sovereignty. Here, the Commission applied its legislative initiative to try to re-align power in the policy-making network (giving the EP greater procedural power and sidestepping unanimity), building a new coalition to counteract the limitations placed on EU tax policy by member states. While legal basis battles between the Commission and the Council are not new in EU policy contexts (Cullen and Charlesworth 1999), the nature of tax policy has meant it has rarely been a notable fighting ground. Here, the legal basis struggle over public CBCR represents a direct challenge by the Commission (backed by the Parliament) to the authority of member states and the Council, which, in turn, is seeking to resist such critical challenge by asserting its exclusive powers through classification of the proposal to the tax policy area.[4]

Civil society activists historically, with little formal involvement in EU international tax policy, have been particularly active in promoting the *idea* and the *content* of public CBCR in the broader political space. It was civil society advocates who initially ignited and pushed the very concept of public CBCR onto the global political agenda, including the OECD and the EU agendas (Baden and Wigan 2017; Seabrooke and Wigan 2016; Lesage and Kacar 2013). While the OECD dismissed the idea in BEPS, it was taken up in Europe, and here debate has largely been framed by activist discourse. The Commission's claims that its April 2016 public CBCR proposal was primarily concerned with combating "tax avoidance" is inherited from activists, who argued years before that public CBCR would help hold companies accountable "for paying the tax that those in civil society believe they should pay" (Murphy 2010). Such linkage between activists and bureaucrats has contributed to appealing to a broader audience, enabled by the politicization of EU tax affairs in the post-crisis years. The effect has been strong resistance to watering down of the proposal by concerned member states. In a 2016 letter, activists for instance urged Commission President Juncker to ensure public CBCR as an "effective tool that delivers the transparency urgently needed in the fight against corporate tax avoidance and corruption" (ActionAid et al. 2016). The same type of framing is applied by the European

Parliament, including in its 2015 resolution on tax transparency, which called for the introduction of public CBCR (European Parliament 2015).

In contrast, the Council's initial official response to the proposed Directive removed almost all references to "corporate tax avoidance", while asserting an alternative knowledge claim, focused on "public scrutiny" and "trust", and importantly stressing the primacy of the previously-agreed OECD guidance on what might constitute appropriate use CBCR information disclosed by corporates (Council of the European Union 2017). An equally critical but not wholly similar framing has been adopted by another group of stakeholders – business interests. Here, the focus has been on discussing the publication of the data as a threat to commercial sensitivity, competitiveness, and international investment, largely inherited from the prior OECD discussions (see Christensen 2020). The position paper on public CBCR from BusinessEurope, a key EU business lobby, noted that the proposed EU directive would "undermine the role of the tax authorities who have the expertise, and (…) the information to properly enforce tax rules" and "put companies with an EU presence at a competitive disadvantage and damage the attractiveness of the EU as an investment destination" (BusinessEurope 2016). Moreover, in notable alignment with the Council, businesses have stressed the primacy of the OECD, noting, "We support the OECD recommendations regarding the reporting of financial information to tax authorities by companies on a country-by-country basis" (BusinessEurope 2016).

The heterogeneity of the policy advocacy and network links is evident here. Civil society activists, seeking policy progression in the EU that was previously resisted at the OECD, are trying to manage their lack of formal standing in the EU policy process by appealing to a broad political audience and broad popular political themes, specifically the politicized and high-profile media issue of "corporate tax avoidance". In the face of procedural resistance from the Council and member states, the Commission and the Parliament have copied and amplified these policy discourse advanced by activists. Meanwhile, the Council and individual member states have sought to reassert their exclusive powers on tax policy to resist the challengers and frame CBCR in less populist terms, referencing the prior OECD agreement. Businesses have supported this latter approach, emphasizing the primacy of OECD-developed framings, and, in particular, the threat to businesses themselves from potential public disclosure of the CBCR data.

These diverging coalitions and policy arguments around public CBCR in the EU setting stand in sharp contrast to the prior CBCR discussions at the OECD, where the close normative socialization of technical experts across the OECD bureaucracy, national delegates, and other stakeholders (in particular, businesses tax professionals) effectively insulated the policy discussions from broader political surges, benchmarked arguments against a narrow set of appropriateness judgments, and re-framed the debate in specific terms, focused on corporate competitiveness and privacy (Christensen 2020). Notably, in the CBCR policy process at the OECD, many civil society groups deliberately opted *not* to participate in discussions, specifically because they lacked the requisite expertise and did not believe in "greenwashing" a process they would have no influence in. These are well-known dynamics in OECD tax policy-making, where "non-conventional" actors – i.e., those who do not possess a narrow set of expertise – are strongly resisted (Büttner and Thiemann 2017; Sharman 2006; Genschel and Rixen 2015; Sharman 2012; Woodward 2009).

At the time of writing (September 2018), the public CBCR directive was still under discussion in the EU. However, the case illustrates the changing setting and dynamics of EU tax networks, having become far more contested and unstable. This has coincided with a newfound ability to challenge the OECD as the dominant international tax policy-maker. In response to the proposed EU directive and ongoing EU discussion, the OECD (Jeffries 2016) has been openly critical, as have key OECD allies such as the United States (Spencer and Jesse 2016), underscoring the radical nature of these actions by actors in and around the EU. This is a new and more unpredictable world of international tax policy-making, contrasting with the regime's historical stability (Genschel and Rixen 2015).

Conclusion

This chapter has provided a discussion of the context of international tax policy and the policy settings of, in particular, the EU and the OECD, focused on the type and dynamics of different networks. Whereas historically, the OECD was always the dominant cooperative forum for international tax issues, today the EU has evolved into a vibrant arena for tax policy debate amongst issue professionals and concerned organizations, and a key challenger to the OECD. This transformation has been characterized by the evolution of EU tax networks from a narrow, "embryonic" community, marked by little diversity, little breadth, and little contest (both internal and toward the OECD), toward a far more open and adversarial network constellation, with significant heterogeneity, and unstable policy coalitions and unpredictable policy outcomes. In the case of policy discussions on corporate tax transparency, and specifically the idea of public CBCR, this transformation has coincided with diverging policy outcomes, moving away from the historical allegiance to the OECD.

Circling back to the broader topics of this edited volume, the EU tax story is illustrative of the dynamic substance and impacts of issue governance in professional-organizational networks (cf. chapter 3). While at a macro-level glance, the organizational landscape of international tax policy has remained stable for years, the changing professional-organization interactions at the micro-level, especially inside the EU, have radically reworked both the content of contemporary international tax debates and their outcomes. Issue professionals in the EU context have pursued novel strategies, drawing on various professional and organizational resources, to successfully contest the historical "issue control" on global tax matters of professionals in and around the OECD community. Conceptually, these strategies are attempts to assert issue control predominantly through what Henriksen and Seabrooke call "challenging" – where parallel professional-organization networks (here in the EU) push and criticize established issue treatment (here in the OECD).

The broader implications for the global tax regime complex (cf. Chapter 2) and international tax policy, and, in particular, the role of EU tax networks, remains uncertain. In the case of CBCR, the divergence of policy ideas and debates between the OECD and EU settings arguably creates further uncertainty and threatens the overall coherence of the international tax regime complex, which was historically ensured stability through the OECD's dominance. These developments, however, do not stand alone, and must be viewed in light of the general process of politicization of international tax affairs and the consequent explosion of issue salience, as well as institutional crises of the EU itself, which have all contributed to the changing background context and the overall prospect for transformation of the EU tax networks and policy-making. Beyond the CBRC issue, similar dynamics of divergence and uncertainty are visible in other high-profile contemporary international tax policy discussions, such as on taxation of the digital economy (OECD 2018; Kelpie 2018). These conflicts provide peculiarly contrasting developments in an era where EU-OECD cooperation is otherwise increasingly close and strong (Carroll and Kellow 2012).

Notes

1 The clash between the EU and the OECD in international tax policy is particularly noteworthy given the general trend of lessening competition and increasing cooperation between the two organizations (Carroll and Kellow 2012).
2 While CBCR is a prominent case of tax policy controversy and OECD-EU divergence, the post-crisis years have witnessed several similarly diverging policy discussions, including recent debates around the taxation of the digital economy (Kelpie 2018; Christensen and Hearson 2019).
3 The Council conclusions of 14 June 2010 specifically encouraged the EU and its member states to work toward *"exploring country by country reporting as a standard for multinational corporations, by encouraging the OECD to pursue its work on country-by-country reporting (…). In addition, Member States should support ongoing consultation work by the IASB (International Accounting Standard Board) on a country-by-country reporting requirement in IFRS 6 (International Financial Reporting Standard 6)"* (cited in European Commission 2010, 3).
4 More broadly, the Commission has recently sought to problematize the general unanimity requirement in EU tax policy, arguing that it unduly constraints effective and necessary political action (Barbière 2017).

References

ActionAid et al. 2016. "Letter to President Juncker on Commission Proposal on Disclosure of Income Tax Information by Certain Multinational Corporations." Brussels. http://www.eurodad.org/Juncker-letter-CBCR.

Arras, Sarah, and Caelesta Braun. 2017. "Stakeholders Wanted! Why and How European Union Agencies Involve Non-State Stakeholders." *Journal of European Public Policy*, April 1–19. https://doi.org/10.1080/13501763.2017.1307438.

Baden, Adam, and Duncan Wigan. 2017. "Professional Activists on Tax Transparency." In *Professional Networks in Transnational Governance*, edited by Leonard Seabrooke and Lasse Folke Henriksen, 130–146. Cambridge: Cambridge University Press.

Barbière, Cécile. 2017. "Juncker Challenges Unanimity on Fiscal Policy." *Euractiv.Com* (blog). September 18. https://www.euractiv.com/section/future-eu/news/juncker-challenges-unanimity-on-fiscal-policy/.

Berg, Chris, and Sinclair Davidson. 2017. "'Stop This Greed': The Tax-Avoidance Political Campaign in the OECD and Australia." *Econ Journal Watch* 14 (1): 77–102.

BusinessEurope. 2016. "Position Paper: Public Country-by-Country Reporting." https://www.businesseurope.eu/sites/buseur/files/media/position_papers/ecofin/2016-07-06_cbcr_position_paper.pdf.

Büttner, Tim, and Matthias Thiemann. 2017. "Breaking Regime Stability? The Politicization of Expertise in the OECD/G20 Process on BEPS and the Potential Transformation of International Taxation." *Accounting, Economics, and Law: A Convivium*. https://doi.org/10.1515/ael-2016-0069.

Carroll, Peter, and Aynsley Kellow. 2012. "The OECD." In *Routledge Handbook on the European Union and International Institutions: Performance, Policy, Power*, edited by Knud Erik Jørgensen and Katie Verlin Laatikainen, 1st ed., 247–258. Routledge. https://doi.org/10.4324/9780203083642.

Chonghaile, Clár Ní. 2016. "'A System of Privilege and Benefits': Is a Global Tax Body Needed?" *The Guardian*, April 11, sec. Journal of Global Development. http://www.theguardian.com/global-development/2016/apr/11/system-privilege-benefits-global-tax-body-oecd.

Christensen, Rasmus Corlin. 2020. "Elite professionals in transnational tax governance". *Global Networks*. https://doi.org/10.1111/glob.12269.

Christensen, Rasmus Corlin. 2021. "Transparency." In *Global Wealth Chains: Asset Strategies in the World Economy*, edited by Leonard Seabrooke and Duncan Wigan. Oxford: Oxford University Press.

Christensen, Rasmus Corlin, and Martin Hearson. 2019. "The New Politics of International Tax: Taking Stock a Decade after the Financial Crisis." *Review of International Political Economy* 26 (5): 1068–1088. https://doi.org/10.1080/09692290.2019.1625802

Christensen, Rasmus Corlin, and Leonard Seabrooke. 2020. "Global Tax Governance: Is the EU Promoting Tax Justice?" In *Governance and Politics in the Post-Crisis European Union*, edited by Ramona Coman, Amandine Crespy, and Vivien Schmidt. Cambridge University Press: 294-311

Christians, Allison. 2010. "Taxation in a Time of Crisis: Policy Leadership from the OECD to the G20." *Northwestern Journal of Law & Social Policy* 5 (1): 1-23.

Cobham, Alex, Petr Janský, and Markus Meinzer. 2018. "A Half-Century of Resistance to Corporate Disclosure." *Transnational Corporations* 25 (3): 26.

Commission of the European Communities. 1992. *Report of the Committee of Independent Experts on Company Taxation*. Luxembourg: Office for Official Publications of the European Communities.

Council of the European Union. 2017. "Proposal for Directive of the European Parliament and the Council Amending Directive 2013/34/EU as Regards Disclosure of Income Tax Information by Certain Undertakings and Branches (CBCR) – State of Play – 10525/17." http://data.consilium.europa.eu/doc/document/ST-10525-2017-INIT/en/pdf.

Cullen, Holly, and Andrew Charlesworth. 1999. "Diplomacy by Other Means: The Use of Legal Basis Litigation as a Political Strategy by the European Parliament and Member States." *Common Market Law Review* 36: 1243.

Dallyn, Sam. 2016. "An Examination of the Political Salience of Corporate Tax Avoidance: A Case Study of the Tax Justice Network." *Accounting Forum*, December. https://doi.org/10.1016/j.accfor.2016.12.002.

Dover, Robert. 2016. "Fixing Financial Plumbing: Tax, Leaks and Base Erosion and Profit Shifting in Europe." *The International Spectator* 51 (4): 40–50. https://doi.org/10.1080/03932729.2016.1224545.

Eccleston, Richard. 2013. *The Dynamics of Global Economic Governance: The Financial Crisis, the OECD, and the Politics of International Tax Cooperation*. Cheltenham: Edward Elgar Pub.

Eccleston, Richard, and Richard Woodward. 2014. "Pathologies in International Policy Transfer: The Case of the OECD Tax Transparency Initiative." *Journal of Comparative Policy Analysis: Research and Practice* 16 (3): 216–229. https://doi.org/10.1080/13876988.2013.854446.

Edwards, Sophie. 2017. "The G77 Will Push for 'tax Justice' through a UN Tax Body, Says Ecuador's Foreign Affairs Minister." *Devex*, January 13. https://www.devex.com/news/sponsored/the-g77-will-push-for-tax-justice-through-a-un-tax-body-says-ecuador-s-foreign-affairs-minister-89442.

Eurodad. 2016. "An Intergovernmental UN Tax Body – Why We Need It and How We Can Get It." https://www.eurodad.org/globaltaxbody

European Commission. 2010. "Public Consultation on Country-by-Country Reporting by Multinational Companies." http://ec.europa.eu/finance/consultations/2010/financial-reporting/docs/consultation_document_en.pdf.

European Commission. 2016a. "Impact Assessment Assessing the Potential for Further Transparency on Income Tax Information." https://eur-lex.europa.eu/legal-content/EN/TXT/PDF/?uri=CELEX:52016SC0117&from=EN.

European Commission. 2016b. "Common Consolidated Corporate Tax Base (CCCTB)." https://ec.europa.eu/taxation_customs/business/company-tax/common-consolidated-corporate-tax-base-ccctb_en.

European Parliament. 2015. "Bringing Transparency, Coordination and Convergence to Corporate Tax Policies - Resolution 2015/2010(INL) of 16 December." http://www.europarl.europa.eu/sides/getDoc.do?type=TA&language=EN&reference=P8-TA-2015-0457.

European Parliamentary Research Service. 2017. "Public Country-by-Country Reporting by Multinational Enterprises." *Briefing*. http://www.europarl.europa.eu/RegData/etudes/BRIE/2017/595867/EPRS_BRI(2017)595867_EN.pdf.

Forstater, Maya, and Rasmus Corlin Christensen. 2017. "New Players, New Game: The Role of the Public and Political Debate in the Development of Action on International Tax Issues." European Tax Policy Forum Research Paper.

Genschel, Philipp, and Markus Jachtenfuchs. 2011. "How the European Union Constrains the State: Multilevel Governance of Taxation: How the European Union Constrains the State." *European Journal of Political Research* 50 (3): 293–314. https://doi.org/10.1111/j.1475-6765.2010.01939.x.

Genschel, Philipp, and Thomas Rixen. 2015. "Settling and Unsettling the Transnational Legal Order of International Taxation." In *Transnational Legal Orders*, edited by Terence C. Halliday and Gregory Shaffer. New York: Cambridge University Press: 154-184.

Hearson, Martin. 2018. "'Futile and Unrewarding': The Wilderness Years of the International Tax Regime." *Martin Hearson* (blog). June 28. https://martinhearson.wordpress.com/2018/06/28/futile-and-unrewarding-the-wilderness-years-of-the-international-tax-regime/.

Hix, Simon, and Bjørn Høyland. 2013. "Empowerment of the European Parliament." *Annual Review of Political Science* 16 (1): 171–189. https://doi.org/10.1146/annurev-polisci-032311-110735.

Jeffries, Joelle. 2016. "EXCLUSIVE: OECD's Saint-Amans Discusses EC Push to Force MNEs to Publish CbCR Data on Their Websites." *TP Week*, April 12. http://www.tpweek.com/Article/3545055/EXCLUSIVE-OECDs-Pascal-Saint-Amans-discusses-EC-push-to-force-MNEs-to-publish-CbCR-data-on-their.html.

Jogarajan, Sunita. 2018. *Double Taxation and the League of Nations*. Cambridge Tax Law Series. Cambridge: Cambridge University Press.

Kelpie, Colm. 2018. "OECD Warns over Interim Moves to Curb Tax Avoidance." *The Irish Independent*, February 26. https://www.independent.ie/business/world/oecd-warns-over-interim-moves-to-curb-tax-avoidance-36642540.html.

Lesage, Dries, and Yusuf Kacar. 2013. "Tax Justice through Country-by-Country Reporting: An Analysis of the Ideas' Political Journey." In *Tax Justice and the Political Economy of Global Capitalism, 1945 to the Present*, edited by Jeremy Leaman and Attiya Waris, 1 ed., 262–282. New York: Berghahn Books.

Lips, Wouter. 2019. "The EU Commission's digital tax proposals and its cross-platform impact in the EU and the OECD". *Journal of European Integration*, https://doi.org/10.1080/07036337.2019.1705800.

Moore, Mick. 2014. "Tax Justice Campaigning: Is Tough Always Smart?" *The International Centre for Tax and Development*. http://www.ictd.ac/blog/tax-justice-campaigning-is-tough-always-smart/.

Morriss, Andrew P., and Lotta Moberg. 2012. "Cartelizing Taxes: Understanding the OECD's Campaign against Harmful Tax Competition." *Columbia Journal of Tax Law* 4: 1.

Murphy, Richard. 2003. "A Proposed International Accounting Standard: Reporting Turnover and Tax by Location." Association for Accountancy and Business Affairs.

Murphy, Richard. 2010. "Time to Act on Tax Transparency." *The Guardian*, June 30, sec. Opinion. http://www.theguardian.com/commentisfree/2010/jun/30/tax-transparency-country-by-country-reporting.

OECD2011. Outcomes from the Second Meeting of the Informal Task Force on Tax and Development: Paris, 11–12 April 2011.

OECD2018. Tax Challenges Arising from Digitalisation – Interim Report 2018.

Oei, Shu-Yi, and Diane Ring. 2018. "Leak-Driven Law." *UCLA Law Review* 65 (3): 1-87.

Ougaard, Morten. 2011. "Civil Society and Patterns of Accountability in the OECD." In *Building Global Democracy?: Civil Society and Accountable Global Governance*, edited by Jan Aart Scholte, 1 ed. Cambridge: Cambridge University Press: 163-181

Owens, Jeffrey. 2002. "Taxation in a Global Environment." *OECD Observer* 230. http://oecdobserver.org/news/archivestory.php/aid/650/Taxation_in_a_global_environment.html.

Picciotto, Sol. 1992. *International Business Taxation: A Study in the Internationalization of Business Regulation*. New York: Praeger.

Puchala, Donald J. 2013. *Fiscal Harmonization in the European Communities: National Politics and International Cooperation*. Bloomsbury Publishing.

Radaelli, Claudio. 1997. *The Politics of Corporate Taxation in the European Union: Knowledge and International Policy Agendas*. 1 ed. London : Routledge.

Radaelli, Claudio. 1999. "The Public Policy of the European Union: Whither Politics of Expertise?" *Journal of European Public Policy* 6 (5): 757–774. https://doi.org/10.1080/135017699343360.

Roland, Aanor. 2019. "Multiple streams, leaked opportunities, and entrepreneurship in the EU agenda against tax avoidance". *European Policy Analysis*. https://doi.org/10.1002/epa2.1069

Salzman, James. 2005. "Decentralized Administrative Law in the Organization for Economic Cooperation and Development." *Law and Contemporary Problems* 68 (189): 189–224.

Scheve, Kenneth, and David Stasavage. 2016. *Taxing the Rich: A History of Fiscal Fairness in the United States and Europe*. Princeton: Princeton University Press.

Seabrooke, Leonard, and Duncan Wigan. 2013. "Emergent Entrepreneurs in Transnational Advocacy Networks: Professional Mobilization in the Fight for Global Tax Justice." GR:EEN Working Paper No. 41. Centre for the Study of Globalisation and Regionalisation, University of Warwick. http://www.greenfp7.eu/papers/workingpapers.

Seabrooke, Leonard, and Duncan Wigan. 2016. "Powering Ideas through Expertise: Professionals in Global Tax Battles." *Journal of European Public Policy* 23 (3): 357–374.

Sharman, J.C. 2006. *Havens in a Storm: The Struggle for Global Tax Regulation*. 1 ed. Ithaca: Cornell University Press.

Sharman, J.C. 2012. "Seeing Like the OECD on Tax." *New Political Economy* 17 (1): 17–33. https://doi.org/10.1080/13563467.2011.569022.

Skjærseth, Jon Birger. 1994. "The Climate Policy of the EC: Too Hot to Handle?" *JCMS: Journal of Common Market Studies* 32 (1): 25–46. https://doi.org/10.1111/j.1468-5965.1994.tb00483.x.

Spencer, Emery-Kevin, and Justin Jesse. 2016. "Preparing for Country-by-Country Reporting in 2016." *Lexology*, March 30. http://www.lexology.com/library/detail.aspx?g=9b356fe2-cbc3-4cca-a042-2359306f88d2.

Tax Justice Network. 2005. "Tax Us If You Can: The True Story of a Global Failure." Briefing Paper.

Tax Justice Network. 2016. "An Informal History of TJN and the Tax Justice Movement." *Tax Justice Network* (blog). http://www.taxjustice.net/5828-2/.

Thompson, Linda A. 2018. "EU Proposals About Money, Not Tax Fairness: Former OECD Official". *Bloomberg BNA*. June 21.

Vega, Alberto. 2012. "International Governance through Soft Law: The Case of the OECD Transfer Pricing Guidelines." http://papers.ssrn.com/sol3/papers.cfm?abstract_id=2100341.

Wojcik, Dariusz. 2012. "Shining Light on Globalization: The Political Economy of Country-by-Country Reporting." Employment, Work and Finance Working Paper No. 12-07. University of Oxford, St. Peter's College. https://papers.ssrn.com/sol3/papers.cfm?abstract_id=2163449.

Woodward, Richard. 2009. *The Organisation for Economic Cooperation and Development (OECD)*. Routledge Global Institutions Series. Oxford: Routledge.

Ylönen, Matti. 2015. "Reinventing the Wheel? The Rise and Fall of the Early Initiatives against Corporate Tax Avoidance from the 1960s to the 1980s." Draft. University of Helsinki.

7

TRANSNATIONAL NETWORKS OF THE SOVEREIGN DEBT RESTRUCTURING REGIME

Nicholas Haagensen

Introduction

The European Union was struck by the Eurozone sovereign debt crisis in 2010, with the Greek state being acutely affected and only recently emerging from the last economic adjustment program in August 2018. There were a large variety of complex issues that EU actors had to deal with during the crisis, but the Greek debt restructuring stands out as particularly complex and difficult. States engage in a debt restructuring in order to regain access to international capital markets. However, this process can be costly, drawn-out, and detrimental for its citizens. Over the last couple of decades, there have been many sovereign debt restructurings, most notably the Latin American countries in the 1980s, and other emerging market economies in the Global South (Das, Papaioannou, and Trebesch 2012). However, the Greek debt restructuring stands out as not only one of the largest in history (€206 billion), but also the first advanced economy to restructure its debt since the end of World War II (Zettelmeyer, Trebesch, and Gulati 2013). The Greek debt restructuring was achieved with a debt exchange in March/April 2012, as well as a buyback of a large amount of Greek bonds in December 2012, but the path to get there included one failed attempt and an about-face: some Euro area members and the ECB denied the need for a sovereign debt restructuring for a long time, but eventually realized that it was inevitable.

One of the objectives of this volume is to assess whether the networked capacity of the EU amounts to more policy coherence in complex global issues. Using the Greek debt restructuring as a case study, I look at the role of social networks concerned with sovereign insolvency, in which EU and European actors are embedded, and to what degree policy cohesion is achieved as well as how professionals compete over controlling the issue of sovereign debt restructuring. Based on my analysis, I find that the high degree of contestation over sovereign debt restructuring inhibits policy cohesion, despite the EU being part of key networks on this issue. I further point to the central role of legal professionals embedded in expert networks in controlling the issue of how sovereign debt restructuring should unfold through their reflexive professional activities (see Henriksen & Seabrooke in this volume), while they cooperate across opposing institutional visions of the issue of sovereign debt.

Legally, sovereign debt restructuring has often been highly problematic in terms of triggering drawn-out litigation which can have serious adverse effects on the economy of the sovereign state (Das, Papaioannou, and Trebesch 2012), let alone the citizens themselves. When it comes to resolving sovereign debt crises, there is no international legal mechanism or framework (Lastra 2016), and in terms of litigation, it is for national courts to adjudicate in this area as all sovereign bonds indicate a jurisdiction that is based on national law. In practice, this means either the bonds are issued under local law (i.e., the sovereign's own law) or the law of a reputable financial jurisdiction, most often English law or New York law. Thus, national law plays a large role in this transnational policy issue. It may be unusual that a state, which is obviously sovereign, can be sued in a foreign national court. This idea is based on the restrictive theory of sovereign immunity, i.e., states are not immune to commercial court proceedings. It started with the US codifying the theory into law with the 1976 Foreign Sovereign Immunities Act (FSIA), the UK following in 1978 with the State Immunity Act of 1978, after which other countries followed suit (Schumacher, Trebesch, and Enderlein 2018).

Historically, the international organizations (IO) that have dealt with sovereign debt management and crises in the global economy are the IMF and the World Bank. The IMF, considered one of the "world's most powerful agents of economic reform" (Halliday and Carruthers 2007: 1137), offers financial assistance to states that are struggling to service their debt on the condition of structural reforms. The World Bank, among other activities, offers guidance to states in the area of debt management to ensure debt sustainability in the long run. When it comes to the specific issue of debt restructuring, however, a market-based approach prevails, which is articulated in a number of codes of conduct as well as various forms of contractual clauses inserted into bond issuances, which essentially means that the creditors and the sovereign have to work out a deal when negotiating a possible debt restructuring. In that way, this legal regime is characterized by private law contracts on a case by case basis, with no legal certainty as to how each case will turn out, i.e., it is down to the negotiations. Thus, part of the complexity of this regime (for more on complexity see Pattberg and Widerberg, this volume) is based on the proliferation of bond contracts based in various jurisdictions, which could be the sovereign's domestic law, or often New York law or English law. More specifically, the outcomes of one negotiation between a sovereign and its bondholders (i.e., an interaction between some elements in the overall system) could have spill-over effects in the form of new legal constructs being created that may or may not become a new legal norm, for example, novel contract terms, with other contracts incorporating the new terms and thereby changing the overall system over time.

But how does such a process of diffusion and change unfold? What are the specific connections or interactions that enable change in a complex system? Pattberg and Widerberg (Chapter 2 of this volume) point to the utility of network theory to unpack the structures of complex systems, such as the one posited above, by, for example, locating central actors vis-à-vis peripheral actors as well as clusters of actors around specific issue topics of the regime. More specifically, Henriksen and Seabrooke (Chapter 3 of this volume) take this further by exploring and conceptualizing the dynamics of professional actors who traverse various social networks existing in the interstices between their organizational affiliations and professional affiliations in the struggle to control how a salient issue is governed in any given regime. In the regime of sovereign debt restructuring, we see clear articulations of issue control by various professional actors, primarily between lawyers and bankers and policymakers. I argue that the technical expertise and experience of the legal professionals plays a central role in organizing the problems and the solutions of the issue of sovereign debt restructuring.

In what follows, I first outline the literature on sovereign debt restructuring and point out the lack of empirical work on the actors and networks in the area, after which I argue for a theoretical approach that locates networks and professionals as key in controlling the issue of sovereign debt restructuring. I then turn to the case of the Greek debt restructuring to analyze the networks implicated thereof and show how they are connected to other networks of the regime of sovereign debt restructuring.

Literature and theory

In the literature, the evolution of the regime of sovereign debt restructuring is often characterized by, on the one hand, a statutory approach based on the creation of an international legal mechanism, and on the other, by a market-based approach comprised of two elements: first, specific legal clauses (commonly known as Collective Action Clauses or just CACs); and second, a code of conduct (Gelpern and Gulati 2006). CACs refer to a variety of clauses, but the specific ones that are commonly promoted fall into two categories: a collective modification clause, enabling a certain portion of the bondholders to accept a debt restructuring such that the whole group is bound; and a collective acceleration clause, preventing demands for full payment by a single bondholder following a default and instead requiring approval via a minimum bondholder vote (Weidemaier and Gulati 2013). The second element of a code of conduct simply refers to soft law norms that are recommended regarding how the sovereign debt restructuring process should unfold in terms of principles such as fairness, transparency, and cooperation.

The use of CACs for sovereign debt restructuring has been a point of much debate in the literature with scholars looking at various dimensions of this contractual approach: the rise and diffusion of CACs despite how difficult standardized contract change can be (Gelpern and Gulati 2006; Gelpern and Gulati 2008; Weidemaier and Gulati 2013); the effectiveness of CACs as a contractual device in sovereign debt restructuring (Weidemaier and Gulati 2013; Gelpern and Gulati 2013); and technical aspects of CACs, e.g., whether they affect sovereign bond yields (Bardozzetti and Dottori 2014; Richards and Gugiatti 2003). In contrast, there is scant literature on the codes of conduct element in sovereign debt, besides Ritter (2010) and Kalaitzake (2017). Finally, some literature touches on the dialectical interplay between the contractual approach, on the one hand, and the statutory approach, on the other (Eichengreen, Kletzer, and Mody 2003; Gelpern and Gulati 2006).

This latter area of literature looks at the evolution of sovereign debt restructuring in terms of a dynamic action-reaction between the institutional visions of a market-based approach and an international statutory approach. This narrative points to the IMF's attempt in the period 2001–2002 to introduce a Sovereign Debt Restructuring Mechanism (SDRM) as the point when CACs became heavily promoted as a counter-proposal to the IMF's statutory approach. Essentially, the IMF wanted to create "a predictable legal mechanism" (Krueger 2002: 4) with the most crucial element being a provision that binds all creditors to a debt restructuring agreement via the acceptance of a qualified majority of creditors (ibid.). The SDRM was not well received by market players and some emerging market sovereigns, who worried that any interaction with such a mechanism would signal default and lead to a self-fulfilling prophecy (Gelpern and Gulati 2006). Furthermore, many were worried about the politicization of what they saw as a market function and even saw a conflict of interest for the IMF as it was often a distressed sovereign's largest creditor (ibid.). The alternative to the SDRM, essentially Collective Action Clauses (CACs), were then heavily promoted at the same time by some at the US Treasury, most notably Under Secretary for International Affairs, John Taylor. Subsequently, the IMF acknowledged the lack of feasibility relating to the SDRM at that time (Ritter 2010), and the market-based approach started to gain traction with Mexico issuing New York law bonds with CACs in 2003 (Drage and Hovaguimian 2004; Weidemaier and Gulati 2013) and other emerging markets following suit (Weidemaier and Gulati 2013). In sum, until the IMF made a serious attempt to introduce a statutory mechanism, market actors and emerging market sovereigns had not really attempted to promote CACs.

On the point of a code of conduct, the most prevalent have been the "Principles for Stable Capital Flows and Fair Debt Restructuring in Emerging Markets" (hereinafter the *Principles*), which were agreed upon between public sector actors, private creditors, and sovereign debtors in 2004 under the auspices of the Institute of International Finance (hereinafter the IIF) – an association for financial institutions (Ritter 2010). The *Principles* were started in 2004, and a report regarding their implementation is released annually. This report is overseen by a Group of Trustees (hereinafter GoT), comprising "former and current leaders in international finance, with exceptional experience" (IIF 2006: 7), who meet once a year to check the progress of the implementation of the *Principles* within the regime of international finance. Furthermore, the GoT oversees the work of the Principles Consultative Group (hereinafter PCG), "a select group of finance and central bank officials with senior representatives of the private financial community tasked with monitoring and encouraging the practical application of the *Principles*" (IIF 2016: 6). The role of the IIF is to act as a secretariat, and consult "with members of the PCG as well as other market participants as to which countries should be included in PCG discussions" (IIF 2006: 7). Crucially, the *Principles* are seen as complementing the use of CACs, which are framed in the *Principles* as an important element of resilience and stability in the financial system. In sum, the *Principles* together with the CACs represent a comprehensive soft norm market approach.

What the literature does not look at comprehensively is the role certain actors and their networks (the GoT and the PCG amongst others) have played in the area of sovereign debt restructuring, the rise of CACs and the *Principles* (but see Kalaitzake (2017) for a political power conception of the PCG and GoT), and a possible statutory approach. At the transnational level, the social space of sovereign debt restructuring is "thin" (Seabrooke 2014), meaning there are less social actors, less mechanisms of socialization, and less professional constraints than at the national level; however, this "thin" environment is becoming more complex as more actors appear and new norms emerge, i.e., it can be characterized as an international complex regime (Alter and Meunier 2009). As Pattberg and Widerberg (Chapter 2 of this volume) assert, network theory can help the researcher render complexity and complex systems by unpacking the elements of the system into various components and their interconnections. Given that I am looking at actors and social networks, Henriksen and Seabrooke (Chapter 3 of this volume) offer a conceptual toolbox for conceiving and analyzing the role of a certain type of actor embedded in social networks that deal with complex regimes.

Henriksen and Seabrooke (2015) look at how professionals located in two-level (organizational and professional) networks use the uncertainty of transnational contexts to control issues beyond "profession jurisdictions or organizational mandates" (ibid.: 14). The authors establish an ideal type actor dubbed an *issue professional* defined as an actor "seen as 'knowing well' within an issue-specific field of governance and source of recognition among their professional peers is often based on a combination of specialized technical expertise and institutional mobility" (Henriksen and Seabrooke, Chapter 3). Based on the dynamic conditions afforded by the nexus of professional and organizational networks, we can expect that actors embedded in the regime of sovereign debt restructuring will have clear professional identities connected to the issues of sovereign debt, which is most clearly articulated in their work experience in the area; their work will entail peer recognition; they will have high technical expertise and complex institutional experience; and hybridity will characterize some of the location of their interactions, i.e., central bankers and policymakers working with private financiers and lawyers. Once we have established the existence of issue professionals and their networks, we can then look at expected behavior. Given the highly technical and narrow nature of sovereign debt restructuring, and given that Henriksen and Seabrooke (this volume) assert that in cases where issues are very technical and narrow, professional expertise and tasks will be coupled to transnational issue control, I have created two propositions appropriate for my case in order to test the empirical material:

Proposition I: *Given the highly technical and narrow nature of sovereign debt restructuring, we expect to see expertise and professional tasks play a large role in controlling and organizing the issue.*

Proposition II: *Given the mixture of actors from various expert areas – central banking, financial investment, and law – we expect to see professionals compete over control of the issue using their expertise.*

In the next section, an analysis of the networks around the Greek debt restructuring will be carried out to explore the degree to which these can be characterized as issue networks and to ascertain the control efforts by issue professionals in the area of sovereign debt restructuring, as well as to consider to what degree the EU's participation in these networks affords policy cohesion.

The Greek debt restructuring

Based on the conceptual framework above, the Principles Consultative Group (PCG) and their Group of Trustees (GoT) can be conceived of as issue networks, as they are focused primarily on the issue of sovereign debt restructuring. The actors in these networks are a mixture of central bankers, private bankers, lawyers, financial advisors, and policymakers from finance ministries and treasuries, all of whom come from Western and Eastern Europe, the US, Asia, and Africa. This indicates a high level of institutional hybridity in the actors' interactions. Based on the actors' credentials, it is clear that they have expertise in their various areas, as well as institutionally complex careers, most notably, moving between public and private organizations, e.g., Jacques de Larosiére, who has worked at the IMF, the European Bank for Reconstruction & Development, as well as the French bank BNP Paribas. Notably, there are few lawyers in these networks, with most professionals coming from banking and finance. It was Jean-Claude Trichet (President of the ECB from 2003 to 2011) who originally proposed a code of conduct for sovereign debt restructuring back in 2001 when he was Governor of the Banque de France (Couillault and Weber 2003). At the IMF Annual Meeting in 2002, he made an official proposal and G-7 officials worked on a report with the private sector and issuers. From there it was taken up by the

IIF together with key public and private officials to create the *Principles*. The narrative regarding the *Principles* is essentially about the need for "transparency and the timely flow of information between debtors and creditors…to ensure close debtor-creditor dialogue and cooperation" (Ritter 2010: 225) with a clear focus on "good-faith negotiations" and "fair treatment" for creditors.

When Greece started having financial difficulties, the networks of the PCG and the GoT had connections to actors who would go on to be directly involved in the restructuring of Greek debt (see Figure 7.1 below). Most notably, Jean-Claude Trichet, President of the ECB, was the Chair of the GoT and played a key role in the Greek debt negotiations.[1] Also on the GoT were Fabrizio Saccomanni, deputy governor of the Bank of Italy, and alternate member on the ECB's Governing Council; Jörg Asmussen,[2] State Secretary of the German Finance Ministry, and who then sat on the executive board of the ECB from the beginning of 2012, and who was directly involved in the negotiations for the restructuring (Kalaitzake 2017); and Ramon Fernandez, Head of the French Treasury. Moreover, key members of the PCG and GoT also represented some of the systemically significant banks and asset managers who owned substantial amounts of Greek bonds at the time. Specifically, BNP Paribas (France) with €5 billion and represented by Jacques de Larosière; Commerzbank (Germany) with €2.9 billion and represented by Klaus-Peter Müller; Deutsche Bank (Germany) with €1.6 billion and represented by Caio Koch-Weser; Bayern LB (Germany) by Elaine Murphy; Greylock Capital (USA) by Hans Humes; HSBC (UK) by Robert Gray; and Intesa San Paolo (Italy) by Gyorgy Suranyi (Zettelmeyer, Trebesch, and Gulati 2013). The IIF coordinated these members to make a Creditor Committee of 32 banks, insurers, and asset managers to represent the creditors of Greece in the negotiations over the debt restructuring with the Creditor Committee, then making a smaller Steering Committee to do the negotiations with Greece's lawyers. The chairs of the Steering Committee were Charles Dallara, then Managing Director of the IIF, Jean Lemierre of BNP Paribas, and Hans Hume of Greylock Capital (Kalaitzake 2017; Zettelmeyer, Trebesch, and Gulati 2013). Notably, both Jacques de Larosiére and Jean Lemierre are well-known to the EU, with both having been President of the European Bank for Reconstruction and Development (EBRD) (see IIF 2011, 2012). Larosiére had also been the Managing Director of the IMF, as well as part of the European Commission task force on the financial crisis (Kalaitzake 2017: 11–12).

When the EU sovereign debt crisis struck in 2010, EU policymakers had to act quickly to implement a variety of legal mechanisms to aid member states in financial distress, while the ECB engaged in a number of monetary instruments, such as sovereign bond-buying programs. At that time, there was a huge amount of contention in the EU on the issue of sovereign debt restructuring. Angela Merkel and Nicolas Sarkozy had declared at Deauville in 2010, their intention for private-sector involvement in debt restructuring. However, in the period from 2010 to 2012, many EU policymakers were very much against the idea (Kalaitzake 2017). In a 2013 report, the IMF suggested that a debt restructuring

134 Nicholas Haagensen

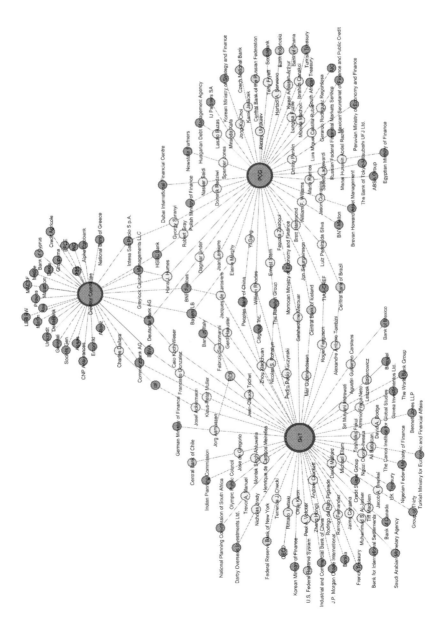

FIGURE 7.1 Network diagram of connections between EU/European actors and PCG and GoT and the Creditor Committee coordinated to negotiate with the Greek government.

with Private-Sector Involvement (PSI) from the onset would have been best for debt sustainability for Greece, but as they state "debt restructuring had been considered by the parties to the negotiations but had been ruled out by the euro area" (IMF 2013: 34). The ECB was notable in this regard, with Jean-Claude Trichet being very much against it from both an institutional and market perspective. Institutionally, the view was that a debt restructuring in euros would undermine the ECB's mandate to safeguard the currency's integrity. From a market perspective, the view was that such an event would affect market confidence, and many feared contagion to other distressed sovereigns.[3] Given that many of the actors involved in the debt restructuring (key European bankers and ECB officials, most notably Jean-Claude Trichet) are also part of the sovereign debt networks of the GoT and PCG, it could be expected that there would be a relatively high level of policy cohesion relating to how the Greek debt restructuring should unfold. As discussed above, though, this was not the case, most obviously because of the reluctance of the ECB to allow a restructuring given its organizational mandate; EU actors being part of these networks did not translate into more policy cohesion.

In July 2011, private-sector creditors – 39 financial institutions holding Greek debt – offered to be involved in a voluntary debt exchange, with the Institute of International Finance (IIF) stating in a press release that the debt exchange would translate to a "21 percent Net Present Value (NPV) loss for investors" (Zettelmeyer, Trebesch, and Gulati 2013: 7). The July 2011 debt exchange, together with the official sector financial assistance, failed to materialize as the EU and IMF had difficulties agreeing on a structural reform package with the Greek government, leading to rising yields in secondary markets. It was later acknowledged that Greece needed a larger debt reduction (Zettelmeyer, Trebesch, and Gulati 2013). On October 26, 2011, a Euro Summit statement invited "Greece, private investors and all parties concerned to develop a voluntary bond exchange with a nominal discount of 50 percent on notional Greek debt held by private investors".[4] However, as stated by the Greek government's key lawyer in the negotiations, Lee Buchheit, the process was far from "voluntary" in that "Greece was commanded to restructure what was left of its debt in the hands of private-sector creditors (about EUR 206 billion)" (Buchheit 2016: 48).

The second PSI would again be done by drawing on the IIF to coordinate a Creditor Committee. This deal was successfully completed, and was characterized by a variety of novel elements. A key feature of the deal was negotiated by Jean Lemierre on the side of the creditors and Michele Lamarche from Lazard on the side of Greece. This was a "co-financing" option which bound the public creditors (Euro-area member states) with the private creditors, as the financing for the debt exchange came via the European Financial Stability Facility (itself funded by the Euro-area member states) in the form of €30 billion worth of new bonds for the private creditors. Essentially, the "co-financing" element meant that if Greece defaulted on its payments to the private creditors, it would also default on the loan from the EFSF and thereby to the public creditors. This component was apparently critical in getting the private creditors to agree to the deal, as it put them on a more equal footing with the public creditors.[5] Importantly, the legal elements of the creation of the EFSF and the bond exchange were handled by lawyers from the law firm Clifford Chance.

An even more crucial feature of the final deal was the decision by Greece, on the advice of its lawyer, Lee Buchheit, to retroactively put CACs into Greek law issued government bonds, thus binding the creditors owning these bonds through legislation (Buchheit and Gulati 2010). This was possible because approximately 93% of outstanding Greek bonds were governed by Greek law (Buchheit 2016). This was seen as a controversial move, but it worked to the degree that Greek bondholders were bound to the new specifications, "if holders of at least 50% in aggregate principal amount of the Greek law-governed GGBs voted either in favour or against the proposed amendment and at least two-thirds of the principal amount voted accepted the terms of a debt restructuring" (Buchheit 2016: 49). In the end, this move enabled Greece to restructure the majority of its domestic law debt, which was crucial for the overall restructuring.

Following the difficulties of the debt restructuring, the GoT and PCG networks engaged in issue control. Essentially, this was manifest in attempts to reinforce their market-based approach of using CACs in bond contracts and following their soft norm code of conduct, the *Principles*. In many ways, the creation of the *Principles* and the annual reports by the PCG and GoT on sovereign debt issues can be seen as issue control by banking and finance professionals embedded in two-level networks – that of their formal organization, e.g., finance ministries, central banks, private banks, law firms, or asset management firms – and that of the professional network – the GoT and the PCG. Every year, they analyze sovereign debt issues and implementation of the *Principles*, all of which is framed by their market-based approach, and given these actors' organizational seniority, as well as the promotion of the *Principles* by the IIF – a politically powerful financial industry association (Kalaitzake 2017) – the market-based approach on sovereign debt has enjoyed policy consensus and convergence (up until the Greek experience), in contrast to the IMF's failed attempt in 2002 at a statutory/international law approach. Subsequently, the IMF has observer status in the PCG meetings, and the *Principles* aims for synergies with the IMF's policies (IIF 2006), indicating the distance the IMF has taken from the statutory approach.

In terms of the Greek debt restructuring, the most clear manifestation of issue control by the GoT in 2012, when, together with the IIF, they organized the Joint Committee on Strengthening the Framework for Sovereign Debt Crisis Prevention and Resolution (hereinafter the Joint Committee) to create a report which took account of the Greek sovereign debt restructuring and the degree to which the *Principles* were followed or deviated from it (IIF 2012), with participation from many of the same actors from the PCG and GoT. This Joint Committee also involved key EU actors such as Thomas Wieser (then President of the Euro Working Group and the EU's Economic Financial Committee),

Klaus Regling (Managing Director of the ESM), and Gerassimos Thomas (then a Director at ECFIN) as well as key lawyers who worked on the side of the Steering Committee (i.e., the private creditors).

Essentially, the report attempts to frame the eventual success of the Greek experience as being tied to a market-based approach, for example, by stating that the Greek experience "has clearly demonstrated that a voluntary, market-based approach is more effective and appropriate than a unilateral, top-down approach to debt restructuring" (IIF 2012: 4). This is misleading. As mentioned, the first PSI attempt failed because there was not enough debt relief, and it was also mainly a private initiative as the French banks had drafted it. Furthermore, the second PSI was said to be far from voluntary as asserted by Greece's lawyer and even by Philip Wood, a lawyer to the Steering Committee; rather, it was an order from the public sector that there should be at least 50% debt relief. Despite Wood affirming that "[t]here was not a lot of negotiation. It was essentially an imposed solution",[6] he still appears on the Joint Committee report. Finally, the deal was ultimately a success for Greece because it could change its domestic law to include CACs in domestic law Greek bonds – an obviously unilateral action. On this, the report states, "Retroactive legal changes to unilaterally modify the terms and the conditions of financial contracts may undermine the integrity of financial markets and the sanctity of contracts and should be avoided" (IIF 2012: 15), although they do say it may be warranted in exceptional cases. The report further criticizes the fact that the ECB's portion of Greek bonds was not part of the restructuring, which indicates the ECB having preferred creditor status over private creditors. However, as Jörg Asmussen – by then a member of the ECB Executive Board – stated, the ECB is forbidden to take part in a debt restructuring, as it amounts to monetary state financing. Yet, Asmussen was part of the 2012 PCG report on the *Principles*, in which this point of the ECB's senior creditor status was critiqued.[7]

The report further states that the *Principles* "have usefully contributed to the development of the modalities for engaging with the private sector (summarized in the March 2011 "Term Sheet") of the European Stability Mechanism (ESM)" (IIF 2012: 3), thus claiming a certain amount of policy cohesion between the PCG and GoT networks' view and the Euro-area policymakers. A clearer indication of this is the inclusion of CACs in Euro-area bonds from January 2013, as stipulated in the ESM Treaty. However, the ESM Treaty also asserts preferred creditor status over private creditors, which the Joint Committee report frames as being an obstacle to "full access to private capital markets" and "fair burden sharing" (IIF 2012: 15). This indicates a policy divergence between the ESM Treaty and Euro-area policymakers and the PCG and GoT, despite the fact that Thomas Wieser, the President of the Eurogroup Working Group, and the EU's Economic and Financial Committee, was a Co-Chair on the Joint Committee report.

In sum, the Joint Committee attempted to control the issue by framing the success of the Greek debt restructuring as being based on a voluntary, market approach, while critiquing aspects which were considered unilateral or gave preferential treatment to public creditors. It also attempted to connect its framing of the issue of sovereign debt with the policy position of the Euro area in terms of the ESM Treaty (besides the preferential creditor status aspect). Overall, this framing follows on from the GoT and PCG's *Principles* annual reports, but the result of the Joint Committee report is ambiguous, since the report praises the success of the debt restructuring, while noting key elements such as the unilateral action of Greece as negatively impacting financial markets. In that way, the market narrative fails to control the issue as it fails to resolve the ambiguities between why the deal was successful on the one hand, and why some elements of the deal were potentially negative, while insinuating policy consensus on these issues among the various actors – from the PCG, GoT, EU officials, and Steering Committee members of the creditors – who were involved in making the report. Finally, none of the legal or financial professionals working on the side of Greece worked on this report, which in some way makes sense because actors like Buchheit would disagree with the Joint Committee on a few points, e.g., the degree to which the deal was voluntary (see Buchheit 2016).

Post-Greek debt restructuring: The rise of competing expert networks

Greek debt restructuring – together with developments in Argentina – re-ignited interest in sovereign debt restructuring globally, with the US Treasury and the United Nations initiating expert groups, in which we see the participation of key legal professionals who were involved in the Greek debt restructuring, but who were not involved in the Joint Committee report. In this section, I analyze these expert networks and the professionals embedded in them, as well as the outcomes of these networks in order to see how they differ from the PCG and GoT networks.

Following the Greek debt restructuring, the US Treasury became interested in Greece's use of CACs, which although successful on the domestic law issued bonds, still led to hold-outs for some of the foreign law issued bonds. Critically, these developments worried them because the implications were renewed interest in a statutory approach and a threat to New York as a dominant jurisdiction in international finance (Sobel 2016). In a report published by the Chair of the US Treasury-led initiative, Mark Sobel,[8] he writes "[t]he effort was premised on the US retaining its long-standing reservations about statutory approaches ... Treasury staff made clear that the US did not support work on statutory approaches" (Sobel 2016: 6). They thus initiated a Sovereign Debt Roundtable (hereinafter the Roundtable) to improve foreign law CACs, and thereby secure the market-based approach to debt restructuring and New York's dominance as a major financial district.

After three meetings and numerous conference calls, a draft model of the aggregation clause was achieved. This was the culmination of work by legal experts, specifically Lee Buchheit (from Cleary Gottlieb and former lawyer for Greece), Anna Gelpern, Ben Heller (Hutchin Hill Capital), Brad Setser (Treasury), Deborah Zandstra (from Clifford Chance and worked on the EFSF debt buy back during the Greek debt restructuring) and Sean Hagan (General Counsel for the IMF) (Sobel 2016). Once the Roundtable had agreed on their model clauses for CACS, in 2014, an industry association for capital markets, the International Capital Market Association (ICMA), offered to develop the legal text for the models. Deborah Zandstra from the law firm Clifford Chance was the primary drafter with the help of Leland Goss, Managing Director and General Counsel for ICMA, and Robert Gray, of HSBC (who has also been part of the PCG and GoT) and the Chair for ICMA's Regulatory Policy Committee. These ICMA model clauses subsequently became the industry standard and were endorsed by the IMF (Sobel 2016). The US Treasury's Roundtable was also supported by Jean Lemierre (of BNP Paribas and key negotiator in the Greek debt restructuring) and Hung Tran (of the IIF).

Mexico became the first country to use the new CACs under New York law. Mexico's Finance Minister participated in the Roundtable, which obviously facilitated the issuance (Sobel 2016). Despite this seeming success for the US Treasury staff involved, as well as the legal actors who participated in the Roundtable, the report by their Chair ends with the following challenge:

> Some country representatives, especially at the United Nations, continue to push for development of a statutory mechanism, even though the statutory approach has found little support in the IMF and G20, and has been rejected by the USA and UK, the key centres in which over three-quarters of foreign law bond issuance takes place. Implementation of the new CACs underscores the innovativeness of the contractual framework and once again shows why work on statutory approaches is unlikely to be needed or gain traction in financial policy circles.
>
> *(Sobel 2016: 10)*

Further evidence of this explicit contestation is found in the United Nations Conference on Trade and Development's (UNCTAD) report published in the same year – 2014 – on their initiative for a statutory mechanism, where they argued that they did not believe that CACs would solve the problem of "vulture funds" initiating litigation and that an international mechanism was necessary: "UNCTAD's remarks were appreciated by the IDB [Inter-America Development Bank] and some participating countries (UK and Dominican Republic), but the IMF and US Treasury representatives were reluctant to open a debate on these broader systemic issues" (UNCTAD 2014). These reservations also came up in the report by the US Treasury initiative from 2013: "the IMF representatives also made clear that the Fund had no intention of pursuing work on statutory approaches" (Sobel 2016: 6). The interesting link between these two approaches is that they are both premised on the cooperation of the very same group of key legal experts, most notably, Anna Gelpern, Law Professor (Georgetown University); Lee Buchheit (from Cleary Gottlieb); and Deborah Zandstra (from Clifford Chance). As mentioned above, both Lee Buchheit and Deborah Zandstra were involved in the Greek debt restructuring, as well as being in key legal networks, such as the International Law Association's Sovereign Bankruptcy Study Group, and the Financial Markets Law Committee's Sovereign Bond Scoping Forum.

Another expert group was formed in 2012, the Expert Group on Sovereign Debt Restructuring, but this time under the auspices of the United Nations Department of Economic and Social Affairs (UNDESA) together with the Centre for International Governance Innovation (CIGI). They were pursuing a renewed interest in the possibility of an international statutory mechanism, along the lines of the IMF's failed SDRM. Here we see Deborah Zandstra, Lee Buchheit, and Anna Gelpern, who all participated in the US Treasury's Sovereign Debt Roundtable, and UNCTAD's initiative, and we also see Daniel Cohen, an economist who was part of Greece's debt restructuring negotiating team with advisors from Lazard.

The culmination of these working groups has not amounted to a statutory mechanism. However, two different sets of principles have been created and endorsed: first, UNCTAD's Principles on Promoting Responsible Sovereign Lending and Borrowing in 2012, and the UN Generally Assembly's Basic Principles for Sovereign Debt Restructuring Processes in 2015. UNCTAD's work on a debt mechanism has amounted to a report published in 2015 called "Sovereign Debt Workouts: Going Forward Roadmap and Guide", with its own set of principles as well as calls for the creation of an international institution, a Sovereign Debt Workout Institution (DWI). Here we see competition in terms of the UN entities producing two sets of principles, both of which are anchored in the market-based approach, meaning they compete with the IIF's *Principles*.

The competition and contestation over the right approach to sovereign debt restructuring presented above flow from the level of the formal organizations from the official sector (the US Treasury and the United Nations), but this does not seem to be a problem for the professionals as they move between the networks and cooperate with the opposing sides, organizing the issue in line with their expertise. We see a few very central actors who are involved in a high number of expert networks, for example, both Lee Buchheit (from Cleary Gottlieb) and Deborah Zandstra (from Clifford Chance) have participated in eight, which indicates a high level of centrality, as shown in Figure 7.2 below. An interesting finding is the centrality of legal academics: Anna Gelpern from the University of Georgetown is the most central actor, having participated in all (12 in total) the meetings of UNCTAD, UNDESA, and the US Treasury Roundtable, making her the most central actor, while Michael Waibel from the University of Cambridge has participated in nine meetings, and Matthias Goldmann from Goethe University Frankfurt has participated in six. The centrality of these actors indicates a large interest in academic legal knowledge as an input to these

The EU sovereign debt restructuring regime 141

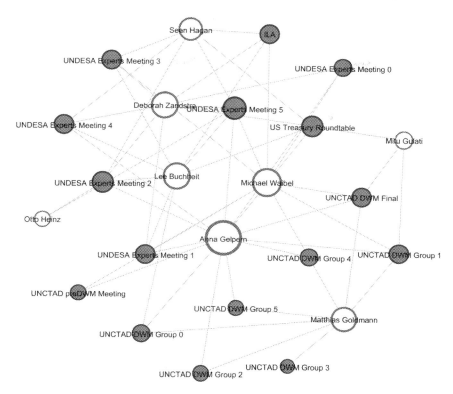

FIGURE 7.2 Main legal professionals embedded in various expert networks on the issue of sovereign debt restructuring.

expert groups, a characteristic that was absent from the PCG and GoT networks. There is limited participation from the EU, with Otto Heinz, a legal expert for the ECB who has also been head of the Financial Law Division of the ECB, having participated in two expert network meetings.

In terms of issue control, the issue of sovereign debt restructuring is highly technical and narrow; thus the professional tasks and control of the issue transnationally are tightly coupled (Henriksen and Seabrooke in this volume). The professional tasks, namely, the legal construction of the financial instrument (bond), which informs the market; the drafting of legal texts and finally practising law, in this case negotiating the legal points of a debt restructuring, go hand in hand with controlling the issue. Legal expertise plays a significant role in the clarification of the technical problems as well as their solution. Bracketing any institutional preference, the legal experts can engage in competing visions of a market approach on the one hand versus a statutory approach on the other, because it is their expertise and professional tasks that inform how they deal with, and control, the issue, which, in turn, organizes the issue. The contestation between the organizations of the US Treasury and UNCTAD organized the issue of sovereign debt restructuring into two opposing visions of how to deal with it; while the cooperation of the legal professionals organized the content of the issue, i.e., the strengthened ICMA model CACs part of the US Treasury's vision of a continuing market approach on the one hand, and further investigation into the feasibility of a statutory mechanism at the level of international law on the part of UNCTAD. Later, competition to the IIF's *Principles* arose both from UNCTAD's Principles on Promoting Responsible Sovereign Lending and Borrowing in 2012, and the UN Generally Assembly's Basic Principles for Sovereign Debt Restructuring Processes in 2015. In sum, our first proposition is confirmed in that the highly technical and narrow nature of the issue is tightly coupled to professionals' tasks and expertise, primarily of the lawyers. Our second proposition sees legal expertise as being the main driver in organizing the issue following the Greek debt restructuring as the most central actors in the expert networks of US Treasury, UNCTAD, and UNDESA are the legal actors. Moreover, the high centrality of legal academics indicates an interest in academic knowledge as an input to these expert networks.

Although there is quite a bit of representation of EU and European actors on the PCG and GoT, the EU seems to play a more limited role in the above-mentioned networks. One partial explanation is that the EU had already gotten the necessary policy in place with the Treaty of the European Stability Mechanism (ESM), which is an international public law treaty, stating that all Euro-area bonds would include CACs from January 1, 2013. Furthermore, the EU's Economic and Financial Committee (EFC) has a sub-committee called the Sub-Committee on EU Sovereign Debt Markets (hereinafter the Sub-Committee) who have investigated the issue of CACs for the EFC.[9] In a way, the Sub-Committee is the EU's own network on sovereign debt. However, it is made up of debt managers from the member states, who play a different role to legal professionals. As Gelpern and Gulati (2013) have shown, these debt managers see their work as having very little to do with legal issues and they are seen as highly conservative. They are not trying to control the issue of sovereign debt restructuring; rather, they are trying to distance themselves from it altogether. They hired legal firm Cleary Gottlieb's London office to assist them with the introduction of CACs in Euro-area bonds in the ESM Treaty.[10] In any case, the actors from the Sub-Committee could not be located in any of the legal networks, expert groups, or the GoT and PCG networks. Thus, I explain the involvement of the ECB lawyers in the UN expert groups as being an attempt to get information about possible policy movements, as opposed to trying to outright influence them given that the EU has already included CACs in Euro-area government bonds as part of the ESM Treaty in 2012. These Euro-area CACs – as well as the experience in Greece – then inspired further development of CACs in other jurisdictions as seen above in the creation of the ICMA model CAC by the legal professionals and interest by the expert groups in a possible statutory mechanism. The 2014 ICMA model includes the choice of "single-limb" voting, meaning all the bondholders across multiple series in a bond can be bound through a majority vote, while the Euro-area bond CACs are "series by series", meaning a higher possibility of one of the series having a minority of hold-outs (Gelpern, Heller, and Setser 2016). However, the Eurogroup, as of December 2018, decided to introduce single-limb CACs into Euro-area bonds by 2022.[11] Given that the ICMA model has been available since 2014, it is striking that it has taken so long for the EU to catch up and points to the lack of speed regarding Eurozone reform.

Conclusion

The findings in this chapter point to certain ambiguities for the EU's capacity to navigate and manage complex issues such as sovereign debt restructuring. Firstly, before the Greek debt restructuring, the PCG and GoT networks that the EU is part of had pursued a stable narrative about the utility of the *Principles* – the code of conduct – and CACs in instances of sovereign debt restructuring. Given the complexity of the Greek experience, the accounting of the events that transpired between the EU actors, the private creditors, and Greece in the GoT's Joint Committee report pointed to incoherence. The report claimed a successful restructuring based on a voluntary, market approach, while critiquing key elements of the restructuring, as well as EU legal obligations. In sum, the implication is that these networks are not able to enable coherence for EU actors, given the complexity of the Economic and Monetary Union, nor can they control the issue as manifest in the divergences between the report and what some of the actors have said of the Greek experience.

The legal professionals that worked on the Greek restructuring went on to be central figures in expert networks focused on exploring alternatives to sovereign debt restructuring in the form of a possible statutory mechanism and alternative codes of conduct to the *Principles*. The analysis of these expert networks indicated the role of legal expertise in controlling the issue of sovereign debt even when the solution envisioned for dealing with the problems of sovereign debt restructurings was framed by two different institutional visions. The possibility that the same group of legal experts can contribute to two competing institutional visions of sovereign debt, i.e., a market-based approach in the form of private contract law versus a statutory approach based on international law – speaks to the particular nature of legal expertise in controlling issues. Law is often adversarial, especially in the US tradition, and it is thus possible for legal experts to entertain potentially opposing institutional setups and work toward their manifestation, especially in the sense of legal scale: market-based activities being governed by contract law at a micro-level (e.g. bond contracts), and a statutory international law mechanism functioning at a more macro-level (e.g. an international organizations as third party dispute resolver). For example, the legal technique of jurisdiction works to separate such scales to avoid clashes of governance (Valverde 2009), thereby enabling the existence of potentially incommensurate legal realities that only come into application when activated by jurisdiction. Further research could look more specifically at how legal techniques, such as jurisdiction, play out in empirical cases of sovereign debt restructuring, and more specifically look at the various layers of jurisdiction that have been used to deal with the Eurozone crisis and whether these pose difficulties for EU law. Furthermore, more systematic analyses of the social networks of the abovementioned actors could be done to locate less central actors that may act as bridges between networks and ascertain to what degree these actors may be brokers between different domains.

Notes

1 In 2012, he was replaced as GoT Chair by Christian Noyer, former ECB Vice-President, who was the governor of the Bank of France at the time.
2 In the diagram, all special characters such as *ö* or *è* are simply inputted as *o* or *e* given formatting issues with the network program.
3 Jean-Claude Trichet interview with Wolfgang Proissl, Financial Times Deutschland (July 14, 2011); online at: https://www.ecb.europa.eu/press/key/date/2011/html/sp110718.en.html.
4 See Euro Summit statement dated 26 October 2011 at https://www.consilium.europa.eu/uedocs/cms_data/docs/pressdata/en/ec/125644.pdf.
5 See https://www.bloomberg.com/news/articles/2012-04-19/a-lazard-banker-is-the-greeks-financial-goddess.
6 See http://www.ifre.com/greek-tragedy-averted/21052459.fullarticle.
7 See https://www.reuters.com/article/us-ecb-asmussen-idUSBRE88O11N20120925.
8 Mark Sobel chaired the US Treasury Sovereign Debt Roundtable: "He has served in the US Treasury for over three decades, including as Deputy Assistant Secretary for International Monetary and Financial Policy, as well as prior to that, inter alia, as Director of the Offices of International Monetary Policy and Former Soviet Union Nations" (Sobel 2016: 3).
9 For more information on the Sub-Committee, see https://europa.eu/efc/about-sub-committee_en.
10 Cleary Gottlieb's services here were completely separated from their services to Greece (Gelpern and Gulati 2013).
11 https://www.consilium.europa.eu/en/press/press-releases/2018/12/04/eurogroup-report-to-leaders-on-emu-deepening/.

References

Alter, Karen J. and Sophie Meunier. 2009. "The Politics of International Regime Complexity—Symposium." *Perspectives on Politics* 7(1): 13–24.
Bardozzetti, Alfredo and Davide Dottori. 2014. "Collective Action Clauses: How Do They Affect Sovereign Bond Yields?" *Journal of International Economics* 92(2): 286–303.
Buchheit, Lee C. 2016. "The Greek Debt Restructuring of 2012." In ESCB Legal Conference 2016. European Central Bank.
Buchheit, Lee C. and G. Mitu Gulati. 2010. "How to Restructure Greek Debt." (Working paper, Duke University Law School, May), http://papers.ssrn.com/sol3/papers.cfm?abstract_id=1603304.
Couillault, Bertrand and Pierre-François Weber. 2003. *Towards a Code of Good Conduct on Sovereign Debt Re-Negotiation*. Banque de France Financial Stability Review No. 2 (June): 154–162.

Das, Udaibir S., Michael G. Papaioannou and Christoph Trebesch. 2012. *Sovereign Debt Restructurings 1950–2010: Concepts, Literature Survey, Data, and Stylized Facts.* http://www.imf.org/external/pubs/cat/longres.aspx?sk=26190.0.

Drage, John and Catherine Hovaguimian. 2004. *Collective Action Clauses (CACS): An Analysis of Provisions Included in Recent Sovereign Bond Issues.* London: Bank of England.

Eichengreen, Barry, Kenneth Kletzer and Ashoka Mody. 2003. *Crisis Resolution: Next Steps.* IMF Working Paper WP/03/196, Washington, DC.

Gelpern, Anna and Mitu Gulati. 2006. "Public Symbol in Private Contract: A Case Study." *Washington University Law Quarterly* 84(7): 1627–1715.

Gelpern, Anna and Mitu Gulati. 2008. "Innovation after the Revolution: Foreign Sovereign Bond Contracts since 2003." *Capital Markets Law Journal* 4(1): 85–103.

Gelpern, Anna and Mitu Gulati. 2013. "The Wonder-Clause." *Journal of Comparative Economics* 41(2): 367–385.

Gelpern, Anna, Ben Heller and Brad Setser. 2016. "Count the Limbs: Designing Robust Aggregation Clauses in Sovereign Bonds." In Guzman, Martin, José Antonio Ocampo, and Joseph E. Stiglitz (eds.), *Too Little, Too Late: The Quest to Resolve Sovereign Debt Crises.* New York: Columbia University Press.

Halliday, Terence C. and Bruce G. Carruthers. 2007. "The Recursivity of Law: Global Norm Making and National Lawmaking in the Globalization of Corporate Insolvency Regimes." *American Journal of Sociology* 112(4): 1135–1202.

Henriksen, Lasse and Leonard Seabrooke. 2015. "'Transnational Organizing: Issue Professionals in Environmental Sustainability Networks." *Organization*: 1–21. doi:10.1177/1350508415609140

Institute of International Finance. 2006. "Principles for Stable Capital Flows and Fair Debt Restructuring in Emerging Markets." Report on Implementation by the Principles Consultative Group, Washington, DC.

Institute of International Finance. 2012. "Report of the Joint Committee on Strengthening the Framework for Sovereign Debt Crisis Prevention and Resolution." Washington, DC.

Institute of International Finance. 2016. "Principles for Stable Capital Flows and Fair Debt Restructuring in Emerging Markets." Report on Implementation by the Principles Consultative Group, Washington, DC.

International Capital Market Association. 2014. *Standard Collective Action and Pari Passu Clauses for the Terms and Conditions of Sovereign Notes.* ICMA. https://www.icmagroup.org/Regulatory-Policy-and-Market-Practice/Primary-Markets/primary-market-topics/collective-action-clauses/

International Monetary Fund. 2011. "Greece: Fourth Review." IMF Country Report No. 11/175. Washington, DC.

International Monetary Fund. 2013. "Greece: Ex Post Evaluation of Exceptional Access under the 2010 Stand-By Arrangement." Washington, DC.

Kalaitzake, Manolis. 2017. "The Political Power of Finance: The Institute of International Finance in the Greek Debt Crisis." *Politics and Society* 45(3): 389–413.

Krueger, Anne. 2002. *A New Approach to Sovereign Debt Restructuring.* Washington, DC: International Monetary Fund.

Lastra, Rosa Maria. 2016. "How to Fill the International Law Lacunae in Sovereign Insolvency in European Union Law?" In ESCB Legal Conference 2016. European Central Bank.

Richards, Anthony and Mark Gugiatti. 2003. "Do Collective Action Clauses Influence Bond Yields? New Evidence from Emerging Markets." *International Finance* 6(3): 415–447.

Ritter, Raymond. 2010. "Transnational Governance in Global Finance: The Principles for Stable Capital Flows and Fair Debt Restructuring in Emerging Markets." *International Studies Perspectives* 11(3): 222–241.

Schumacher, Julian, Christoph Trebesch and Henrik Enderlein. 2018. *Sovereign Defaults in Court*. CESifo Working Paper no. 6931. Munich.

Seabrooke, Leonard. 2014. "Epistemic Arbitrage: Transnational Professional Knowledge in Action." *Journal of Professions and Organization* 1(1): 49–64.

Sobel, Mark. 2016. "Strengthening Collective Action Clauses: Catalyzing Change—The Back Story." *Capital Markets Law Journal* 11(1): 3–11.

United Nations Conference on Trade and Development. 2014. "Project on Promoting Responsible Sovereign Lending and Borrowing And Debt Workout Mechanism."

Valverde, Mariana. 2009. "Jurisdiction and Scale: Legal 'Technicalities' as Resources for Theory." *Social and Legal Studies* 18(2): 139–158.

Weidemaier, Mark and Mitu Gulati. 2013. "A People's History of Collective Action Clauses." *Virginia Journal of International Law* 54(1): 51–95.

Zettelmeyer, Jeromin, Christoph Trebesch, and Mitu Gulati. 2013. "The Greek Debt Restructuring: An Autopsy." *Economic Policy* 28(75): 513–563.

8
ENVIRONMENTAL GOVERNANCE NETWORKS

Climate change and biodiversity

Claire Dupont

Introduction

Global environmental governance is characterized by increasing complexity over time, with greater numbers and types of actors, institutions, interactions, interests, and governance modes. Since environmental issues came onto the political agenda in the mid-20th century, there has been an explosion of international and supranational norms, rules, and institutions in response that have developed into a collection of fragmented but overlapping, governance regimes (Biermann, Pattberg, van Asselt, & Zelli 2009; see also the contributions by Orsini and Godet and by Pattberg and Widerberg, in this volume).

The literature on global environmental governance highlights the complexity of many environmental issues as a clear driver for such governance developments. The causes of, and solutions to, many environmental issues are situated in multiple sectors of society, involve multiple levels of governance, and are transboundary, requiring multilateral (and perhaps also polycentric) responses (Biermann & Pattberg 2008; Jordan, Huitema, van Asselt, Rayner, & Berkhout 2010). Environmental issues are thus characterized as particularly complex to resolve, and are often declared "wicked" problems (Levin, Cashore, Bernstein, & Auld 2012). When action is not taken across all the sectors, actors, and levels of governance involved, it is less likely to be effective in solving the environmental problem. This combination of interest distribution, uncertainty, linkages, problem diversity, and political difficulties (Keohane & Victor 2011, pp. 12–13) has contributed to the development of multiple institutions covering various, but overlapping, aspects of environmental governance, which are sometimes in conflict, but often mutually reinforcing (Oberthür, Dupont, & Matsumoto 2011).

Yet, despite the growth of global environmental governance efforts, many of the indicators used to assess the quality of the environment report worsening trends – putting the effectiveness of decades of top-down governance into question. The United Nations Environment Programme's Emissions Gap Report 2018 highlighted the technical knowledge and feasibility of achieving goals to combat climate change, but that it is the policy plans that remain insufficient (UN Environment, 2018). In addition to the proliferation of bi- and multilateral governance regimes, we also see evidence of a combination of bottom-up, public-private, transnational initiatives with top-down, intergovernmental modes of governance. Scholars have built on the foundational research of Elinor Ostrom on "polycentric governance" to study these latest trends in global environmental governance (Jordan, Huitema, van Asselt, & Forster 2018; Jordan et al. 2015). In this context, research on the coherence and effectiveness of multiple sources and types of governance in international environmental networks is in its infancy.

In this chapter, I analyze the role of the EU in international environmental networks, focusing on questions of coherence and effectiveness. I assess the ability of the EU to engage strategically, effectively, and coherently in global environmental governance networks on climate change and biodiversity. I find that the EU has managed to adapt its internal coherence and has engaged in more coordination and coherent action with third country partners. However, I conclude that determining effectiveness is problematic. Effectiveness can be understood from an "output" perspective, with the agreed action (at EU or at international level) aligning with the stated goals (goal achievement). Or, effectiveness can be understood from an "outcome" perspective, with the agreed action resulting in an actual improvement in the state of the global environment. From the "output" perspective, the EU's effectiveness has generally improved over time in global environmental governance, but it has fluctuated. From the "outcome" perspective, we cannot yet say that actions taken in global environmental governance networks, or the EU's role therein, have been effective. I suggest that the varying degrees of effectiveness are related to the broader internal and external context within which the EU operates: the institutional, political, and broader governance contexts pose challenges to more effective action.

The chapter proceeds as follows. First, I outline the context for the EU's role in global environmental networks. Second, I analyze the evolution of the EU's role in two global environmental networks over time: climate change and biodiversity. Third, I discuss the findings of the analysis, underlining certain trends in the shift in the EU's role in global environmental networks. Finally, I present some concluding remarks and highlight avenues for further research.

Understanding the EU's role in environmental networks

The EU's position in international environmental networks depends on the convergence of internal and external dynamics. First, the EU's internal political interest and policy development in an issue area is a key part of the motivation of the EU to engage, but also a central element of the credibility of the EU as an actor in these networks (Bretherton & Vogler 2006; Vogler 2017). If the EU has successfully adopted and implemented far-reaching internal policies in an environmental issue area, then this plays a role in how the EU is perceived and received as a legitimate actor in international environmental networks. This, in turn, depends on the internal political, institutional, and economic context at the time of policy negotiations. Furthermore, the EU's internal political dynamics lead to more or less coherent, stable, and effective engagement in international environmental networks. As the EU has developed better tools to speak with one voice in international negotiations, for example, it has been perceived as an important and coherent partner in combating environmental problems (da Conceição-Heldt & Meunier 2014; van Schaik 2010).

Second, the balance of power and/or interests within an international environmental network interacts with the ability of the EU to engage strategically in international environmental networks. In the context of environmental networks, sources of power can stem from the weight of an actor as the cause of an environmental problem, from its economic and technological advancement, and from its ability to persuade or coerce partners to follow its preferred policy options (often subsumed under an actor's negotiating capacity) (Birchfield 2015; Goldthau & Sitter 2015). The dominance of different interests in a network can also change as the global political order shifts, or in response to shocks in the global system (Nohrstedt 2006).

Because of this interaction of internal and external dynamics, the EU's role in global environmental networks has changed over time. As global environmental governance has shifted toward a networked approach, including a multitude of actors, issues, norms, and ideas, the EU has remained a relevant, sometimes crucial, international actor (Adelle, Biedenkopf, & Torney 2018; Bäckstrand & Elgström 2013). At the same time, the EU loses considerable flexibility due to its internal institutional structure and political culture. Nevertheless, the EU has shown a certain degree of adaptability in responding to shifts in context, both internally and externally, to continue acting strategically (Adelle, Biedenkopf, & Torney 2018).

The EU moved from taking little action on environmental issues in the 1980s to becoming a major international actor, with a considerable environmental *acquis*, in the 2000s. Such developments are often linked to entrepreneurial policy-linking by the European Commission and strong support from the European Parliament over the years (Burns & Carter 2010; Skjærseth & Wettestad 2010). By linking environmental policy action to the EU's competence on the internal market, the Commission could embed environmental action into the core work of the EU. The Parliament's constant efforts to increase environmental policy ambition led to compromises with member states in the

Council that were higher than, or more than, the lowest common denominator. International negotiations' timetables, and EU ambition to be a global leader, also motivated EU action (Oberthür & Roche Kelly 2008).

Development of the EU's role in climate and biodiversity networks

In this section, I analyze the EU's role in two cases of international environmental networks: climate change and biodiversity. In both cases, international governance has moved from intergovernmental negotiations to a complex regime of (sometimes overlapping) institutions, laws, and regulations, owing to the expansion of the network: a growth in the number and type of actors, interests, and norms (see chapters by Orsini and Godet; Pattberg and Widerberg; and Seabrooke and Henriksen). Global regimes on climate change and biodiversity are more or less fragmented collections of institutions and actions, although interlinkages across policy fields have also been increasingly recognized, and new tools of governance have been developed over time (Biermann & Pattberg 2012; Keohane & Victor 2010; Oberthür & Rabitz 2014).

I explore two connected questions throughout the case study analysis: (1) how has the EU's role within the network changed over time? And (2) have the observed changes led to increased effectiveness and/or coherence? For the first question, I provide a historical overview of the development of the EU's role in climate and biodiversity networks. I focus on examples of contestation, cooperation, and competition within the network. For the second question, I loosely follow a framework proposed by Camilla Adelle, Katja Biedenkopf, and Diarmuid Torney (2018) to identify the governance tools used by the EU to promote coherence and effectiveness in international environmental networks (or EU external environmental policy). These include active participation in international negotiations; dialogues; providing incentives or punishments ("manipulating utility calculations") in bilateral/multilateral relations; and supporting capacity building. I also draw on the distinction between output and outcome effectiveness, as described above (Oberthür & Groen 2015).

International climate change network

The international network for climate change has developed from an intergovernmental negotiating process to a multi-actor, multi-sector, and multi-institution global network.

The 1970s and 1980s were decades of limited international action on climate change. Climate change became an issue of political importance in the wake of the 1972 UN conference on the human environment in Stockholm, but there was little movement on the issue until the 1980s.

> **BOX 8.1: INTERGOVERNMENTAL PANEL ON CLIMATE CHANGE (IPCC)**
>
> The main international institution in global climate governance is the United Nations' Framework Convention on Climate Change (UNFCCC), which is supported by the Intergovernmental Panel on Climate Change (IPCC).
>
> Established in 1988 by the World Meteorological Organization and the United Nations Environment Programme, the IPCC is tasked to assess the latest science on climate change. Every five to seven years, the IPCC releases a report compiled by thousands of scientists, synthesizing research. The findings of the reports are synthesized further, in cooperation with government representatives, to produce a "summary for policymakers". While this is policy-relevant, the IPCC should steer clear of providing "policy prescriptive" content.
>
> IPCC Assessment Reports have been published in 1990, 1996, 2001, 2007, and 2013–2014. The IPCC has also engaged in producing "Special Reports" that delve into specific issues. In October 2018, it published a report on "Global Warming of 1.5°C", which outlined the impacts of global warming of 1.5°C, and the pathways of greenhouse gas (GHG) emissions reductions required to stay within that threshold.
>
> IPCC reports play an important role in framing the international negotiations on climate change, and the EU, in particular, highlights the necessity of agreeing on adequate action based on scientific evidence.
>
> All reports of the IPCC are available online at www.ipcc.ch.

The founding of the Intergovernmental Panel on Climate Change (IPCC) in 1988 – a body charged with the task of reviewing and reporting on the latest scientific knowledge on climate change – was a major step toward acknowledging the breadth of the climate problem (see Box 8.1). The periodic reports of the IPCC continue to play a significant role in keeping climate change high on the political agenda (Dupont & Groen 2018).

In 1992, the United Nations Framework Convention on Climate Change (UNFCCC) was adopted at the Earth Summit in Rio de Janeiro (see Box 8.2). The main objective of the UNFCCC is to stabilize the concentration of greenhouse gases (GHGs) in the atmosphere at a level that would "prevent dangerous anthropogenic interference with the climate system" (Art. 2). The Convention also lays down the general principles to achieve this objective, including that countries should act based on their "common but differentiated responsibilities and respective capabilities", that "developed countries should take the lead in combating climate change", and that parties should take "precautionary measures" where there is scientific uncertainty (Art. 3). Since 1992, negotiations to agree on commitments and implementing measures to achieve the goal of the UNFCCC based on the overarching principles have resulted in two main international agreements: the 1997 Kyoto Protocol and the 2015 Paris Agreement. While the 1997 Kyoto Protocol laid down specific commitments for developed country parties, with a top-down compliance system, the Paris Agreement is a bottom-up system to which all parties submit their own commitments, with dialogues and stocktakes in the future to encourage adequate and improved action (Dröge 2016; Oberthür 1999).

The adoption of these international agreements was fraught with challenges, especially linked to the principle of "common but differentiated responsibilities and respective capabilities". Negotiating the Kyoto Protocol was politically challenging, with the US and China at loggerheads over respective action. In 2001, President George W. Bush withdrew the US from the Kyoto Protocol, putting its entry into force at risk. Negotiations on a follow-up agreement to the Kyoto Protocol should have been completed in 2009 at the, now infamous, 15th Conference of the Parties (COP15) in Copenhagen. Instead, COP15 adopted a non-binding "Copenhagen Accord" in a context of division and mistrust among the parties (Dimitrov 2010; Groen & Niemann 2013). It took a further six years before the negotiating parties picked up the pieces to adopt the Paris Agreement in 2015. In the intervening years, disillusionment and disappointment with the intergovernmental negotiation arena led to a further proliferation of other types of action, governance modes, and interconnections with private and NGO actors (Bäckstrand, Kuyper, Linnér, & Lövbrand 2017; Jordan et al. 2015).

The EU's own position within the international climate regime shifted from being one party among many to becoming a major player and initiative-taker. In the 1990s, the EU already made rhetorical statements about its ambition to lead the world on climate change. However, with little credible internal policy on the issue, it was not successful in taking up such a leading role. A combination of new internal action in the early 2000s and the EU's efforts to ensure the Kyoto Protocol entered into force, despite the US withdrawal, moved it into a credible leadership role: it became a leader-by-example. The late 2000s again saw a shift in the EU's role. The combination of the severe financial and economic crisis and the failure of the 2009 Copenhagen COP led to a weakening of the EU's leadership role. This was largely owing to a change in the political commitment among certain EU member states, who had to give attention rather to responding to what was to become a convergence of crises (Falkner 2016). The EU then became a mediator among other party positions, working to ensure international agreement, and was less busy with agreeing its own unilateral exceptional action (Bäckstrand & Elgström 2013; Dupont, Oberthür, & Biedenkopf 2018; Oberthür & Roche Kelly 2008).

This changing role of the EU was characterized at different times by contestation over its assumed leadership role and by efforts to build cooperative relationships. While it cannot be said that there was competition among parties to assume a leadership role in international climate politics, competing norms have been pushed by the EU and other actors.

Contestation over the EU's leadership role was implicit in the 1990s, when few other actors accepted the EU's declared leadership role, especially considering the lack of credible internal policy action in the EU (Dupont & Oberthür 2015; Oberthür & Roche Kelly 2008). The contestation gave way to acceptance in the mid-2000s as the EU improved its unity of message and developed internal policies (van Schaik, 2010). This shifted once more toward contestation, as the EU's leadership style leading up to and during COP15 in Copenhagen in 2009 demonstrated a considerable degree of disconnection from the fundamental issues of fairness (in the procedure and in the commitments) raised by other parties. In the wake of COP15, the EU took time to regroup and change its leadership and international engagement style from top-down, leadership-by-example, to one of engagement and cooperation with other partners (Bäckstrand & Elgström 2013; Dupont & Oberthür 2017).

The new role for the EU as a cooperative partner can be seen in the tools it employs in its external climate policy. First, the EU (and its member states) is the largest provider of climate finance. It provides this finance through its competence to deploy development aid, and through multilateral funds — specialized international climate funds (such as the Global Environmental Facility), the World Bank, and the UN Development Programme, for example — and through bilateral channels. Bilateral funding mechanisms also serve the purpose of providing incentives to partners to act on climate change, or to punish them if they do not ("manipulating utility calculations").

Second, the EU engages in capacity building efforts with third countries. The funds described above also serve the purpose of building the capacity of partners to act on climate change: financing policy action is essential for building knowledge and experience. Capacity building also takes place through targeted climate diplomacy with partners, such as training efforts or bilateral dialogues to prepare countries for international negotiations, or helping countries to draw up their national climate plans.

Finally, the EU engages with other partners to connect its internal policies on climate change to their jurisdictions. A prominent example is the EU's efforts to help other countries or regions develop emissions trading systems — exporting EU knowledge on how (not) to design such systems (Dupont, Oberthür, & Biedenkopf 2018).

With these shifts in the EU's role, we can see that the EU has managed to increase coherence to a certain extent. Over the years, it became a more unified actor in international climate politics, and it has also managed to connect climate objectives to other areas of external policy (Dupont, Oberthür, & Biedenkopf 2018). At the same time, the EU has successfully implemented GHG emission reduction policies internally. The EU is the first region in the world to reduce consistently its emissions, even when emissions related to consumption are taken into account (Eurostat 2019). The EU reduced its reported GHG emissions by about 23% between 1990 and 2015 (EEA 2017).

However, while it has become a more coherent international partner, successful in reducing its own emissions, and sometimes effective in achieving some of its own goals for global climate governance (Groen & Niemann 2013), it has been less successful in pushing global action to follow suit. World emissions of GHGs increased from about 30 Gigatonnes of CO_2 equivalent ($GtCO_2e$) in 1990 to nearly 46 $GtCO_2e$ in 2014 (CAIT data, World Resources Institute). The UN intergovernmental processes have shown their limitations, leading also to the complex governance arrangements in place today.

It remains to be seen whether new "polycentric" governance arrangements will be more effective on a global scale, and whether the EU can continue to adapt its climate diplomacy in response to the bottom-up, multi-actor climate regime in place under the Paris Agreement. At the EU level, some action has been taken to engage in a bottom-up approach to climate policy development, but the effectiveness of these approaches remains to be assessed. While I do not analyze the EU's role in global environmental governance from a polycentric perspective in this chapter, initial studies of polycentric approaches to climate governance suggest that these approaches have not (yet) necessarily led to more effective, substantive action. The EU has engaged in such efforts by supporting city and municipality networks, for example (see the Covenant of Mayors, the Mayors Adapt initiative, among others). Further empirical research on polycentric and/or bottom-up governance approaches in the EU and globally are required (Jordan, Huitema, van Asselt, & Forster 2018; Jordan et al. 2015).

International biodiversity network

As with the international climate change network, efforts to protect biodiversity at an international level have led over the years to a proliferation of actors, institutions, sectors, and interests. The complex regime for biodiversity includes regulation on conservation, trade, and fairness in accessing and benefiting from genetic materials. The EU's role in the wider biodiversity network has also changed – from a disengaged actor in the early years of international biodiversity governance to a leader or facilitator in more recent years.

International biodiversity governance is regulated, first and foremost, by the Convention on Biological Diversity (CBD), adopted at the Earth Summit at Rio de Janeiro in 1992 (see Box 8.2). The main objectives of this Convention are outlined in Article 1:

> the conservation of biological diversity, the sustainable use of its components and the fair and equitable sharing of the benefits arising out of the utilization of genetic resources, including by appropriate access to genetic resources and by appropriate transfer of relevant technologies, taking into account all rights over those resources and technologies, and by appropriate funding.

BOX 8.2: THE EARTH SUMMIT

In 1992, 172 states came together in Rio de Janeiro, Brazil at the "Earth Summit": a global meeting dedicated to the environment and sustainable development. The results of this summit included:

1. United Nations Framework Convention on Climate Change
2. United Nations Convention on Biological Diversity
3. Rio Declaration on Environment and Development
4. Statement of Forest Principles

The Earth Summit provided momentum in the development of global environmental governance and helped put environmental issues on the broader agenda of the global political community.

In 2012, the so-called "Rio+20" Summit on Sustainable Development tried to recreate some of this early momentum and led to the agreement of 17 Sustainable Development Goals (SDGs).

See: https://sustainabledevelopment.un.org/?menu=1300

The development of global governance on biodiversity followed a similar pattern as climate governance, with negotiations after the adoption of the Convention on appropriate tools to achieve the overarching objectives. In 2000, the parties adopted the Cartagena Protocol on biosafety, aiming to ensure the safe handling and transport of living organisms. In 2012, the Intergovernmental Science-Policy Platform on Biodiversity and Ecosystem Services (IPBES) was set up to provide updated scientific knowledge on the state of biodiversity to policymakers. In 2014, the Nagoya Protocol on access to genetic resources and the fair and equitable sharing of benefits arising from their utilization was adopted. In addition, the Convention on international trade in endangered species of wild flora and fauna (CITES), adopted in 1975, is another link in the complex regime for biodiversity protection.

The EU's engagement in international biodiversity governance is a mix of its own internal policy objectives, its aim to be a major global environmental player, and the broader international context. The EU's Birds Directive was first adopted in 1979 – the oldest EU environmental legislation (79/409/EEC, amended in 2009 to become Directive 2009/147/EC). It forms the cornerstone of EU conservation legislation and was complemented in 1992 with the Habitats Directive (92/43/EEC), which set up Special Protected Areas in the EU (part of the Natura 2000 network of protected sites). In addition to internal legislation, the EU adopted its biodiversity strategy in 1998. This strategy – updated in 2006 and 2011 – outlines the ultimate objective of EU biodiversity policy to halt the loss of biodiversity by 2020 (European Commission, 2011b). The strategy has a strong external orientation. It lists specific EU actions to contribute to meeting this goal at the global level, including reducing the impact of EU consumption patterns on global biodiversity; funding global biodiversity actions; screening EU action on development cooperation to reduce negative impacts on biodiversity; making sure that benefits from genetic resources are equitably shared (Target 6).

In addition to its internal policies, EU interest in engaging in international biodiversity governance shifted over time: from simply maintaining the status quo in international biodiversity governance until the mid-2000s to engaging more in the second half of the 2000s. This shift can be attributed to more openness to cooperation with, especially, developing countries in the negotiations leading to the adoption of the Nagoya Protocol, and a more assertive engagement of the EU generally (Groen 2016; Oberthür & Groen 2015). It was also motivated by the EU's growing biotechnology sector, and its interest in moving biodiversity negotiations forward in its favor. To achieve this aim, it moved from a disinterested to an engaged actor in international biodiversity networks from about 2006 onwards (Oberthür & Rabitz 2014).

But the EU's role in biodiversity networks includes both multilateral and bilateral action. First, the EU aims to integrate biodiversity objectives into its negotiation of free trade agreements ("manipulating utility calculations"), both by referring explicitly to the international legal framework on biodiversity and by including arrangements to monitor sustainable development indicators as relevant to biodiversity. EU internal instruments also regulate trade in favor of protecting biodiversity: Forest Law Enforcement, Governance and Trade action (FLEGT), related Timber Regulations, and the EU Wildlife Trade Regulations (implementing CITES). Thus, actors wishing to access the EU market are expected to change their practices to meet certain biodiversity criteria (Kettunen 2018).

Second, the EU engages in considerable capacity building efforts to support biodiversity protection efforts. As outlined above, integrating biodiversity objectives into development cooperation policies is an objective of the EU's biodiversity strategy. As a result, the EU adopted an initiative in 2014 called Biodiversity for Life (B4Life), which aims to protect biodiversity in third countries by supporting the good governance of natural resources; promoting ecosystem conservation for food security; and, promoting ecosystem-based solutions for the green economy (Kettunen 2018). These objectives are part of overarching strategies for the EU's internal policy development, as well as objectives toward third countries (European Commission 2011a).

When it comes to coherence and effectiveness, the record of the EU is lower than assessed under the climate regime. On coherence, efforts have been made to integrate biodiversity objectives into the EU's external policy – especially its trade and development cooperation policies. However, the EU has had limited success in integrating biodiversity objectives into its own internal policies over the years, and a degree of political commitment has been lacking (Jordan & Lenschow 2010). On effectiveness, reports on the state of biodiversity protection show worsening trends, both in the EU and globally (Kettunen 2018). If we understand effectiveness as the EU's achievement of its own goals in international negotiations, then we see a mixed record (Groen 2018). The EU was long a disinterested actor on biodiversity. It did not push for effective action at the international level until the mid-2000s, and even then, it was part of a new constellation of internal interests. It had little ambition to push for strong policy measures, although it did have the ambition to play a major role in international biodiversity policy. While the EU's internal biodiversity strategy is relatively strong, it lacks clear legal instruments for internal development and strong political backing. In terms of effectiveness, measured as a positive impact for protecting biodiversity, the EU does not fare well on its own internal policies. The goal to halt the loss of biodiversity has been missed and simply pushed to a later date. This is hardly a credible position for an aspiring leader (Kettunen 2018; Oberthür & Dupont 2011).

Discussion

The analysis above points to several general trends in the role of the EU in global environmental regimes or networks. First, the EU has adapted its engagement in international climate and biodiversity regimes over time. In climate change, the EU declared quite early in the development of the international governance regime that it intended to play a "leading" role. However, it took some time for the EU to demonstrate credible leadership with a combined strategy of internal policy development and external engagement. This process led to heightened coherence in EU internal and external action on climate change, and a degree of effectiveness in climate outcomes within its own territory (reduction of GHG emissions). It also had some effectiveness in terms of output, or "goal achievement" in the international climate regime (Groen & Niemann 2013). In the biodiversity network, the EU has been less engaged and less inclined to take on a leadership role. However, the EU has also increased its coherence in biodiversity networks over time, particularly through cooperation with third countries. In terms of effectiveness, the EU's internal biodiversity policies have not resulted in a halt in the loss of biodiversity, and the EU's goal achievement in the global network has been mixed (Groen 2018). The EU has shifted its role in climate and biodiversity networks over time, and has increased coherence, but this has not necessarily led to sufficiently effective outcomes and outputs.

Second, the EU's adaptation has benefited from increased unity of vision *within* the EU, as well as an increased recognition by international partners of the importance of the EU in global environmental governance. Over time, the EU has become a more reliable and recognized international actor in its own right (Vogler 2017). Its ability to adopt internal policy and to prepare international strategies, its increased coherence in its messages to third countries, and its adaptation in negotiations have led to more coherent and cooperative interactions with partners (Adelle, Biedenkopf, & Torney 2018; van Schaik 2010). In climate and biodiversity governance, the EU builds its internal strategies in line with international engagement, and vice versa. However, the EU's unity of vision internally has been under stress in recent years, as a result of financial/economic, migration, and political crises that have led to environmental issues receiving less political attention (Burns & Tobin 2018; Burns, Tobin, & Sewerin 2018).

Third, the shifts in the EU's engagement have not necessarily led to similar responses from international partners. Most environmental problems are transboundary or global in nature, requiring a global response. Not all states are equally engaged in dealing with environmental problems, and the EU's adaptation toward a more coherent, cooperative actor has not been sufficient to gain "followers" (Burns, Tobin, & Sewerin 2018). Most importantly, the United States remains a reluctant or disengaged partner in both the climate and biodiversity regimes. As one of the major countries responsible for environmental problems (historically), but also because of its economic and political clout, a disengaged US is a point of considerable weakness for the reach and effectiveness of global environmental networks.

It can, therefore, be argued that while the EU has made efforts to adapt to the increasing complexity of environmental governance, there are still points to be improved. The EU has updated its internal policy efforts and its external strategies for engaging with partners. It has become a more coherent actor internationally. It has had some (but insufficient) effectiveness in both achieving its goals in global environmental networks and in policy outcomes. However, on the global scale, we are still missing a sufficient net benefit for the environment from the EU's role in these international environmental networks.

Conclusions

Global environmental governance is characterized by increasing complexity toward a series of overlapping complex, sometimes contradictory, regimes. Scholars today refer regularly to the notion of "polycentric" governance to describe the networks and modes of governance surrounding these regimes. While it is challenging for the EU to find a natural role in a "polycentric" governance system – as a hierarchical governance institution itself – EU engagement in international environmental networks has shifted over time in response to this evolution. The EU has long specifically supported multilateral action to deal with environmental problems (Oberthür & Roche Kelly 2008). It has had to adapt its role toward more coherence internally and externally on environmental issues and diplomacy. This adaptation has led to the recognition of the EU as an important actor and has resulted in some effective outputs (and outcomes). While coherence has increased, this has remained insufficient given the scale of the environmental issues. In particular, the EU has faced increased challenges internally to maintain the interest in ambitious environmental action and has not succeeded in bringing other key international actors on board.

The future remains uncertain, both in terms of the effectiveness of global environmental regimes to tackle the issues at hand and in terms of the development of the EU's role. What is certain is that the EU's adaptive capacity will be further tested, especially in the context of "polycentric" governance regimes. But the importance of the EU as an actor in such regimes is not in doubt. Strategies to overcome or mitigate (potential) institutional and political barriers to effective action must, therefore, be emphasized. Such strategies can build on the strengths of the EU (some of which have not been discussed here), including emphasizing its political clout in bilateral and multilateral relations or diffusing its policies through its trade relations. Other strategies may require a reorientation of priorities. A global turbulent governance system (Ansell, Trondal, & Øgård, 2016) may present the EU with the opportunity to push forward with considerable purpose on the transition to sustainability, as the region of the world representing compromise and stability. Reaping the benefit of turbulence requires continuous EU-level political commitment to leading action in international environmental networks. Further research is needed on potential strategies to heighten the EU's effectiveness in global environmental governance during turbulent times.

References

Adelle, C., Biedenkopf, K., & Torney, D. (Eds.). (2018). *European Union External Environmental Policy*. Houndsmills: Palgrave MacMillan.

Ansell, C., Trondal, J., & Øgård, M. (2016). Turbulent governance. In C. Ansell, J. Trondal, & M. Øgård (Eds.), *Governance in Turbulent Times* (pp. 1–26). Oxford: Oxford University Press.

Bäckstrand, K., & Elgström, O. (2013). The EU's role in climate change negotiations: From leader to 'Leadiator'. *Journal of European Public Policy*, 20(10), 1369–1386.

Bäckstrand, K., Kuyper, J.W., Linnér, B.O., & Lövbrand, E. (2017). Non-state actors in global climate governance: From Copenhagen to Paris and beyond. *Environmental Politics*, 26(4), 561–579.

Biermann, F., & Pattberg, P. (2008). Global environmental governance: Taking stock, moving forward. *Annual Review of Environment and Resources*, 33, 277–294.

Biermann, F., & Pattberg, P. (2012). Global environmental governance revisited. In F. Biermann & P. Pattberg (Eds.), *Global Environmental Governance Reconsidered* (pp. 1–23). Cambridge, MA: MIT Press.

Biermann, F., Pattberg, P., van Asselt, H., & Zelli, F. (2009). The fragmentation of global governance architectures: A framework for analysis. *Global Environmental Politics*, 9(4), 14–40.

Birchfield, V.L. (2015). Coercion with kid gloves? The European Union's role in shaping a global regulatory framework for aviation emissions. *Journal of European Public Policy*, 22(9), 1276–1294.

Bretherton, C., & Vogler, J. (2006). *The European Union as a Global Actor*. London: Routledge.

Burns, C., & Carter, N. (2010). Is co-decision good for the environment? An analysis of the European Parliament's green credentials. *Political Studies*, 58(1), 123–142.

Burns, C., & Tobin, P. (2018). The limits of ambitious environmental policy in times of crisis. In C. Adelle, K. Biedenkopf, & D. Torney (Eds.), *European Union External Environmental Policy: Rules, Regulations and Governance Beyond Borders* (pp. 319–336). Houndsmills: Palgrave MacMillan.

Burns, C., Tobin, P., & Sewerin, S. (2018). *The Impact of the Economic Crisis on European Environmental Policy*. Oxford: Oxford University Press.

da Conceição-Heldt, E., & Meunier, S. (2014). Speaking with a single voice: Internal cohesiveness and external effectiveness of the EU in global governance. *Journal of European Public Policy, 21*(7), 961–979.

Dimitrov, R.S. (2010). Inside Copenhagen: The state of climate governance. *Global Environmental Politics, 10*(2), 18–24.

Dröge, S. (2016). *The Paris Agreement 2015: Turning Point for the International Climate Regime*. SWP Research Paper. Berlin.

Dupont, C., & Groen, L. (2018). Framing in het EU-klimaatbeleid: De rol van expertise. *Vlaams Tijdschrift Voor Overheidsmanagement (VTOM), 2018*(2), 51–63.

Dupont, C., & Oberthür, S. (2015). The European Union. In E. Lövbrand & K. Bäckstrand (Eds.), *Research Handbook on Climate Governance* (pp. 224–236). Cheltenham: Edward Elgar Publishing Ltd.

Dupont, C., & Oberthür, S. (2017). The Council and the European Council: Stuck on the road to transformational leadership. In R.K.W. Wurzel, J. Connelly, & D. Liefferink (Eds.), *The European Union in International Climate Change Politics: Still Taking a Lead?* (pp. 66–79). London: Routledge.

Dupont, C., Oberthür, S., & Biedenkopf, K. (2018). Climate change: Adapting to evolving internal and external dynamics. In C. Adelle, K. Biedenkopf, & D. Torney (Eds.), *European Union External Environmental Policy: Rules, Regulations and Governance Beyond Borders* (pp. 105–124). Houndsmills: Palgrave MacMillan.

EEA. (2017). *Trends and Projections in Europe 2017. Tracking Progress Towards Europe's Climate and Energy Targets*. Copenhagen: European Environment Agency.

European Commission. (2011a). *Communication from the Commission: A Resource-Efficient Europe - Flagship Initiative under the Europe 2020 Strategy*. COM(2011), 21.

European Commission. (2011b). *Our Life Insurance, Our Natural Capital: An EU Biodiversity Strategy to 2020* (No. COM(2011) 244 final).

Eurostat. (2019). *Greenhouse Gas Emission Statistics - Carbon Footprints*. https://ec.euro pa.eu/eurostat/statistics-explained/index.php?title=Greenhouse_gas_emission_stat istics_-_carbon_footprints&oldid=398157#Carbon_dioxide_emissions_associated _with_EU_consumption. Accessed: 2 April 2019.

Falkner, G. (2016). The EU's problem-solving capacity and legitimacy in a crisis context: A virtuous or vicious circle? *West European Politics, 39*(5), 953–970.

Goldthau, A., & Sitter, N. (2015). Soft power with a hard edge: EU policy tools and energy security. *Review of International Political Economy, 22*(5), 941–965.

Groen, L. (2016). *The Importance of Fitting Activities to Context: The EU in Multilateral Climate and Biodiversity Negotiations* (PhD thesis). Brussels: Vrije Universiteit Brussel.

Groen, L. (2018). Explaining European Union effectiveness (goal achievement) in the convention on biological diversity: The importance of diplomatic engagement. *International Environmental Agreements: Politics, Law and Economics*. https://doi.org/10.1 007/s10784-018-9424-y

Groen, L., & Niemann, A. (2013). The European Union at the Copenhagen climate negotiations: A case of contested EU actorness and effectiveness. *International Relations*, 27(3), 308–324.

Jordan, A., & Lenschow, A. (2010). Environmental policy integration: A state of the art review. *Environmental Policy and Governance*, 20(3), 147–158.

Jordan, A., Huitema, D., van Asselt, H., Rayner, T., & Berkhout, F. (Eds.). (2010). *Climate Change Policy in the European Union: Confronting the Dilemmas of Mitigation and Adaptation?* Cambridge: Cambridge University Press.

Jordan, A., Huitema, D., Hildén, M., van Asselt, H., Rayner, T.J., Schoenefeld, J.J., ... Boasson, E.L. (2015). Emergence of polycentric climate governance and its future prospects. *Nature Climate Change*, 5(11), 977–982.

Jordan, A., Huitema, D., van Asselt, H., & Forster, J. (Eds.). (2018). *Governing Climate Change: Polycentricity in Action?* Cambridge: Cambridge University Press.

Keohane, R.O., & Victor, D.G. (2010). *The Regime Complex for Climate Change*. Discussion paper 2010-33. Cambridge, MA: Harvard Project on International Climate Agreements.

Keohane, R.O., & Victor, D.G. (2011). The regime complex for climate change. *Perspectives on Politics*, 9(1), 7–24.

Kettunen, M. (2018). Biodiversity: Strong policy objectives challenged by sectoral integration. In C. Adelle, K. Biedenkopf, & D. Torney (Eds.), *European Union External Environmental Policy: Rules, Regulations and Governance Beyond Borders* (pp. 147–166). Houndsmills: Palgrave MacMillan.

Levin, K., Cashore, B., Bernstein, S., & Auld, G. (2012). Overcoming the tragedy of super wicked problems: Constraining our future selves to ameliorate global climate change. *Policy Sciences*, 45(2), 123–152.

Nohrstedt, D. (2006). External shocks and policy change: Three Mile Island and Swedish nuclear energy policy. *Journal of European Public Policy*, 12(6), 1041–1059.

Oberthür, S. (1999). *The Kyoto Protocol. International Climate Policy for the 21st Century*. Berlin: Springer.

Oberthür, S., & Dupont, C. (2011). The Council, the European Council and international climate policy: From symbolic leadership to leadership by example. In R.K.W. Wurzel & J. Connelly (Eds.), *The European Union as a Leader in International Climate Change Politics* (pp. 74–91). London: Routledge.

Oberthür, S., & Groen, L. (2015). The effectiveness dimension of the EU's performance in international institutions: Toward a more comprehensive assessment framework. *Journal of Common Market Studies*, 53(6), 1319–1335.

Oberthür, S., & Rabitz, F. (2014). On the EU's performance and leadership in global environmental governance: The case of the Nagoya Protocol. *Journal of European Public Policy*, 21(1), 39–57.

Oberthür, S., & Roche Kelly, C. (2008). EU leadership in international climate policy: Achievements and challenges. *The International Spectator*, 43(3), 35–50.

Oberthür, S., Dupont, C., & Matsumoto, Y. (2011). *Managing policy contradictions between the Montreal and Kyoto Protocols*. In S. Oberthür and O. Schram Stokke (Eds.), Managing Institutional Complexity: Regime Interplay and Global Environmental Change. Cambridge, MA: MIT Press, pp. 115–141.

Skjærseth, J.B., & Wettestad, J. (2010). Making the EU emissions trading system: The European commission as an entrepreneurial epistemic leader. *Global Environmental Change*, 20(2), 314–321.

UN Environment. (2018). *Emissions Gap Report 2018.* https://www.unenvironment.org/resources/emissions-gap-report-2018

van Schaik, L. (2010). The sustainability of the EU's model for climate diplomacy. In S. Oberthür & M. Pallemaerts (Eds.), *The New Climate Policies of the European Union: Internal Legislation and Climate Diplomacy* (pp. 251–280). Brussels: VUB Press.

Vogler, J. (2017). Global climate politics: Can the EU be an actor? In R.K.W. Wurzel, J. Connelly, & D. Liefferink (Eds.), *The European Union in International Climate Change Politics: Still Taking a Lead?* (pp. 20–33). London: Routledge.

9
GLOBAL COMPLEXITY, CIVIL SOCIETY, AND NETWORKS

Manfredi Valeriani

In the first chapter of this volume Godet and Orsini highlight an interesting characteristic of the relationship between policy outcomes and networks. If it is true that networks can affect policy outcomes, then it is legitimate to ask wider and more general questions relating to the nature of this relationship. More specifically, in relation to the focus of this chapter, what do networks offer to Civil Society Organisations (CSOs) in terms of achieving their goals and objectives? This chapter zooms in on the case of a specific Italian CSO (Lunaria) and the European network in which it operates to probe the relationship between networks and their members and shed greater light on how members navigate and engage within and through such networks to achieve their goals.

Lunaria is a relatively small CSO promoting peace, social and economic justice, equality, democracy, bottom-up participation, social inclusion, and intercultural dialogue. Above any other, its main activity is the creation and management of voluntary camps in Italy and abroad, where the organization has a series of partners with which it exchanges volunteers. Lunaria is an example of the organizations that populate the Italian third sector that, as surveyed by the Italian National Statistic Institute (Istat), is typical of a large number of small and medium organizations (Istat 2014). From a theoretical perspective, the relative size of Lunaria means that it is extremely exposed to external influence and constraints. At the same time, the incredible international outreach of the organization suggests that Lunaria has efficiently navigated the complex regimes it has faced over the years. Among the networks that Lunaria engages with in order to achieve its goals, the Alliance of European Voluntary Service Organizations represents a highly formalized network that enables a small organization to engage in transnational dynamics through the creation of partnerships, exchange of volunteers, and management of resources. The Alliance is a formalized network of partner organizations that has the main objective of representing and facilitating coordination and higher efficiency among its members. The Alliance is the largest network of its kind and it is supported by the European Union[1] and the Council of Europe.[2]

This chapter is structured in the following way. The first theoretical section shows how the complexity of the international system has given birth to a series of challenges for CSOs. It also formalizes the reasons why CSOs choose to operate through networks to address these challenges. The sections that follow have the objective of understanding the relationship between the network and its members. Mapping the structure of a specific network (the Alliance) and investigating the role of one of its members (Lunaria), the chapter will show how organizations can craft and navigate large networks, retaining great agency over them and over their very essence.

The chapter proceeds with a mixed method sequential approach, where a more quantitative-descriptive network analysis is utilized to inform the qualitative analysis for the purpose of more effective verification. The final results suggest – certainly in relation to the specific case at hand – that organizations retain a considerable level of agency power over the networks in which they navigate. Furthermore, the analysis also suggests that the strategic choices within networks are influenced by the goals and mission of the organization. In this sense, and contrary to Henriksen and Seabrooke (Chapter 3 of this volume) where the focus is on the different strategies through which professionals establish control over issues, professionals are considered more as an instrument for collaboration rather than actors with strong agency. This chapter thus aims to uncover dynamics at a meso-level. That is, where organizations interact with each other in a structured and restricted environment, even though the analysis does have certain implications for both the micro and macro level.

Civil society and networks: Reasons to engage

Beyond the debate over its existence, effects and value, globalization has increased global complexity, creating more and faster flows and global networks than ever (Appadurai 1996; Held & McGrew 2003; Marchetti 2016; Scholte 2005). Global actors are active and passive players in this scheme. While international actors can actively promote globalization by reducing barriers and conducting transnational activities, they are also subject to the phenomenon and they can rarely escape the implications globalization has on them.

At the institutional level, globalization can threaten internal equilibria, but it can also create opportunities for national actors or governments' international strategies. Multinational Corporations (MNCs) can access wider markets, but they also face wider competition. Civil Society Organizations (CSOs) can advocate globally, but they are more likely to engage with hostile legal environments. Globalization offers a series of challenges and opportunities for the players that it touches. In this realm, civil society and its organizations navigate a series of different regimes whose complexity is constantly increasing. For example,

Pattberg and Widerberg (see Chapter 2 in this volume) show how the growing role of non-state actors has brought complexity into the area of forestry governance. These considerations are not strictly related to a specific issue area, but they spread across different sectors. Abbott and Snidal's "Governance Triangle" indeed shows how CSOs (referred to as NGOs in their case) take part in several governance schemes (2009). Additionally, the complexity that CSOs face is not only related to the variety of actors that they interact with or to the plurality of sectors they operate in. Complexity is given also by increasing competitiveness and limited resources.

The number of CSOs has increased exponentially over the years (Figure 9.1 below) (Anheier, Kaldor, & Glasius 2005; Ehrenberg 2011; Keane 2003; UIA 2017).

The growing number of organizations operating globally and the limited resources available to them has led to a situation of extreme competitiveness (Brown & Troutt 2004) where CSOs are asked to navigate a system that does not always accept them. Forced competitiveness is recognized to be a constraint for CSOs that may have to diverge from their original strategies and missions in order to secure resources and repel competitors (Cooley & Ron, 2010). Excessive competition can also damage CSOs due to their inability to reorganize their mission efficiently. Once a CSO has set its directions and is extensively operating in a specific sector, changing it may be too costly and practically impossible (Marchetti, 2016). Furthermore, if it is true that CSOs are gaining relevance on the international stage, it is also true that they are generally at a bargaining power disadvantage compared to other actors. While many international CSOs efficiently surf globalization channels to conduct transnational activities across the globe, national states are increasingly restricting their space for action. States have increased the regulations that directly limit the space for civil society often through constraining legislation (Dupuy, Ron, & Prakash 2016).

In short, beyond the complexity highlighted by interconnection across sectors and global activities, CSOs face increased competitiveness, limited resources, and constraining environments. There are no easy escape routes from these

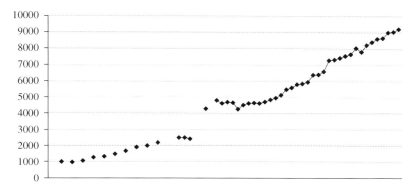

FIGURE 9.1 Yearbook of International Organizations – number of NGOs 1951–2017.

dynamics. If a globalized and interconnected world has allowed for a growing relevance of the civil society sector, it has also strengthened and increased its dependency on the other two sectors. The three sectors coexist and interact at different levels in an equilibrium that sees the three complementing each other (Anheier, Kaldor, & Glasius 2005). Resource scarcity also has other effects on CSOs. For instance, while CSOs are by definition outside of market dynamics (due to their non-profit orientation), they still need resources in order to sustain themselves (Doh & Teegen 2002; McCarthy & Zald 1977; Pfeffer & Salancik 2003; Prakash & Gugerty 2010; Teegen, Doh, & Vachani 2004). The lack of resources has two main implications for CSOs. First, it deprives the organizations of the freedom they need to conduct their activities and achieve their goals. Resources are needed in order to gather new and further resources. Second, the unequal distribution of resources creates asymmetries between small and large organizations. With generally limited income sources, the former struggle to adapt while, having a broader set of possibilities for income, the latter can redirect resources more freely.

In this realm of adverse conditions, organizations often create or engage in networks that can foster their activities. However, it is difficult to determine whether these networks are freely created by organizations to achieve higher efficiency or if instead they are forced on them by external factors. This doubt becomes extremely relevant when considering small organizations with a scarce possibility to influence or change the system. Nevertheless, beyond structural or organizational limits, it is shown in this chapter that even small CSOs can have access and use extensive and large networks, retaining a high level of agency over them. Civil society exhibits a networked structure at many different levels.

Many authors have focused on the networked structure of civil society (Cohen & Arato 1994; Larry 1994). In an attempt to overcome structural limits imposed by power asymmetries with the state, organizations may rely on international networks to bypass national constraints and mobilize international communities as theorized by Keck & Sikkink's renowned "boomerang effect" (1998). Organizations can also try to overcome resource scarcity through strategic actions where networks are used to create organizational ties with partners to increase comparative advantages in terms of resources and power (Doh & Teegen 2002). Furthermore, the networked structure of civil society is not represented only by its *external ties*. Civil society engages with a series of *internal* networks as well. CSOs usually interconnect with a plurality of constituencies whose preferences often affect the organization's activities. For instance, donors are needed in order to support the organization economically, and trustees represent the CSOs' constituency that the organization activates to pressure the actors it intends to influence (Borzaga & Defourny 2001; Handy 1995; Lewis 2001; Prakash & Gugerty 2010). Moreover, CSOs extensively rely on volunteers, making them relevant parts of internal networks as well (Anheier 2014).

CSOs are in a central position when linking various groups and constituencies. A CSO coming into a network is likely to bring many more counterparts into the network than just itself. These conditions could alter the creation of networks, since the effects of admitting a new member in the network may not be foreseeable by the old ones. Trust and mistrust can mark the difference between relations based on control or cooperation, simplifying or complicating the creation of partnerships (Van Puyvelde, Caers, du bois, & Jegers 2012). Therefore, even when dealing with external ties and networks, it is always important to keep the door open for the implications and effects that internal ties may have.

Focusing on external networks, an interesting classification is offered by Baldassarri and Diani (2007) that divides civil society's relationships into two categories: *transactions* and *social bonds*. The former qualifies those exchanges necessary to achieve shared goals. Transactions will be shown to be extremely relevant for this chapter. Beyond material resources, the results of the analysis show a great relevance given to what I call *networked* and *homologated* mission.

With networked mission I indicate the fact that a specific mission requires a networked structure in order to be properly achieved.

In this specific case, it is shown that the goal of promoting international volunteering initiatives incentivizes organizations to act through a network. In addition, homologated mission describes the fact that core components of the organization's mission are shared among the other members of the community, facilitating the creation of networks and the sharing of information, resources, and know-how. The relevance of mission homologation is also shown by the case study when briefly describing other networks Lunaria is engaging with for some of its activities. Both networked and homologated mission are concepts that closely relate with the one proposed by Baldassarri and Diani, especially with the concept of transactions. It could be said that transactions are those relations that are necessary to achieve a networked mission. Offering a better understanding of the reasons behind the choice to engage in networks, these concepts allow for a better construction of the network analysis. Networks are created because they offer solutions to challenges created by the system and its changes. As summarized in the following table (Table 9.1), networks offer specific opportunities to strengthen actors' capabilities and to improve their own management.

First, networks respond to increased competitiveness through establishing collaborative relations, turning competitors into allies and allowing for higher specialization of their members without precluding them access to relevant issue areas. Second, networks mitigate resource scarcity by allowing resource sharing within them and allowing their members to access resources that without a network form would be inaccessible. Third, networks can help in overcoming power asymmetries and restricting environments by creating alternative channels of operation and communication.

TABLE 9.1 Challenges and network solutions

Challenges	Networked solutions
Increased competitiveness	• Partnership and alliances, moving from competition to collaboration
	• Specialization and shared know-how
Limited resources	• Exchange of resources within the network
	• Access to otherwise inaccessible resources
Power asymmetries and constraining environments	• Coalition and higher impact through collective action
	• Different action routes through international channels

From this perspective, networks are indeed a positive phenomenon that enhances CSOs' possibilities and facilitates their operations. However, while the beneficial effects of networks are well established in the literature, their possible side effects are often left out. The following sections of this chapter are dedicated to understanding whether networks have side effects on organizations, forcing them to accept choices they would not otherwise take, leaving them with limited or absent agency over the network itself. The results for the selected case show that networks do not seem to have restrictive effects, with organizations able to have their role and participate in the network notwithstanding their resources or capabilities. Furthermore, interviews show that the beneficial effects of networks here summarized are consistent with the organization's experience.

The next section will describe the network Lunaria is a member of, the Alliance of European Voluntary Service Organisations. The network analysis that has been conducted has served the double purpose of providing a picture of the organizational structure of the Alliance and of assessing the structure of the network and the relative position Lunaria has in it. The Alliance is a network consistent with those described in this section, where transnational ties are created to foster common activities beyond a single actor's capacities.

Mapping CSOs' transnational networks: The Alliance of European Voluntary Service Organizations

A mixed method approach (Creswell & Plano Clark 2018) perfectly serves the scope of this chapter. The integration of quantitative and qualitative analysis allows for a better understanding of the subject in question. On the one hand, the network analysis alone would be unable to uncover the relations among the actors involved. On the other hand, without the preceding network analysis, the qualitative research would lose in structural coherence and argumentative strength. Therefore, the mixed method approach is used for the purpose of complementarity and development (Greene, Caracelli, & Graham 1989). The former purpose aims at obtaining more complete understanding of the issue, and the latter entails the use of one method to inform the use of the other (Valeriani & Plano Clark 2019). Timing of integration is also an important aspect of mixed method research (Guest 2013). The two methodological strands were mixed in two phases of the analysis, during the data-gathering phase when more qualitative data was used to construct the network analysis and during the final phase, where results of the interviews were compared to the results of the previous analysis.

The network analysis was conducted over the Alliance of European Voluntary Service Organizations, a CSO founded in 1982 that includes a series of national organizations operating in the promotion of intercultural education, understanding and peace through means of voluntary service.[3] The Alliance was chosen among the different networks Lunaria engages with because it is the most structured one. The high level of formalization has allowed for the proper drawing of the networked governance of the Alliance through its core bodies and committees. The network comprises organizations from 28 countries; it sees the participation of around 13,000 volunteers per year divided in around 1,200 camps organized by its members, making it the largest European network for volunteers' exchanges. Stressing the added value of volunteering, the Alliance promotes annual programs of International Voluntary Projects in the member's countries and exchanges of volunteers between the members. The Alliance's Plan on Action is fostered through working groups (WGs), committees, and task forces (TFs) that act as collaborative and management bodies sustaining the organization's structure. With an actual workforce of just a few employees, the governance of the organization is left in its governing bodies. The Alliance prides itself on the achievement of guaranteeing the widest and most democratic participation of its members, allowing them to reach higher levels of quality, effectiveness, and sustainability of their projects and membership. There are no organizational hierarchies in the Alliance, and members interact equally in the different management bodies. Although it is sometimes contested (Faul 2016) the absence of hierarchy is a generally recognized key element of networks (Finnemore & Sikkink 1998).

Starting with seven original organizations, the Alliance now sees 43 full members and a series of associate and candidate members in addition to several partners. Among the full members, at the time of writing, two thirds are involved in committees and WGs.[4] Committees, WGs, and TFs have organizational freedom for their work, meetings, and seminars. The adherence to these bodies was chosen to formalize the ties between the organizations for the network analysis. Due to their relevance for the management and the activities of the Alliance, membership in these bodies entails the possibility to actively participate and possibly to influence the networks. The bodies, their activities, and their members are also fully described in the Alliance reports, providing good and solid data to build the network analysis upon. The data was gathered from the Alliance Annual Report for 2017, the last available at the time of writing.

Organizations were linked according to participation in different committees, WGs, and TFs. Each project was analyzed, and its members were linked together.

When the link was overwriting a pre-existing one, the edge was weighted by one additional unit. The resulting network shows an intricate set of connections, underlining the reiterated nature of some interactions. It is not rare to find the same organizations operating in different bodies. The cooperative spirit that lies behind such an active participation by the members in the governing bodies suggests that the Alliance follows the structure of a mandating network of issue control as presented by Henriksen and Seabrooke (Chapter 3 in this volume). Indeed, members are not aiming at moving issues from one group of organizations to another. Instead, they attempt to embed their priorities within the existing group of organizations through active representation in the governing bodies. In this framework, professionals involved in the mechanism become instrumental for the participation and interaction of the organization, but they do not engage in specific conflicts with other groups. This can be derived from the theory and the review of the governance documents of the Alliance and was also confirmed by the interviews conducted with members of Lunaria who confirmed the cooperative attitude of its representatives in the Alliance.

I considered eight different bodies in total. They include one committee, two tasks forces, and five working groups. These bodies represent the totality of the governing bodies of the Alliance except one committee and one task force whose members were not reported in the annual report. Besides functioning as operating bodies of the organization, these projects and the networks they compose are instrumental to specific functions, allowing the Alliance to tackle a series of challenges. Each committee, WG, and task force has specific objectives, ranging across different issues, from management and enlargement to sustainability and global challenges. The Alliance Development Committee (ADC) is a permanent body focusing on the strategic development of the Alliance. Similar to a think tank, the committee develops long-term proposals for the further development of the network. The committee operates to promote the external development of the organization as well as its enlargement. The ADC can also address and be addressed by other projects in the implementation phase. The Access for All Working Group (A4AWG) is a WG with the scope of strengthening the inclusion of volunteers with lower opportunities in the network. The WG creates tools and activities to promote the active participation of the volunteers and to create richer experiences for them. The Environmental Sustainability Working Group (ESWG) works in the field of sustainability, promoting it in the camps and among the volunteers of the Alliance. Providing advice and information, and promoting common events, the WG encourages awareness and implementation of sustainability in offices, camps, and everyday life. The WG also works as a bridge between the Alliance and other networks active in the field, recognizing the importance of a networked action in order to face the global challenges to which sustainability gives rise. The Staff Development Working Group (SDWG) is a quality reviewer operating within the network, serving as a supportive body for members' needs and challenges. The WG monitors and evaluates the members' activities, offering tools and support systems in order to facilitate them. The

Training Needs Working Group (TNWG) maps and addresses the needs related to training and education at the Alliance level as well as the member level. The WG works as a strategic partner for the other committees, WGs, and TFs to support their training needs. In the same area it works as a consultant for various Alliance organizations. The Gender Equality Working Group (GEWG) has the objective of promoting gender equality as one of the values of the Alliance. As other WGs it also serves as an information and planning provider in its area of interest. The Global Action Task Force (GATF) and the Volunteers' Engagement Task Force (VETF) are two TFs working respectively on migration and decreasing volunteering engagement.

The variety of issues that these bodies tackle shows how the networks allow for a subdivision of the tasks in an attempt to reach higher efficiency. Once the organizations were divided according to the different bodies they take part in, a simple network analysis was conducted to better understand the basic structure of the relations involved. In conformity with the information retrieved about the Alliance, slightly less than two-thirds of the members are not part of any committee, WG, or TF. They remain outside the network and were not plotted. The network analysis is an indicator for the interview-based qualitative analysis. Due to their limited descriptive value for this aim, these outliers were excluded from the representation of the network. Their absence does not affect the analysis of the position of active members, namely Lunaria, within the network and their presence reduces the precision of the graphical representations. The network analysis is used to provide a picture of the connections among the members of the Alliance. There are a series of available measures that can be used to map the relations and the relative power of a network's nodes. In this case the choice was to use *degree centrality* as a measurement. While being the simplest form of centrality, degree centrality still provides a good reference measure (Newman 2010). The network based on participation in governing bodies provides a good picture of the governance structure of the Alliance. However, it does not allow elaborating on important assumptions on the values of the ties, their direction, or the objects exchanged through them. Therefore, using other measurements for centrality may be misleading. For example, even though we can assume that participating in the bodies allows for the exchange of information and increases the possibilities of affecting the governance of the organization, using a measure such as betweenness centrality may seem too ambitious (Freeman 1977). Moreover, the undirected nature of the network impedes the use of measures such as authority or hub centrality (Kleinberg 1999). Therefore, degree centrality remains the most appropriate measure. In its simplicity, it gives a consistent picture of the participation in Alliance governance without forcing assumptions on the actual exchanges among the organizations. Indeed, to uncover these exchanges a more in-depth approach is needed that will be used in the qualitative part of this analysis.

The results of the network analysis that show that the Alliance has an average network density value that is assessed around 0.54 and an average path length

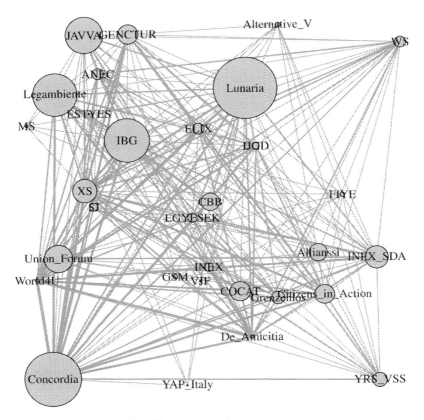

FIGURE 9.2 Mapping the Alliance network.

of slightly less than 1.46. When dealing with centrality it is clear that some organizations have indeed higher centrality compared to others, with Concordia reporting the highest centrality score and with Lunaria, IBG, and XS following after.

The network indicates a cohesive action between the organizations with each member having several chances to interact and collaborate with the others. The intricate network is represented in Figure 9.2, where nodes are sized and colored based on their degree centrality score.

Assessing members' perceptions: The case of Lunaria

After having mapped the characteristics of the Alliance's network, we can move on to the analysis of Lunaria. Lunaria was chosen because of its relatively small size, yet successful operations with high international outreach. The organization also has a relatively important position in the network, without being the most central. The average position of Lunaria in the network makes it a good case to investigate.⁵ Furthermore, beyond being selected for its properties, Lunaria was also chosen due to reasons of data access. Lunaria publishes a series of reports on its activities and social structure that are easily available online. Finally, interviews could be conducted in Italian directly by the author without the need for a translator or other intermediaries.

Lunaria is an Italian organization based in Rome and founded in 1992. Among its objectives are the promotion of peace, social justice, equality, democracy, and bottom-up participation, social inclusion, and intercultural dialogue. Many of the aims and core values resemble those of the Alliance, of which Lunaria has been a partner from 1993 and full member from 2002. Through its advocacy activities, Lunaria promotes processes of change at a local, national, and international level. Its social action is based on international volunteering, youth policies, migration, and the fight against racism. Lunaria also conducts analyses of budgetary, economic, and social policies. Lunaria is an apolitical association that funds itself through member contributions as well as public funding from the EU and national institutions. The organization carries out several international activities, positioning itself as a member of a series of national and transnational networks. One of these is the Alliance. Although Lunaria's issue areas and the geographical range are extremely wide, the organization only relies on a staff of 13 people and on extensive support from volunteers. The small dimension of the organization in comparison with its outreach is an additional factor in favor of its selection as a case study.

Lunaria is indeed a case of success, and understanding its relations and impact within the networks it navigates offers great insight with regard to the overall aims of this chapter. Lunaria is active in a series of projects that can be summarized as follows: international volunteering, youth exchange, migration, and the fight against racism, the "Sbilanciamoci!" campaign. International volunteering activities is the area where the cooperation with the Alliance network is the highest. Since its foundation, Lunaria has involved more than 24,000 Italian and foreign volunteers in its volunteering camps. In 2017 alone, Lunaria sent 520 volunteers to international camps and hosted 297 international volunteers in the camps organized in Italy. Lunaria started to be involved with youth exchanges, training, and youth initiatives in 1993, promoting non-formal education activities for young people at the local, national, and European level (Lunaria 2017).

In 2017, Lunaria involved around 350 youth workers in its training and exchange initiatives (Lunaria 2017). Among these initiatives, the projects conducted within the framework of the Alliance are extremely relevant. Relations with the network and with specific partners are not rare in Lunaria's reports, indicating the organization's continuous and solid relations with its networks. In the area of migration and the fight against racism, Lunaria has promoted research activities, awareness-raising campaigns, and information spreading activities since 1996. Finally, since 1999, Lunaria has initiated the "Sbilanciamoci!" campaign where a series of different CSOs come together with the aim of creating an economy of justice and a new model of development based on the values of rights, peace, and environmental preservation. The campaign publishes an annual report that analyzes the State Annual Budget Law and makes proposals for alternative policies.

The just described projects highlight the variety of issue areas and initiatives that Lunaria deals with. All of the projects appear to be conducted through the use of networks. Understanding the agency of the organization within these networks is the core driver of the qualitative analysis.

Interviews with two high members of the Alliance and with two high members of Lunaria were conducted in autumn 2018. Although the Alliance is a vast network of organizations, its own staff is extremely limited. At the same time, as emerged from the description of the working group's structure, different personnel of the member organizations operate at different levels of the Alliance structure. The interviews were based on a semi-structured form to give the interviewee maximum freedom of explanation. During the interviews, particular attention was given to the issues related to Lunaria's transnational activities and to the cooperation status within the Alliance. The interviews aimed at understanding the organization's perception of its position and relations with the network. Interviews were conducted face-to-face in Italian, or remotely when necessary.

Lunaria recognizes itself as being among the most central members; at the same time, it recognizes the higher centrality of other organizations, namely Concordia. However, the interesting result is also that at different levels, the interviewees stressed the lack of importance of the practical dimensions of the organizations in affecting their roles within the network. In fact, the interviewees linked the relative importance of the organizations to the organizations' voluntary engagement with the network, beyond their material characteristics. This response suggests that organizations retain considerable agency over the network they engage with. The history of Lunaria's role within the Alliance is, in this sense, emblematic. Joining it after more than ten years after the foundation of the Alliance, and becoming a full member after 20, Lunaria soon moved from the role of a newcomer to one of the most important members. This climb was indeed voluntary, as emerged during the interviews. The interviews have highlighted that Lunaria's vision of the Alliance has influenced its decision to play a more central role in the network, a decision that was not constrained or influenced by any external or structural condition.

Interviews also show that inter-organizational networks indeed serve the purposes summarized in the first section. Acting through a network offers wider opportunities and access to resources and objectives otherwise unachievable. For instance, it was remarked during the interviews that, having members in Brussels, the Alliance allows its members to have direct access to information and advocacy possibilities with regard to the EU. The network also creates a solid cooperative environment. Indeed, the interviewees did not refer to any competition among members. Possible differences and divergences were related only to the vision over the network future and structure. The idea of the networks as tools to achieve better results, overcome power asymmetries, create cooperative frameworks, and accessing various resources seems confirmed. Furthermore, from this result, a dimension above all seems to emerge: the mission. The distinction presented in the first section between networked and homologated mission originates from this result.

The idea of networked mission, that is, a mission that requires a network to be efficiently achieved (i.e., international volunteer exchanges), does not seem to limit the organization's freedom of engagement and decision. The history of Lunaria within the Alliance has shown that even if engagement is needed for the sake of higher efficiency, organizations that are willing to do so can freely integrate in the network beyond material constraints. The concept of homologated mission is better represented by another initiative that Lunaria promotes: "Sbilanciamoci!". This initiative focuses on the analysis and the proposition of alternatives to the Italian national budgetary law. The campaign has been successfully conducted since 1999 through a national network that sees the participation of 48 CSOs. The campaign is also undergoing a process of internationalization at the European level. However, budgetary laws' differences in timing, format, and regulation across European countries make the network creation process more challenging.

According to interviewees, the process is still at its preliminary phase, where different organizations operating on the same issue get to know each other and set the basis for a common agenda. Starting from national orientation and undergoing an internationalization process for the sake of collaboration, mission homologation becomes a facilitator, if not a requirement, of the network creation process. In this sense, networks appear to be established or engaged strategically by the organizations. CSOs operate strategically and develop the network-building process according to the specific characteristics that the issue they work on presents. On the other side, the idea of mission homologation also lies in the fact that common ideological grounds create stronger networks and ties. Interviewees reported that networks could be created *ad hoc* to satisfy external requests such as the conditions posed to access EU funding. However, they also stressed the precarity of these networks, which rarely go beyond the immediate objectives they are created for, limiting the returning benefits of its members.

Instead, an inverted process is often encouraged. In fact, beyond the instrumental benefits that networks such as the Alliance have, these networks also offer the opportunity to establish cooperation and partnership that allow for a more solid creation of sub-networks, if necessary. This is coherent with the idea that trust and mistrust play a crucial role in the establishment of networks. Reiterated exchanges within a network solidify relations among the members that are indeed more prone to use these experiences to build up future structures when needed.

The importance of the mission, and its intrinsic value for the organization, offers a good avenue for further research in this sense. The hybrid nature of the third sector makes it highly subject to the continuous struggles and integration between interests and values (Abbott & Snidal 2002). In fact, the literature on civil society has started attributing its objects of study, elevated normative values. For instance, the literature on social movements (Della Porta & Diani 1998), in its analysis of civil society and its relationship to political change, underlines the movements' principled importance. In recent years, this approach has been contrasted by more rational-oriented explanations. Economic models have been applied to CSOs, from organizational theories (Daft, Murphy, & Willmott 2010; DiMaggio & Powell 2016; Eikenberry & Kluver 2004; Luxon & Wong 2017), to those that focus on resource dependency (Chang 1997; McCarthy & Zald 1977; Pfeffer & Salancik 2003). At the same time, more comprehensive approaches have also made their way into the debate. Collective action (Olson 2002; Prakash & Gugerty 2010), social enterprises (Borzaga & Defourny 2001), and social capital (Adler & Kwon 2002) are examples of more mitigated approaches.

The results of this analysis go in the direction of the more comprehensive approaches. It has emerged that organizations indeed act strategically, but it is not possible to overlook their value-oriented side and the intrinsic power of their mission and dedication to it. Further evidence for this conclusion is the answer given by one of the interviewees, who played a great role for Lunaria's activities in the Alliance, on whether or not Lunaria would have joined the network anyway, had it been a larger organization with more resources at its disposal. The answer was positive, stressing the fact that more resources would have implied the possibility of an even larger engagement and investment in the network. This answer is a clear example of how values and mission affect CSOs' behavior. Resources are needed but are strategically used to achieve the final goal of the organization. This final conclusion opens the door for further research. While resource dependency theories may assume that larger organizations with larger resources may not need to engage in networks, the results of this analysis seem to suggest that the CSOs' principled orientation may mitigate this behavior. Further studies may provide a deeper understanding of CSOs' nature and behavior on these questions.

Furthermore, interviews also showed possible trends in professionals' behavior within CSOs. Of those people interviewed, all had decades of experience in the field, from volunteers to highly experienced managers. All the interviewees – perhaps not surprisingly – showed great dedication and affiliation to the cause of the organization. At the same time, they appear to be well aware of the benefit of a networked action through the Alliance. In this situation, where the goals of the members are aligned with the goals of the network, professionals are able to advance both organizational structures, with this becoming central to their activities. This fits well with the model advanced by Henriksen and Seabrooke in this volume, where professionals retain relevant roles in the framing of the related issues. Moreover, while the micro approach adds value to the analysis of Lunaria, the macro framework addressed by Orsini and Godet in Chapter 1 is also of some relevance. Indeed, this case also demonstrates how sectors of society build networks outside of the influence and sphere of the state, building intricate webs of action that give birth to new and deep dynamics. Thus, whilst the existence of this web does not have any link with the debate over a decreasing role of the state on the international stage, it does highlight how vast and intricate the international space for action is. With a plurality of actors engaging in transnational activities, networks proliferate, representing bridges and opportunities for entities (such as Lunaria) that would otherwise be unable to have the outreach they achieve through networked action.

Conclusions

This chapter offered a wider understanding of the relations between networks and their members. In order to do so, it developed a mixed method analysis of a defined CSO and one of the international networks it engages with. Civil society was chosen as the sector of investigation due to its natural propensity to operate through networks. At the same time, the choice of a small CSO originated from the idea that with its limited relative power, it is extremely exposed to the challenges created by growing complexity.

Theories show that networks offer several solutions to navigate this complexity. However, the real impact of the members of these networks on the networks and vice versa is rarely investigated. In its double-stage analysis, this chapter defined the outlines of the international network in question, and then focused on the perceptions of one of its members in order to draw out certain conclusions in relation to CSO engagement and action in such networks. The results show overall that the member is well aware of its position within the network, it retains a good level of agency over it, its engagement is not limited by material constraints and its organizational mission and dedication appear to be the main drivers of the engagement. The analysis also offers important insight for the debate relating to the principled versus interest-driven nature of civil society. Indeed, the broader implication of the analysis from this case study is that although organizations operate strategically, the principled goals and the organization's values remain central drivers of their operations.

This conclusion highlights how civil society can address complexity while dealing with the internal struggle between resource dependency and mission achievement. Under such conditions, CSOs have proved to build networks to increase their efficiency and efficacy. Where the system requires alliances, organizations build networks to share costs and benefits. This conclusion provides a basis for further research that looks at CSOs using a framework that balances between excessively rational or normative approaches. Moreover, the chapter could also represent a base for further studies on the management of networked organizations, looking at the working group structure for different networks, and studies on the resilience of CSOs networks. If networks are so useful to navigate complexity, what happens in times of crisis or risk for the network? How does the network and its members respond to it? Asking such questions going forward will no doubt shed further light and further inform the debate on how CSOs navigate, manage, and influence networks.

Notes

1 Through the Erasmus + programme.
2 http://www.alliance-network.eu/about-us/.
3 Information and data were retrieved on the Alliance's website: http://www.alliance-network.eu.
4 http://www.alliance-network.eu/committees-and-working-groups/ (retrieved on 27/09/2018).
5 Lunaria's density score was of 26 well above the third quartile (20). Its centrality score was of 0.7, still above the third quartile (0.56).

References

Abbott, K.W., & Snidal, D. (2002). Values and interests : International legalization in the fight against corruption. *The Journal of Legal Studies, 31*, 141–177.
Abbott, K.W., & Snidal, D. (2009). The governance triangle: Regulatory standards institutions and the shadow of the state. In W. Mattli & N. Woods (Eds.), *The politics of global regulation* (pp. 17–40). Princeton, NJ: Princeton University Press.
Adler, P.S., & Kwon, S.-W. (2002). Social capital: Prospects for a new concept. *Academy of Management Review, 27*(1), 17–40.
Alliance of European Voluntary Service Organisations. (2017). *Annual report 2017.*
Anheier, H.K. (2014). *Nonprofit organizations: Theory, management, policy.* London and New York: Routledge.
Anheier, H.K., Kaldor, M., & Glasius, M. (2005). *Global civil society.* London.
Appadurai, A. (1996). *Modernity al large: Cultural dimensions of globalization* (Vol. 1). Minneapolis: University of Minnesota Press.
Baldassarri, D., & Diani, M. (2007). The integrative power of civic networks. *American journal of sociology, 113*(3), 735–780.
Borzaga, C., & Defourny, J. (2001). *The emergence of social enterprise.* London: Routledge.
Brown, L.K., & Troutt, E. (2004). Funding relations between nonprofits and government: A positive example. *Nonprofit and Voluntary Sector Quarterly, 33*(1), 5–27.
Chang, M. (1997). Civil society, resource mobilization, and new social movements theoretical implications for the study of social movements in Taiwan. *Chinese Sociology & Anthropology, 29*(4), 7–41.
Cohen, J., & Arato, A. (1994). *Civil society and political theory.* Cambridge: MIT Press.
Cooley, A., & Ron, J. (2010). The political economy of transnational action among international NGOs. In Prakash, A., & Gugerty, M. K. (Eds.), *Advocacy organizations and collective action* (p. 205). Cambridge: Cambridge University Press.
Creswell, J.W., & Plano Clark, V. (2018). *Designing and conducting mixed methods research* (III). London: Sage Publications Inc.
Daft, R.L., Murphy, J., & Willmott, H. (2010). *Organization theory and design.* Boston: Cengage learning EMEA.
Della Porta, D., & Diani, M. (1998). *Social movements: An introduction. 2006.* Malden.

DiMaggio, P., & Powell, W. (2016). The iron cage revisited : Institutional isomorphism and collective rationality in organizational fields, *American Sociological Review*, 48(2), 147–160.
Doh, J.P., & Teegen, H. (2002). Nongovernmental organizations as institutional actors in international business: Theory and implications. *International Business Review*, 11(6), 665–684.
Dupuy, K., Ron, J., & Prakash, A. (2016). Hands off my regime! governments' restrictions on foreign aid to non-governmental organizations in poor and middle-income countries. *World Development*, 84, 299–311.
Ehrenberg, J. (2011). The history of civil society ideas. In M. Edwards (Ed.), *The Oxford handbook of civil society* (pp. 15–27). Oxford University Press.
Eikenberry, A.M., & Kluver, J.D. (2004). The marketization of the nonprofit sector: Civil society at risk? *Public Administration Review*, 64(2), 132–140.
Faul, M.V. (2016). Networks and power: Why networks are hierarchical not flat and what can be done about it. *Global Policy*. http://doi.org/10.1111/1758-5899.12270
Finnemore, M., & Sikkink, K. (1998). International norm dynamics and political change. *International Organization*. http://doi.org/10.1162/002081898550789
Freeman, L.C. (1977). A set of measures of centrality based on betweenness. *Sociometry*, 40, 35–41.
Greene, J.C., Caracelli, V.J., & Graham, W.F. (1989). Toward a conceptual framework for mixed-method evaluation designs, *Educational Evaluation and Policy Analysis*, 11(3), 255–274.
Guest, G. (2013). Describing mixed methods research: An alternative to typologies. *Journal of Mixed Methods Research*, 7(2), 141–151.
Handy, F. (1995). Reputation as collateral: An economic analysis of the role of trustees of nonprofits. *Nonprofit and Voluntary Sector Quarterly*, 24(4), 293–305.
Held, D., & McGrew, A.G. (2003). The global transformations reader: An introduction to the globalization debate. *Booksgooglecom*. http://doi.org/GLOB HELD/G.T.R.
Istat. (2014). *Non-profit institution profile based on 2011 census results*. Rome.
Keane, J. (2003). *Global civil society?* (Vol. 23). Cambridge: Cambridge University Press.
Keck, M.E., & Sikkink, K. (1998). *Activists beyond borders: Advocacy networks in international politics*. Ithaca: Cornell University Press.
Kleinberg, J.M. (1999). Authoritative sources in a hyperlinked environment. *Journal of the ACM (JACM)*, 46(5), 604–632.
Larry, D. (1994). Rethinking civil society: Toward democratic consolidation. *Journal of Democracy*, 5(3), 4–17.
Lewis, D. (2001). *The management of development organizations*. London and New York: Routledge.
Lunaria. (2017). *Annual report*. Rome.
Luxon, E.M., & Wong, W.H. (2017). Agenda-setting in greenpeace and amnesty: The limits of centralisation in international NGOs. *Global Society*, 31(4), 1–31.
Marchetti, R. (2016). *Global strategic engagement: States and non-state actors in global governance*. Lanham: Lexington Books.
McCarthy, J.D., & Zald, M.N. (1977). Resource mobilization and social movements: A partial theory. *American Journal of Sociology*, 82(6), 1212–1241. http://doi.org/10.1086/226464
Newman, M. (2010). *Networks: An Introduction* Oxford: Oxford University Press.
Olson, M. (2002). *The logic of collective action* (20th ed.). Cambridge: Harvard University Press.

Pfeffer, J., & Salancik, G.R. (2003). *The external control of organizations: A resource dependence perspective*. Stanford: Stanford University Press.

Prakash, A., & Gugerty, M.K. (2010). *Advocacy organizations and collective action*. Stanford: Cambridge University Press.

Scholte, J.A. (2005). *Globalization: A critical introduction*. London: Palgrave Macmillan.

Teegen, H., Doh, J.P., & Vachani, S. (2004). The importance of nongovernmental organizations (NGOs) in global governance and value creation: An international business research agenda. *Journal of International Business Studies, 35*(6), 463–483.

UIA. (2017). *Yearbook of international organizations*. Bruxelles: Brill.

Valeriani, M., & Plano Clark, V. (2020). Mixed methods: Combination of quantitative and qualitative research approaches. In J.F. Morin, C. Olsson, & E.O. Atikan (Eds.), *Key concepts in research methods* (pp. 151–155).

Van Puyvelde, S., Caers, R., du bois, C., & Jegers, M. (2012). The governance of nonprofit organizations: Integrating agency theory with stakeholder and stewardship theories. *Nonprofit and Voluntary Sector Quarterly, 41*, 431–451.

10
MULTI-LEVEL DIPLOMACY IN EUROPE IN THE DIGITAL CENTURY

The case of Science Diplomacy

Luk Van Langenhove and Elke Boers

Introduction

The environment in which diplomacy used to operate has changed dramatically. The world order seems to have been turned upside down and there is little agreement on the shape of the new diplomatic environment. The rejection of a unipolar model has not produced a clear alternative except that it can now be agreed that there is a highly complex diffusion of power (Hocking and Melissen 2012). Parag Khanna even argued that our

> twenty-first-century diplomacy is coming to resemble that of the Middle Ages: Rising powers, multinational corporations, powerful families, humanitarians, religious radicals, universities, and mercenaries are all part of the diplomatic landscape. Technology and money, not sovereignty, determine who has authority and calls the shots.
>
> *(Khanna 2011)*

This statement has become even more true today, as we live in an environment where liberal values are more and more questioned and undermined, where extreme voting behavior has led to the ascent of right-wing and populist parties, and where scientific results are no longer automatically believed to be true. On top of it, the budget cuts for the diplomatic corps have been so dramatic in many countries that their visibility and thus political clout has been reduced drastically. Whilst countries like China are investing more and more in their diplomatic network, the US no longer seems to value its diplomats, but relies even more on its military department. As Farrow (2018) puts it: "first shoot and never ask questions". But whilst, on the one hand, governmental diplomacy seems to have had its best time, on the other hand, diplomacy has been revived in other areas and in other societal layers. This can probably be related to the digitalization of society that not only led to the emergence of "digital diplomacy" but also made it possible for all kinds of actors other than states to engage in diplomacy (Manor 2018). The impact of digital technologies on diplomacy is, therefore, one of the major developments in diplomacy of the last decades that not only changed the nature of diplomacy but also led to a proliferation of diplomatic actors.

Indeed, the diffusion of power has led to an augmented complexity of the global system, with many other actors besides states having a say in decision and policy-making processes. It has led Slaughter (2017) to make the case that in today's world networks play a central role in diplomacy (see also Godet and Orsini, Chapter 1). Within this context the EU and other European diplomatic actors can be regarded as a laboratory of the changing nature of diplomacy. A key question is how in Europe diplomatic actors and networks have sought to navigate, manage, and potentially influence this new diplomatic reality? This question can be illustrated by the case of Science Diplomacy: a new form of diplomacy that networks foreign affairs to scientists and that in Europe involves both states and the EU.

This chapter develops in three parts. The first section will contextualize complexity in diplomacy and argue that we are entering an era of Multilateralism 2.0. Section two then deals with how European and EU actors have been part of these changes, and looks into how they have attempted to navigate the disruptions more generally. This has been done by adding to traditional diplomacy other forms of more networked diplomacy. Finally, the third section will present the case of Science Diplomacy to illustrate the ability of EU and European actors to navigate, manage, and influence through Science Diplomacy networks.

The old paradigm: State to state diplomacy

Diplomacy is often seen as one of the oldest professions, and is supposedly the first human activity that has led humanity to organize itself into a bigger structure than a closed small tribe consisting out of only family members (Harari 2018). As societies grew into cities and cities into kingdoms or empires, diplomacy started to play an even more important role. Merchants and ambassadors being often one and the same profession, as "between kings there is brotherhood, alliance, peace and good words if there is an abundance of precious stones, silver and gold" (Khanna 2011). This interpretation of diplomacy transformed during the 16th century in Europe, at the height of the rivalry of the Italian city-states of Venice, Genoa, and Milan. The Machiavellian chessboard game, penned down in *The Prince*, would emphasize a statecraft that mixed the arts of diplomacy and war. A century later, however, public-corporate agents of imperial expansion such as the Dutch and British East India companies would put themselves on equal footing with other extensive foreign ministries as their power reached far beyond where diplomats had ever carried out negotiations. Merchandise and trade would typically always precede diplomatic endeavors.

The now traditional interpretation of diplomatic one-to-one state affairs took shape after the Peace of Westphalia in the middle of the 17th century, when a new political order arose based on the sovereignty of states. Diplomats, often members of nobility, were seen as representatives of the king, negotiating in the best interest of their country in order to avoid war in the future. This traditional form of diplomacy acted, and still does in some cases, as if there is a neatly lined international environment consisting of clearly identifiable players (Melissen 2005). This principle of sovereignty is until today one of the main concepts in international law and enshrined in the United Nations Charter. Principles of multilateralism could already be linked with the emergence of the "Westphalian world order which was built upon sovereign states and the possibilities and necessities of those states to cooperate with each other" (Van Langenhove 2010). Classical diplomacy thrived in a world of industrial production, bureaucratic efficiency, and limited communication and communication speed. Today, diplomacy takes place in a world of high connectivity and global access of information.

The shift to classic multilateral diplomacy (Multilateralism 1.0)

It could be said that the very first successful modern endeavors to bring together all states in order to cooperate better on an international level was the foundation of the League of Nations and, quickly after that, the United Nations established in 1945, after which many other regional (such as NATO and the OECD) and global (such as the Worldbank, GATT, and IMF) inter-state structures were created in order to deal with emerging world problems. That year was maybe also simultaneously the end of the great power summits, with Yalta in 1945 arguably being one of the last. In this format 1.0, multilateralism referred to institutionalized cooperation among states, serving as the key players in international organizations. This classical multilateral order has been under threat for several years, and most scholars of international relations agree that the Westphalian model of sovereign states is long overdue. This contestation toward great power summits is easily detectible through the huge protests and critique the G20 summits receive yearly.

Several developments have caused this state-centered system to become less efficient. One of those is that since the UN's inception, its member base has almost quadrupled (from 51 to 193 member states), as in 1945 many of the current states were still under colonial rule. Many other states have split or dissolved, as, for example, the Soviet Union. Most of the current states are relatively small, and the more members the UN counts, the more difficult it will become to govern it. With the current separatist movements all over the world, it is likely that this number of UN member states will only increase.

Another factor that diminishes its efficiency is that the world has become more globalized and connected than people had ever imagined in 1945. World trade nowadays only has limited restrictions, and technological advancements have given a new dimension to the word "connectivity". Globalization, however, has also caused a substantial gap between the wealthy and the poor. The benefits of globalization remain highly concentrated among a small number of states, and within those states among a tiny percentage of the population. The multilateral system has developed unevenly. At the same time, intergovernmental and international structures that made the world's most important decisions for decades, like the UN Security Council, are now being perceived as deadlocked and outdated structures, being too bureaucratic and slow in this fast-moving world. The UNSC is perceived as having no political decision-making power and lacking the speed to decide upon fast-evolving conflicts. On top of that, its veto powers still stem from the foundation of the UN when many of the UN's members were still colonial – or satellite – states subject to the veto power states.

Disruptions

Today's world order is going through a lot of changes. Fletcher (2016) mentions four major trends we are living through: the erosion of US hegemony combined with a shift to a period without a lead nation; the collapse, perhaps rapid, of the 20th-century world order; the increased influence of non-state actors and new elites; and the technological empowerment of individuals. These trends all have consequences for multilateralism and diplomacy. And although they affect the whole world, their consequences are perhaps most felt in Europe given the development of the EU as hybrid actor (part intergovernmental organization and part supranational).

The proliferation of governance; toward Multilateralism Mode 2.0

In recent years there has been a significant shift in the power balance between global, regional, national, and local levels of governance. Once the preserve of states, governance is now distributed amongst different types of governance entities that are not states, but do have some statehood properties. As a result of this proliferation of governance, diplomacy is no longer preserved solely for sovereign states; both subnational regions (like Flanders in Belgium) and supranational regions (like the EU) have emerged and are gaining more decision-making power, also in their way of conducting external relations. Subnational actors, both regions and cities, are resonating louder on the international political stage (Van Langenhove, 2011). This is no surprise as they account for a large part of today's cross-border contacts. Even cities are becoming a key feature of the new global political landscape, with mayors sometimes holding just as much power as ministers. With more than half of the world's population living in cities, and the population of megacities having increased tenfold in 40 years, this should not be underestimated. In many ways, cities seem to be way more efficient in governing than national governments. They are often ahead of their governments when it comes to urban regeneration, citizen involvement, energy, and transport. Moreover, whereas cities can even succeed in failed states, no state could survive with failed cities. This thought also resonates well with Parag Khanna's (2011) argument that the world is not run by coherent states, but rather by *islands of governance* instead of effective governments. And these islands are not states, but cities. "Today, just forty city-regions account for two-thirds of the world economy…Cities, more than nations, are the building blocks of global activity today. Our world is more a network of villages than it is one global village" (p. 14).

Regions and cities are not the only non-state actors that have increased influence at the international relations and global governance level. Companies, NGOs, and wealthy individuals or families are playing important roles as well. They not only invest in business, but also in civil society and diplomatic networks. Both the Gates and the Soros families, for example, make huge societal efforts through their foundations, being even called "celebrity diplomats" (Cooper 2008). This raises questions on the future of the state system that has provided the grounds for the international political order in the last centuries. Indeed, the challenge in this new era is not states with too much power, but too little. As Fletcher argued, declining powers are more disruptive than rising ones, and great powers do not seem to want to exert great power anymore. Instead of a balance of power, we are perhaps heading toward a period characterized by the absence of any hegemonic power. States, even the strongest, are discovering the limits of their influence.

So, the state-centered multilateral system, what Van Langenhove called Mode 1.0 of the Multilateral System (Van Langenhove 2010), is gradually transforming into a more open system where non-state actors also play a role (Embassy Lab 2016). Van Langenhove predicts that the Multilateralism 2.0 Mode will be more open, networked, and less state-centered, where globalization has also created a world of greater interdependence between networks and states. This transition, however, also places in front of us a serious power paradox: whilst the policy authority and the problem-solving power lies within the boundaries of the nation-states, the causes – and therefore also the potential solutions – lay with networks, at more global, transnational, and local levels (Thakur and Van Langenhove 2006). This shift can also be witnessed through the commitment of both the UN and the EU to involve more and more stakeholders, like civil society, external experts, and other platforms.

Of course, this changing nature of diplomacy and the environment in which it is conducted doesn't make things easier for career diplomats. As Tom Fletcher (2016, p. 215) acknowledged:

> It is naturally easier for diplomats to understand the world in terms of this great power narrative. The big questions in international affairs since the birth of modern diplomacy in the fifteenth century have been about how states relate to each other. Diplomats found and expanded a natural

niche in that system. It also reinforces our roles – we send ambassadors to Paris and Beijing, not to Google and Apple. Yet foreign ministries have long ceased to be able to monopolize their government's interface with the world, let alone their countries.

The rise of the internet; connectivity; networks

The second big disruption came with the rise of the internet: it gave rise to abundant information and super connectivity; a rise of network diplomacy where networks become diplomatic actors (cf. university alliances) and where diplomatic actors network (cf. association of science advisors). We are moving from a hierarchical toward a networking world, and diplomats' mindsets have to move to networks and coalitions (Embassy Lab 2016).

The digitalization of diplomacy, as Manor (2018) put it, impacts four dimensions of diplomacy: the audience, the institutions, the practitioners, and the practice of diplomacy. The internet has been and still is causing many implications we have to face. It is changing how humans interact socially and economically at a faster pace than at any time in history (Fletcher 2016), and in a more networked than hierarchical manner. So also because of technological advances, diplomacy faces a crisis of legitimacy and trust, and sometimes other non-state actors can do diplomacy more effectively.

Indeed, as Slaughter (2017) has extensively argued, current state "chessboard games" (formal and closed) will have to make way or at least coexist with the fast-moving dynamics of networks and connections (often informal and open) in order to solve global problems of all nature, be it climate, criminal networks, or cybercrimes. The issue within state affairs is that you either reach an agreement with another government or sanction them. You only have x amount of options in state diplomacy, which will not necessarily bring a solution to a problem. If you reach out to networks, you often tap into a way more connected and open world of solutions. This is definitely one big issue within state and intergovernmental diplomacy; they are bound by the limited options of their own chessboard.

So, another way of listing foreign policy problems is to focus on the *nature* of the problems that are currently difficult to solve. Slaughter (2017) has argued that networks can address foreign policy problems of different nature, namely (i) scale, (ii) resilience, and (iii) execution/task problems. The nature of these problems means that sole governments cannot address them (see Chapter 1 of this volume). For Slaughter, it is not individual actors such as a state that need to be mobilized to deal with the three types of problems but specific types of networks. It is evident that science is already playing an extremely important role in these issues, and this will become even more evident.

Scale problems lie in the ability to solve problems on a small scale, and thus to provide micro solutions to existing problems. Science-related examples could be water pollution (when one country filters, but the other still pollutes a river or lake) or air pollution (when one city prohibits the drive-through of high-polluting vehicles, it doesn't mean the other city will be spared from less pollution). Resilience would mean the "resistance to change and the ability to more quickly recover from changes", or as Slaughter quotes Andrew Zolli in her book: "The capacity of a system to maintain its core purpose and integrity in the face of dramatically changed circumstances" (Slaughter 2017).

Increasing resilience is probably one of the most difficult problems to address for a government, as it is inherently linked to networks. Think of cybercrimes and cyberattacks, which are difficult to stop exactly because of their nature. Execution tasks often occur when there is a solution available, but it is too difficult to apply. This could be because of a science-policy gap (when policy-makers do not understand the essence of a problem or do not accept scientists' advice), international unwillingness, or because of a scale problem (clearing all plastic out of the ocean).

We are treating the most significant issues of our time – terrorism, climate change, the economy – as if they are global first and local second. But, in fact, the opposite is true. Many global issues are more rooted in local injustices. The notion of "global poverty", for example, has its own varieties with its own blend of drivers, including overpopulation, geography, and corruption. Making the global ecosystem more resilient will happen through local and regional measures. Generation Y's leaders will likely have five jobs across public, private, and non-profit sectors over the course of their careers, and thus be pragmatic rather than ideological about the role of the state. They see problems functionally, not nationally, and see diplomacy not as vertical and hierarchical, but rather as distributed networks: all are connected, there is no center. In the meantime, NGOs such as Oxfam and the Gates Foundation participate in political agendas without official approval, yet the work is as diplomatic as that of a foreign ministry.

The rise of social media and Public Diplomacy

The last disruption has come with the rise of social media: the projection – and thus also protection – of images has gained more and more importance. Public Diplomacy and the diplomacy of everything has started to make its way (Snow and Taylor 2008). Civil society is engaging more than ever in what was previously seen as state affairs, conducted behind closed walls, and diplomats are looking for approval of the citizens of their country they represent. Social media has accelerated diplomatic activities to a hitherto unseen pace, which has both its advantages and disadvantages. More online engagement is expected from both bottom-up as well as top-down agencies.

Influencing the opinion of people and gaining their approval will of course become more important in this world where even the US President prefers Twitter above official governmental communication channels, and diplomats tweet about negotiations rather than wait for the outcomes. But government officials seem to be tied to their own "chessboard game" as traditional diplomacy often cannot tap into the connected networks that dominate the world more and more. Bottom-up networks usually reach way more people, and act as a many-to-many communication, whereas state diplomacy is often considered as a one-to-one, privileged, and closed practice – maybe one of the reasons why G20 summits receive less attention than before. Besides or in coalition with these bottom-up initiatives, peer-to-peer networks will (Embassy Lab 2016) gain more territory, as these will spread information within the most relevant circles and thus create more understanding and better cooperation.

As diplomats are no longer representatives of the elite but those of the state and its population, they should indeed represent the interests of the population. Tavares argues for a more "humanized" modern diplomacy. "To most countries, the legitimacy of diplomatic presence is still predicated upon anachronistic concepts such as distant representation, closed-door negotiations, exclusive knowledge, or professional nobility" (Tavares 2018).

The emergence and growing importance of Public Diplomacy shows this need for a reaction to the changing nature of diplomacy and the way international relations is conducted in general. Public Diplomacy can be described as the processes by which direct relations with people in a country are pursued to advance the interests and extend the values of those being represented. As Melissen (2005) points out, that definition of Public Diplomacy often leans toward the definition of propaganda (although its intention has a different base and moral starting point). Public Diplomacy is in this context related to the growing importance of soft power and the need to gain more public support of foreign policies, both for state and non-state actors. It is therefore a natural cause and phenomenon of this new approach to global affairs. In parallel, an evolving relationship between science and diplomacy has been taking place, as scientific networks and advice are playing a more and more significant role in diplomatic activities (Figure 10.1).

The *sui generis* case of the EU

Ever since the end of World War II, Europe has been the theatre of a complex process of so-called regional integration where a growing number of states have engaged in a mix of intergovernmental agreements and the building of a supranational entity (Van Langenhove 2011). Through a series of treaties starting with the Treaty of Rome in 1957 (followed by the Treaties of Brussels Maastricht, Amsterdam, Nice, and Lisbon) a complex web has been created that ties the national states into a dense economic and political integrated space. Today, the EU has a legal personality, and although it is not a state, it has several statehood properties, including a diplomatic force that is institutionally embedded in the European External Action Service (EEAS). The result is that governance in Europe can now be described as multi-level governance. But this is more than just a hierarchical set of powers governed by the principle of subsidiarity. The reality is that the situation in Europe is one where all levels of governance are

Multi-level diplomacy in Europe   189

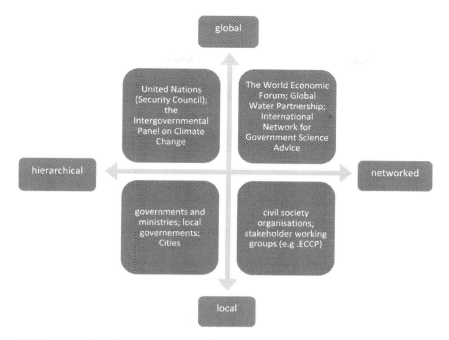

FIGURE 10.1   Multi-level, multi-actor diplomacy.

shaping, implementing, and monitoring policies together. One of the crucial instruments in this is the establishment of a system of "permanent representations" (the so-called COREPER) of the member states to the Brussels institutions. Next to pursuing their official mandate to prepare the meetings of the Council at the ministerial level, the offices of the permanent representations also engage in many activities such as organizing debates and information sessions. Science Diplomacy has recently been such a topic. The unintended consequence of this is that by doing so, Science Diplomacy gains in credibility in the diplomatic milieu.

Van Middelaar (2017) describes the complex structure of the EU's political and institutional infrastructure as follows: there is the inner core of the Union and its European Commission in Brussels; the intermediary circle of the European Council, comprised of the heads of state of EU member states; and the outer circle made up of the states themselves. The outer sphere is where traditional diplomacy takes place between states driven by self-interest. The inner core of the Union comprises a growing field of policy issues listed in the treaties between the states and dealing with common interests. The intermediary circle is where the inner and outer circle meet in the European Council and can be seen as the top of a pyramid of meetings that starts at the bottom with countless national committees of civil servants, followed by the weekly meetings of the representatives (ambassadors) of the member states to the Union, and by the monthly meeting of the ministers that cover specific policy issues such as economic affairs, agriculture, science policy, and so on. To add to the complexity, a number of member states that have a federal structure also bring in civil servants, representatives, and ministers of their subnational regions.

As a result, governance in Europe – on whatever topic – is dispersed over many spaces and has given birth to all kinds of formal and informal networks, as well as to a proliferation of diplomatic actors. Time and again a delicate balance between the Union and the member states needs to be achieved.

Science and Technology is one of the policy domains that in Europe is both a competence of the EU member states and the EU. Through its so-called Horizon 2020 programme the EU has invested approximately 80 billion Euro over the 2014–2020 period. Part of this endeavor has been directed toward the external dimension. Since 2012, a strategic approach has been adopted to enhance and focus the Union's international cooperation activities in science and innovation. In the document COM (2012) 497, it is clearly stated that such international cooperation should support the EU's external polices by coordinating closely with enlargement, neighborhood, trade, and its Common Foreign and Security Policy (CFSP). The same document also states that "Science Diplomacy" has to be used as an instrument of soft power "and as a mechanism for improving relations with key countries and regions". A similar point of view is expressed in COM (2014) 339 Final, where it is stressed that further efforts need to be made in addressing the external dimension of Research and Innovation policy. In a speech delivered at the European Institute in Washington on June 1, 2015, the EU Commissioner for Research, Science, and Innovation boldly stated that he wants "science diplomacy to play a leading role in our global outreach for its uniting power". In that same speech he compared Science Diplomacy to a torch that can "light the way, where other kinds of politics and diplomacy have failed". But, as will be argued in the next section, Science Diplomacy in Europe is still in a formative phase.

The case of Science Diplomacy

Just as there is a shift toward more involvement of citizens in international affairs, there is also a shift in expectations when it comes to science from the side of governments and international organizations. Whereas science was in the past always meant to reach a particular goal, based on products and results, there is now also more attention for the process of Science Diplomacy in the sense that politicians expect to build better relations with other countries when they give more funding for science projects. The rationale behind this strategy would be that scientists can keep communication channels open where politics cannot. In many instances, the use of the term Science Diplomacy by government actors or policy-makers fits into a positioning strategy, making them think instrumentally about science and technological development in terms of contribution to the state interests, in particular their foreign affairs or international relations. Science

Diplomacy then becomes a tool and a rationale in the broader context of the science society social contract. Policy-makers then demand that scientists take up "diplomatic roles", but it still remains to be seen if this way of thinking will be accepted in the scientific community, as only a handful of scientists accept or even *are aware of* their possible positioning as "science diplomats".

On the other side of the spectrum, scientist-driven Science Diplomacy has gained more momentum these past years, with scientists stepping up their efforts in their fight against false facts and limited access to scientific data, which hinders the formation of science-based policy-making. Their societal engagement can easily be situated on both the local and global levels of the more networked side of the spectrum. The worldwide March for Science initiatives are probably one of the best examples of scientists uniting against this phenomenon of non-scientific policy-making: it was a direct reaction against the Trump administration's views on climate change and science, and the exclusion of scientific knowledge in policy decisions. On Earth Day 2017, more than 600 cities held protests, uniting more than 1.07 million people around the globe. Especially this category, promoting science in the fight against fake news, has found its base in the scientific community itself. In this case they surely are public diplomats as they are taking up their role to inform the population and trying to engage with the public, whilst trying to counter the negative stance toward scientific findings.

An emerging new agenda for Science Diplomacy

During the past years, there has been a call for a narrower application of the term Science Diplomacy, as it is seen as a container concept that encompasses nearly all fields of science, and as a catch-all concept in public policy (Rüffin 2018). Not all so-called applications of Science Diplomacy fall within the borders of what is generally accepted as Science Diplomacy (e.g. providing scientific advice in policy-making processes to come to evidence-based decisions), but some clearly do. State-driven – traditional – forms of Science Diplomacy, for example, are clearly a subset of Public Diplomacy, as through the promotion of national science and technology systems, countries are trying to attract more talented human resources to ensure their place on the global science stage. Targeting a particular audience abroad to advance your own country's interest would indeed be one of the core principles of diplomacy. State-driven diplomatic endeavors (track-one diplomacy) will remain of relevance, as many national needs can only be fully represented by these practices. These national needs can be divided into (1) *influence and soft power*, gained through, for example, bilateral relations and development assistance; (2) *security issues*, such as crises, disasters, and threats (cyber, fake news) and the technical aspects of treaties; (3) *economic issues*, such as trade, innovation, and standards; and other (4) *national needs*, such as technical capabilities, access to know-how, and the development of science, technology, and innovation (Gluckman et al. 2017). These applications of Science Diplomacy could, therefore, be situated on the local, hierarchical level as they mostly serve national governments.

However, neither Public nor Science Diplomacy is seen as a unique stately activity as it flows from the developments of the 21st century. As is the case for most other networks, both the theory and practice of Science Diplomacy originated from science organizations and individual scientists. The concept was first coined by the AAAS and the Royal Society, and was soon echoed by several other science academies and organizations. This scientist-driven diplomacy has mostly focused on (1) bridging national divides in order to be able to conduct science, (2) finding solutions to global challenges, (3) bridging the gap between science and policy-making, and (4) advocating for science and resisting digital disinformation challenges (International Association for Media and Communication Research 2018), such as fake news or non-evidence-based policy-making. As all these categories are more than ever actual, science-driven Science Diplomacy will only become more important, and will most likely coexist with state-driven Science Diplomacy. As these scientist-driven forms of Science Diplomacy often address global issues (which can also be traced back to local problems, of course), we could say this is a form of global, both hierarchical (United Nations) and networked (International Network for Government Science Advice) Science Diplomacy.

The praxis of Science Diplomacy within networks

If it is accepted that Science Diplomacy is a concept that refers to a set of tools that foreign policy actors can use to solve problems of world politics, then one should start with listing those problems and reflect on *if* and *how* Science Diplomacy could help in overcoming those problems. One could start by listing some traditional security topics related to conflicts such as peace-making, peacekeeping, peacebuilding, and peace enforcement. Other foreign policy topics should then be added, such as development issues, clashes in national interests, and global problems.

It seems evident that science is already playing an extremely important role in the issues that were identified by Slaughter (2017), and this will become even more evident. This poses a new challenge to foreign policy-makers: what are the tools needed to foster the emergence and development of Science Siplomacy networks? At the time of writing there is no official European answer to this, as the networking approach seems not to be high on the policy agenda of the EU. But nevertheless, Science Diplomacy is increasingly a topic of interest to the many actors of the Brussels European "bubble" as is illustrated by the above-mentioned example of COREPER and the Permanent Representations.

The increasingly networked organization of governance gives a golden opportunity for the application of Science Diplomacy. Some European governments already recognize the growing importance of the roles that both science and private sector actors play. In 2013, for example, France appointed a "special representative of France to international negotiations on the information society and the digital economy". More recently, Denmark has taken unprecedented action in delegating a direct digital ambassador to members of a stateless private sector: Google, Apple, Facebook, and Amazon (GAFA). Such actors represent a world without borders, one in which each enterprise generates as much capital as an average country (Gramer 2017). The active cooperation of these stakeholders with the security services has helped in the monitoring and mitigation of radicalization and cybercrime. However, these companies can also disclose personal information for unwanted purposes, as the recent Cambridge Analytica scandal has shown.

The potential for scientists to become more involved in Science Diplomacy thus constitutes a significant opportunity for the field. The growing interconnectedness of a world linked by applications in information and communications technology (ICT) allows scientists to deepen their global networks. Additionally, some political actors appear to take the values of science seriously as well. The EU, for example, not only supports scientific cooperation across borders but also backs research projects that study Science Diplomacy, a commitment that can only strengthen the "ownership" of Science Diplomacy by the scientific community. The impact of these projects within this formative phase seems to be mostly situated at the level of awareness building.[1]

The increasing involvement by the Science and Technology community in several multilateral environmental agreements, as well as in other global problems, is an example of these newly forming networks. Science Diplomacy can certainly exploit this potential further in the future, as it is already doing to a certain extent through information-sharing, international cooperation, and advocating to close the gap with policy-makers to come to better informed policies and solutions. Van Langenhove argues that these developments started from both sides of the spectrum, as:

> this evolution has been facilitated by two interlinked developments: on the one hand, the gradual opening of the multilateral system to S&T community participation, and on the other, organizational efforts by the S&T community to maximize its participatory power in the global governance system.
>
> *(Van Langenhove 2016)*

But as the involvement of the EU shows, this is not a straightforward process. Often the European Science Diplomacy initiatives are taken at EU level within the Directorate General of Research, Technology, and Development without much interaction with the European External Action Services. On top of that, it is far from clear what the division of labor should be between the EU and its member states, as most of them have developed their own Science Diplomacy policies. And by and large the scientists who should play a pivotal role in deploying Science Diplomacy activities are hardly involved in shaping the Science

Diplomacy policies both at the level of the EU and in the member states.[2] In other words, interaction, dialogue, and networking are still very much needed at the level of the EU.

Conclusion

Diplomacy is not what it used to be. Gone are the Great Ambassadors who acted on behalf of their states as observers and collectors of intelligence and as negotiators of treaties. Originally, diplomacy was "the mechanism of representation, communication and negotiation through which states and other international actors conducted their businesses" (Melissen 2005). What came instead are government officials and political leaders who engage in summits in negotiations as well as non-state actors that engage in "unconventional diplomacy". The latter is related to the need felt by states to employ so-called Public Diplomacy in order to influence perceptions and legitimize their power on the approval of their policies by foreign publics.

States will be around for some time; we haven't yet come up with a better idea. But they are becoming weaker and less trusted. The world faces a more dramatic combination of change and challenge than ever before, and we are overwhelmed by that change. At a time when we have the tools to react globally, we are failing to use them. We face massive global transition at a time when there is a lack of global leadership and a growing realization that we are leaderless (Fletcher 2016). This not only calls for a rethinking of what diplomacy is but also for a new theoretical framework to study the complexity and entanglement of all kinds of networks. The network approach (see Chapters 1 and 2) provides a useful set of concepts and tools for analysis, but in the long run the practice of Science Diplomacy will need to be integrated further into the academic endeavor of International Relations theory (Kaltofen an Acuto 2018).

As for what concerns Science Diplomacy for and by scientists, this seems to be becoming more important as a result of a number of societal developments. First, there seems to be a tendency to present alternative facts or to limit access to scientific data that does not support what governments want to hear. This shows that scientists need to step up their efforts of making available the results of their research to policy-makers, as well as to the general public (Van Langenhove and Boers 2018).

Second, there also seems to be a growing shift toward nationalism and protectionism which may well translate into governments attempting to keep scientific findings within the boundaries of their own country. This would be in direct opposition to the mindset and philosophy of scientific communities, and the networks within which they operate, where openness and the ability to cooperate across borders with other experts is (often) one of the main requirements for excellence in science.

It is often said that we are heading toward a knowledge society. This might include that in the future there will also be global knowledge and data wars. That is why – in line with Slaughter's call that world networks play a central role in diplomacy – Science Diplomacy should not only be the concern of governments. Rather it is also up to the scientific community to realize that it has a major role to play in promoting international cooperation. Science Diplomacy is a practice that can be organized from both the scientists' and the governments' side of the spectrum. On the one hand, it is part of national or regional state structures as it is directly funded by governmental organizations or it resides in national or international companies that one way or another are also embedded in national state systems. On the other hand, science is internationally organized in global epistemic communities. Moreover, all actors could engage in a double Science Diplomacy policy: one that aims to foster international collaboration and one that aims to strengthen national interests. We should not forget that science is a major force of power in the world and that it contributes to the hard and soft power of actors – states, regional organizations, and institutions – as it produces knowledge that can contribute to wealth, trade, and prosperity. Behind the diplomacy-of-everything trend (sports diplomacy, culinary diplomacy, celebrity diplomacy, science diplomacy, and so on), there are the many different epistemic communities or networks of experts with specific knowledge or skills that can be mobilized for this.

In sum, the proliferation of diplomatic practices and diplomatic epistemic networks brings with it a complexity that calls for more knowledge management. States and other diplomatic actors have to mobilize more and more human resources to process the available knowledge and organize the formal and informal relations between different actors. As one of the largest funding agencies in the world, the EU might play an exemplary role here by stepping up a networked approach to Science Diplomacy. In doing so, it would contribute to shaping the diplomacy of the 21st century.

Notes

1 See, for instance, *Examining EU leadership in science and cultural diplomacy*, the summary of the El-CSID project at the CORDIS website: https://cordis.europa.eu/project/rcn/200262/brief/en.
2 This assessment is based upon the research performed within the EL-CSID project of which the results can be consulted at www.el-csid.eu.

References

Cooper, F. Andrew (2008), *Celebrity Diplomacy*, New York and London: Routledge, Taylor & Francis Group, 147p.

Embassy Lab (2016), "Future Diplomacy", http://hybridspacelab.net/project/future-diplomacy/.

Farrow, R. (2018), *War on Peace: The End of Diplomacy and the Decline of American Influence*, New York: HarperCollins Publishers.

Fletcher, Thomas (2016), *The Naked Diplomat*, HarperCollins Publishers, 336p.

Gluckman, Turekian, et al. (2017), "Science Diplomacy: A Pragmatic Perspective from the Inside", *Science & Diplomacy*, Vol. 6, No. 4, http://www.sciencediplomacy.org/article/2018/pragmatic-perspective.

Gramer, Robbie (2017), "Denmark Creates the World's First Ever Digital Ambassador", *Foreign Policy*, https://foreignpolicy.com/2017/01/27/denmark-creates-the-worlds-first-ever-digital-ambassador-technology-europe-diplomacy/.

Hocking, Brian, Melissen, Jan et al. (2012), "Futures for Diplomacy - Integrative Diplomacy for the 21st Century", *Clingendael*, https://www.clingendael.org/sites/default/files/pdfs/20121030_research_melissen.pdf.

https://www.qeh.ox.ac.uk/sites/www.odid.ox.ac.uk/files/DigDiploROxWP2.pdf.

International Association for Media and Communication Research (2018), "Digital Disinformation Challenges", https://iamcr.org/news/challenges_of_digital_disinformation.

Kaltofen, Carolin and Acuto, Michele (2018), "Rebalancing the Encounter between Science Diplomacy and International Relations Theory", *Global Policy*, Vol. 9, No. 3, pp. 15–22.

Khanna Parag (2011), Chapter One: Mega-Diplomacy. In *How To Run the World*, New York: Randan House.

Manor, Ilan (2018), "The Digitalization of Diplomacy: Toward Clarification of a Fractured Terminology, Oxford Digital Diplomacy Research Group", *Oxford Digital Diplomacy Research Group Working Paper Series*, https://www.qeh.ox.ac.uk/sites/www.odid.ox.ac.uk/files/DigDiploROxWP2.pdf.

Melissen, Jan (2005), *The New Public Diplomacy: Soft Power in International Relations*, Basingstoke: Palgrave Macmillan, http://culturaldiplomacy.org/academy/pdf/research/books/soft_power/The_New:Public_Diplomacy.pdf.

Rüffin, Nicolas (2018), "Science Diplomacy- A Catch-All Concept in Public Policy?", 18 April, https://era.ideasoneurope.eu/2018/04/18/science-diplomacy-catch-concept-public-policy/.

Slaughter, Anne-Marie (2017), *The Chessboard and the Web: Strategies of Connection in a Networked World*, Yale: Yale University Press Books, 304p.

Snow, Nancy and Taylor (2008), Philip, *Routledge Handbook of Public Diplomacy*. New York and London: Taylor& Francis, 388p.

Tavares, Rodrigo (2018), "International Diplomacy Needs an Overhaul to Stay Relevant. Here's Why", https://www.weforum.org/agenda/2018/05/international-diplomacy-needs-an-overhaul-to-stay-relevant-here-s-why/.

Thakur, Ramesh and Van Langenhove, Luk, (2006), "Enhancing Global Governance through Regional Integration", *Global Governance: A Review of Multilateralism and International Organizations*, Vol. 12, No. 3, pp. 223–240.

Van Langenhove, Luk (2010), "The Transformation of Multilateralism Mode 1.0 to Mode 2.0", *Global Policy*, Vol. 1, No. 3, https://onlinelibrary.wiley.com/doi/full/10.1111/j.1758-5899.2010.00042.x.

Van Langenhove, Luk (2011), *Building Regions*, London: Ashgate.

Van Langenhove, Luk (2016), "Global Science Diplomacy for Multilateralism 2.0", *Science & Diplomacy*, Vol. 5, No. 3, http://www.sciencediplomacy.org/article/2016/global-science-diplomacy-for-multilateralism-20.

Van Langenhove, Luk and Boers, Elke (2018), "Does Science Diplomacy Needs a New Purpose in the Populist Era?", *Georgetown Journal of International Affairs*, 14 May 2018. https://gjia.georgetown.edu/2018/05/14/does-science-diplomacy-need-a-new-purpose/

Van Middelaar, L. (2017), *De Nieuwe Politiek van Europa*, s-Gravenhage: Historische Uitgeverij.

11
EUROPEAN UNION NETWORKING AGAINST TRANSNATIONAL CRIME

Anja P. Jakobi and Janina Kandt

Introduction

Like in other areas of this book, networks have been a major means for the EU and other actors to fight transnational organized crime: "It takes networks to fight networks" (Arquilla and Ronfeld 2001: 15) – has been one mantra in countering crime. Yet, definitions of networks, of crime and of success in countering crime differ widely. As Orsini and Godet (Chapter 1) show, networks have increasingly been used to govern global problems across many policy areas. The growth of networks can also emerge due to forum shopping of actors, or as an alternative to other forms of governance. This is also visible in global crime governance, where some networks have emerged as an alternative to state-based governance arrangements, for instance, parallel-existing networks with overlapping competencies relating to cybercrime, while other networks have been used to enforce state-based agreements, such as the hierarchically structured networks around global anti-money laundering efforts. While some networks, like those against money laundering, represent a conglomerate of different regional, professional, and thematic networks, other global networks like the G7/8 have pushed forward specific crime policies in contexts of other international organizations (Scherrer 2009). The EU and its member states participate in different networks against transnational crime, but also establish networks themselves. These networks are a consequence of an expansion of global crime governance in which a growing number of actors – both public and private – are involved in countering crime across borders.

Given the huge variety in networks against transnational crime, this chapter examines networking with regard to two transnational crimes that have been codified at the international level, namely (a) money laundering and terrorism financing, and (b) cybercrime (Council of Europe 2001; FATF 2012). Both crimes profit from the fact that the financial system and cyberspace are global and virtual, which means that crimes can be committed rather independently from the actual location of the criminal. This also means that only a few safe havens are sufficient to undermine the effectiveness of global crime governance in these fields. Moreover, both sorts of crimes usually include reliance on non-state actors like banks, Internet companies, or other non-state actors. The EU and its members thus not only need to govern states, but also sub-national entities, and this necessity emerges against a background of large international differences in state interests, data protection, banking secrecy, and policing powers. These areas are thus highly complex to manage for the EU. At the same time, both issue areas have a close link to networks: anti-money laundering efforts formed the first and most prominent international network against crime, and given the similarities of both crimes, it is often discussed as a model for global cybercrime governance (Jakobi 2015).

We apply a broad definition of networks, with both states and international organizations as well as non-state actors like civil society and business organizations as participants. Despite this variety, two general types of networks can be distinguished: those that are mainly a forum for the exchange of ideas and policy development against transnational crime, and those that are concerned with implementation and enforcement of counter-measures. Networking can, therefore, range from establishing legal harmonization to being a practice of law enforcement during international joint investigations, and the role of the EU differs accordingly. As with any other networks, networks against transnational crime can be analyzed quantitatively and qualitatively (Knoke and Yang 2008; Scott 2007), referring to interactions as well as other forms of social relations. In this chapter, we focus on the formal roles of the EU in these networks and less on the informal, daily interactions. Moreover, given the large number of networks against transnational crime, we focus on those that are most important and central to the management of complexity. We first introduce global crime governance and the importance of networks in managing this complexity (see Pattberg and Widerberg, Chapter 2). We then present our two case studies of networking. The concluding section shows the similarities and differences in these fields, and assesses the role of the EU in managing the complexity of transnational crime.

Global crime governance and networks

Governance networks have gained prominence in International Relations (IR) research since the late 1990s, when new forms of governance became prominent in domestic and international politics, a rise of shared governance among private and public actors, as well as new, more informal forms of governance have been established, supplementing or even replacing cooperation in formal organizations like the UN (Rosenau and Czempiel 1992). At the same time, building upon police cooperation, multilateral legal assistance as well as long-established global treaties against drugs, the governance of transnational crime has grown significantly since the 1990s. Global crime governance today includes a myriad of forms on all levels of policy-making. It can be based on bilateral or multilateral activities, formal as well as informal cooperation, market-based instruments as well as prohibitions; and it can result in binding and non-binding treaties (Jakobi 2013a; Andreas and Nadelmann 2006).

Global crime governance is the outcome of political negotiations, and these can also result in functionally suboptimal compromises. At the same time, crime is a highly salient issue, and it is politically difficult not to engage in countering it – regardless of whether this activity results in crime reduction. These factors contribute to some skepticism regarding a reduction of crime through networking. Moreover, success is difficult to measure not only because crime statistics are linked to a high degree of uncertainty, but also because of the substantial differences among countries in defining crime, protecting their internal sovereignty, as well as the resources and capabilities of police forces. The management of complexity thus involves two aspects: (1) establishing a common ground in defining crime, common agendas, or harmonizing criminal laws, and (2) establishing effective international cooperation against crime, including cooperation in law enforcement. Networks against transnational crime – as well as the EU's engagement in these – show both types.

While networks correspond to the need for international cooperation among different judicial systems, their rise is not only due to empirical reasons, but also due to conceptual reasons: the "discovery" of networks does not necessarily mean that networks have been less important or non-existent before. Rather, many forms of social cooperation are today analyzed through a networking lens. This is particularly visible in the study of transnational crime, where networked forms of organization are today much more prominent in analyses than the classical, mafia-style model of organizational hierarchy (Williams 2001; UNODC 2002). Global networking has been facilitated by new forms of communication and mobility, and conceptual questions of what a network is in contrast to other forms of social interaction in groups often remain unclarified. In IR research, different concepts of networks have been put forward, ranging from those linked to public policy and governance studies (Börzel 1998), to networks as forums of governmental specialists (Slaughter 2004), networks as global cooperation of public and private actors (Reinicke 1998), and network analysis as an analytical instrument (Kahler 2009). Governance networks against crime have been mentioned frequently in these contexts. For instance, the Kimberly Process, a network of governmental actors, civil society, and business has initially been an example of how a policy network could curb the illegal market for conflict diamonds in a way that state-based governance alone could not – and even in the absence of a global, formal criminalization of conflict diamonds (Jakobi 2013b; Haufler 2009).

The European Union takes part in many networks against crime, either by being a representative for all member states, or as a self-standing member or observer, depending on the policy areas and the institutional setting of the network. The EU, for instance, has no official role in the G7, but does in the G20. The Council of Europe, as a non-EU institution, has sometimes been more important in countering crime – e.g. with regard to corruption – than the EU. In contrast, Europol today is a more important international police network for many EU countries than Interpol has been. With regard to the competencies of the European Union to counter transnational and organized crime, Title VI of the Treaty of the European Union sets out the legal framework for the EU's actions to combat organized crime (European Union 2012). Following the creation of the Schengen areas, the EU established a common, borderless region that initially lacked corresponding overarching judicial and police cooperation (Betti 2001: 5). The European Council meeting in Tampere (December 1999) prominently targeted trafficking in human beings, high tech crime, money laundering, corruption, and other crimes. The meeting underlined the need for common counter-activities against crime, including comparable charges and penalties in member states. As a consequence, member countries increasingly adopted common rules against crime, as well as investing in judicial cooperation, expanding Europol's mandate, and creating Frontex for border protection.

Taken together, crime governance has expanded significantly since the 1990s, and networks are an important part of it. With the rise of anti-terrorism activities, EU networks have further expanded, bilaterally with the US, multilaterally within international organizations, and internally within the EU. Besides vertical formal networks that implement European decisions, many informal and horizontal law enforcement networks among organizations exist, which creates potential problems for effectiveness as well as legitimacy: effectiveness can be hampered by duplication of structures, in particular if law enforcement prefers informal channels for networking. This preference, however, also decreases legitimacy, because horizontal networks are usually harder to control and influence democratically (Bures 2012; Den Boer et al. 2008). Whether a network is successful can also depend on the perspective and the ultimate goal. For instance, the coordination efforts of the European Union Counter-Terrorism Coordinator are less relevant for EU-internal cooperation, than for cooperation with other, external actors (Mackenzie et al. 2013).

While networking is an integral part of EU activities against crime, the role of the EU and its different agencies differs widely, as do the different national approaches regarding banking secrecy, privacy, and data protection. Particularly after 2001, counter-terrorism efforts have led to the emergence of a common, European security interest that was not necessarily given before this (Kaunert 2010: 54). Externally, the EU traditionally has a strong transatlantic relationship with the US. However, this bilateral cooperation needs to bridge across very different law enforcement traditions (Kaunert 2010: 55–56). Networking helps bring together different institutions, also by establishing new arenas for policy development and multi-level games. Moreover, the large number of networks in countering crime reflects the multifaceted character of transnational crime, yet it also means that networks exist in a large number, with different mandates, institutionalized or personalized, as well as with different impacts.

EU networking against money laundering and terrorism financing

The networking activities against money laundering and terrorism financing represent a hierarchically structured, centralized network with many sub-networks, but clearly defined roles based in governmental agreements. The international activities against terrorism financing themselves have evolved from the anti-money laundering regime, which was established by the G7 and its Financial Action Taskforce (FATF) from 1989 onwards (Nance 2018). While the UN referred to money laundering in its 1988 convention against drug trafficking, the FATF network ultimately developed and promoted comprehensive anti-money laundering and anti-terrorism financing measures. Terrorism financing was added to the FATF agenda after 9/11, yet it had been the subject of a UN Convention in 1999. Only after the terrorist attacks was this convention ratified more widely, and ultimately, the FATF contributed most to formulating criminalizing and monitoring requirements. Individuals who finance terrorism can also be blacklisted in the Security Council, yet the mechanisms by which blacklisting is implemented rely on the earlier established, and wide-ranging, FATF regime (Bierstecker and Eckert 2008; Gardner 2007).

In essence, countering these transnational crimes relies on banks and financial institutions – including those trading with virtual currencies – which are obliged to follow specific oversight and monitoring procedures. Financial intelligence based on banking data has become an important part of countering and prosecuting crime and terrorism. Accordingly, global forums and networks that develop policies or implement these also include the Bank of International Settlements, to SWIFT, global networks of private banks, and financial intelligence organizations or compliance officials (Kingah and Zwartjes 2015; Tsingou 2018). This reflects the global complexity of illicit finance, yet these global and intense efforts also raise the question of whether they correspond to the – still unknown – amount of money laundered in the banking system. While commissions have been established to estimate the amount, there is still little known on the magnitude (Levi and Reuter 2007). For this reason, the global networking of the EU is clearly corresponding to the regulatory efforts in this area, yet how much these activities reduce or inhibit money laundering and terrorism financing remains unknown.

The central, global network FATF is a network hosted in Paris at the OECD, with 38 governmental members – 36 countries, plus the European Union and the Gulf Cooperation Council as regional organizations. The FATF has further established different regional networks all across the world, with the European part being managed by the Council of Europe (Moneyval 2017). The overall structure of the global network follows a top-down logic, with regulations being agreed upon among the limited number of FATF members and being spread to the different regional forums as implementing networks. The European influence on the policy-making process of these regulations is thus more important than in the regional, FATF implementing network. At the same time, the European Union translates FATF recommendations into binding directives against money laundering and terrorism financing, so that members are obliged to follow these policies. The FATF has been influenced mainly by governmental actors, in particular, the US and the G7 network. In recent years, some new members have also increased the G20 influence. Moreover, the position of private actors, like banks, benefits from the data and infrastructure they provide (de Oliveira 2018).

In contrast to other regimes against transnational crime, anti-money laundering and counter-terrorism financing are relatively coherent global norms with strong possibilities of enforcement. Policy development takes place only in a few bodies – mainly the FATF, and to some degree also the UN (which mainly refers to FATF regulations, however). There are thus not many potential sites for effective networking outside the FATF with regard to policy development, and along with some of the EU's member states, the European Commission is a member of the FATF. Still, the major power in this network has been the US, where standards against money laundering have been established early as a means to counter crime and which have often been a nucleus for global anti-money laundering policies (Jakobi 2013a).

By networking with the FATF and by being an "exemplary implementer", European counter-terrorism efforts have increased the role of the European Commission and its bodies toward member states. Responding to the FATF and Security Council requirements, the European Union has established coordinative functions for adequate implementation that benefited both the external partners in the UN Security Council and the FATF, as well as decreasing transaction costs for members (Kaunert and Della Giovanna 2010). Networking complexity – even only as a kind of clearing house – has thus benefited the European Union, internally and externally.

Anti-money laundering is a broad, almost universally applied tool against crime, relying mostly on banks and the supervision of financial flows. With the onset of transnational terrorism in the 2000s, the regime has been expanded, including more actors, and a more comprehensive obligation to monitor and assess risks linked to specific financial transfers or clients. Terrorism is one of the key threats to European security outlined in the European security strategy (European Commission 2015; European External Action Service 2016). Due to its high saliency, a large number of internal networks have been set up against terrorism financing, but existent tools against money laundering have also been strengthened.

For instance, the European Council has three groups working on the preparation of counter-terrorism legislation: the Working Group on Terrorism, dealing with international aspects (COTER); the Working Party on the Application of Specific Measures to Combat Terrorism (COCOP); and the Working Party of Foreign Relations Counselors (RELEX) (Doody 2015: 52). The Council Working Group on Terrorism is a network of representatives from the EU's member states' permanent representations in Brussels which deals with external matters, threat assessments and policy recommendations regarding counter-terrorism, the implementation of UN Conventions and financing of terrorism (Council of the European Union 2004: 2). It serves as central contact point for all information concerning counter-terrorism in the permanent representations and transmitter of documents to the member states (Lugna 2006: 108).

Further internal networks linked to enforcement exist, like Europol, Eurojust, or the European Task Force of Chiefs of Police: Europol established a Joint Liaison Team, analyzing different terrorist threats, including terrorism financing. It is composed of representatives from EU member states and third countries (Council of the European Union 2016). When the EU founded Eurojust in 2002 the member states expressed a need for more intense cooperation in the field of organized crime (Welfens 2016: 137). Yet Eurojust also has the mandate to strengthen cooperation between anti-terrorism magistrates, conveying regular meetings on terrorism with representatives from the EU's member states. The network of European Chiefs of Police is an *ad hoc* group established in 2000, aimed at fostering the exchange of experiences, best practices, and information on cross-border crimes. After 9/11, the network of police chiefs was supplemented with the informal ATLAS network, requested by the European Council to establish cooperation of special intervention units in the European Union. This network currently comprises more than 30 counter-terrorist special intervention units based in the police, gendarmerie, and armed forces of the EU member states and Norway (Block 2007).

Another enforcement network is the "Egmont Group", assembling financial intelligence units all over the world. With some variety due to the national background, these units typically monitor banks' behavior, but they also assess suspicious transactions and aim to develop more effective anti-money laundering and counter-terrorism policies. Since 2017, the European Union and Europol have observer status at the Egmont Group, aiming to facilitate cooperation among European police forces and financial intelligence units worldwide. At the same time, the European Union itself has fostered exchange among national units, creating common networks for data transfer (Europol 2018).

All in all, the European Union is not the most important actor in creating rules against money laundering and terrorism financing, but the Union as well as some member states can influence the FATF decisions that are the ultimate regulations in this field. The centralized network structure determines the main way of influence on the governance of these crimes. This also shows that EU networking depends on the quality of the networks, less on the quantity – there is not much need to create further policy-developing networks if the position in the FATF can be used effectively. The situation is different with regard to enforcement, which mostly relies on internal EU networks that are created and supported by the EU to implement directives effectively. Given the centrality of the FATF as a single actor for global networks, the number of networks in implementation and enforcement with strong EU influence is thus much higher.

EU networking against cybercrime

Recent years have witnessed a growing awareness regarding threats posed by cybercrime, yet the specific nature of the threat can vary widely. It includes many computer-related crimes, including illegal access to data and espionage, taking over computer networks, online fraud, online child sexual exploitation, and attacks against critical infrastructures and information systems. Threats posed by cybercrime can be linked to scenarios of military-style warfare, as well as to crimes like fraud or hacking. As in the case of anti-money laundering, the actual number of cybercrimes is unknown and open to debate, varying also with the definition of what exactly "cybercrime" includes. While cyber-governance and regulation has expanded on the national level, there are fewer global activities compared to anti-money laundering and terrorism financing.

The United Nations plays a central role in the advancement of global networking in the combat of cybercrime. With its resolution 65/230, the UN established the open-ended intergovernmental expert group to analyze the societal and political challenges posed by cybercrime and the responses taken by the member states, the international community, and the private sector. The expert group was established in 2011 and based on resolutions 22/7 and 22/8 of 2013, continued its work. The enhancement of international cooperation, exchange on national legislation and best practices, technical assistance, and the examination of the development of existing or new national and international responses are core interests of the expert group (Commission on Crime Prevention and Criminal Justice 2013b; Commission on Crime Prevention and Criminal Justice 2013a). The network further aims at providing guidance to the work of UNODC as well as assistance to member states (United Nations 2011). Besides UN member states, the private sector and academia were represented and European Union representatives were involved in the group's meetings. The expert group is a public-private partnership with the EU as self-standing member.

When it comes to the investigation of cybercrime, Interpol plays an important role on the global level. The organization coordinates transnational cybercrime investigations and supports member countries in the conduct of such inquiries. Interpol's initiatives comprise cooperation with further actors and the establishment of exchange platforms, such as the Cyber Fusion Center (Interpol 2019b), which brings together experts from law enforcement and industry to provide member countries with actionable intelligence. Interpol, furthermore, collaborates with Europol and launched the annual Interpol-Europol Cybercrime Conference in 2013 to bring together public and private actors for the development of global responses to cybercrime (Interpol 2019a).

Together with the US, the EU has initiated a network via the establishment of a bilateral working group on cybersecurity and cybercrime. The parties have further deepened cooperation through the "EU–US Cyber Dialogue". EU-US cooperation aims to expand joint as well as global cyber incident management response capabilities and to set global standards on cybercrime, engage the private sector in this management, share good practices with the private sector, and launch awareness-raising activities (European External Action Service 2014). The EU and the US have also established a network – the Global Alliance – to combat online child abuse with 54 member countries that aim to enhance victim protection and to prosecute offenders (European Commission 2012). These initiatives strengthen a multi-stakeholder approach as well as a transatlantic approach against cybercrime. Networking has developed among state actors, with the EU being in the role of an initiator.

These important global networking initiatives seem to be of high relevance for the EU. While the EU is actively participating in idea generation in the case of the UN networking and advances global standard-setting in the EU-US partnership, the EU, represented by Europol, is an important partner for Interpol in the development of global responses to cybercrime.

On a pan-European level the Council of Europe Convention against cybercrime from 2001 has been central in shaping the EU's cybercrime governance. The convention sets up a common approach to computer-based crimes like illegal access to data, data and systems interference, as well as content-related offences, including the distribution of materials depicting child abuse (Council of Europe 2001). The convention constitutes the first and most significant multilateral binding international standard to regulate cybercrime to date (de Hert et al. 2018). Based thereon, the EU has together with the Council of Europe initiated two networks against cybercrime (GLACY and GLACY+) aiming at the worldwide implementation of the Cybercrime Convention. Most importantly, international cooperation with eight priority countries in Africa, the Asia-Pacific, and Latin America and the Caribbean region is enhanced to facilitate the provision of judicial training, capacity building, information sharing, and to provide support for implementing cybercrime legislation (Council of Europe 2016). GLACY and GLACY+ are networking initiatives between state actors aiming at the implementation of the Convention. The EU is here, as initiator, an active party ascribing importance to this initiative as an instrument for peace and stability (European External Action Service 2018).

EU-wide cybercrime governance is mainly shaped by the EU's framework decision on attacks against information systems, which emphasizes the importance of converging member states' criminal law related to attacks against information systems (European Parliament and The Council 2013). In 2013, the EU adopted its first Cybersecurity Strategy, under which cybercrime is included in the EC's political priorities (European Parliament and Council of the European Union 2003). Based thereon, the EU developed a common approach to combat cybercrime comprising common objectives and instruments, a multi-stakeholder approach and cooperation with the private sector (European Commission 2007; European Parliament and The Council 2009; European Commission 2013;

European Parliament and Council of the European Union 2016). Cooperation with public actors in the EU's member states was facilitated through the creation of the Cooperation Group and a computer security incident response teams' network (CSIRTs Network) composed of national public servants (Council of the European Union 2016; European Commission 2001; European Parliament and The Council 2004). The teams are responsible for monitoring incidents at the national level, providing early warning alerts and information to relevant stakeholders about potential risks, responding to incidents, and providing a risk and incident analysis in the member states (European Parliament and Council of the European Union 2016). Coordination between the actors is still a challenge when it comes to cross-border incidents and simultaneous attacks on critical information systems (European Commission 2017a), due to very different structural and financial contexts in the member states. Another example for networking efforts with public actors in member states is the European Judicial Cybercrime Network. It was established in 2016 by the Council, following an initiative of Eurojust (European Commission 2017b). The network consists of prosecutors of EU member states that specialize in the area of cybercrime. It is a facilitator for exchange of information and expertise, good practices, and legislative developments and jurisprudence. It is also a forum for discussion and dialogue for the coordination of investigations across member states and cooperation with the EU institutions and agencies (EUROJUST 2017). In both cases, the EU initiated their establishment for idea generation and enforcement.

Cooperation with non-state actors is pursued within various networking initiatives. One example is the enforcement network "European Public-Private Partnership for Resilience", which was established in 2009 to address cross-border security concerns in the telecommunication sector (Irion 2012: 19). The partnership was the first Europe-wide governance framework composed of public and private stakeholders, including representatives from the EU institutions, national public authorities, network infrastructure operators, and European associations representing infrastructure operators for information and communication technologies. In 2013, it was subsumed into the Network and Information Security (NIS) Public-Private Platform (European Commission 2013) which mainly aims at the exchange of information and the identification of technologically neutral best practices to enhance cybersecurity. It further serves as a tool to implement the measures defined in the NIS Directive across the EU in a convergent manner (European Parliament and Council of the European Union 2016; European Commission 2018). Further cooperation with business actors in enforcement takes shape in the EC3, the European Cybercrime Center at Europol. The EC3 aims to overcome the fragmentation of cyber security policies, raise awareness, and build trust between private and public actors (European Commission 2017a). It pools expertise and information, supports criminal investigations, and promotes EU-wide solutions (Christou 2016: 88; Christou 2018). One of the EC3's operations takes shape in the Joint Cybercrime Action Task Force (J-CAT). It is composed of cyber liaison officers based in participating member states as well as in non-EU partner countries and staff from the EC3. They cooperate regularly on case studies with national experts from Eurojust and Europol (Europol 2014). The EU actively advances this network with its widespread activities ranging from idea generation to enforcement and its focus on public-private cooperation. The EU's central role in this network can be explained by the high complexity of cybercrime governance and the EU's Digital Agenda, which responds to this by spelling out the importance to facilitate and enhance global cooperation of the involved actors in the effective combat of cybercrime (European Commission 2010).

Taken together, networks in cybersecurity have a strong emphasis on enforcement, and they involve a large number of private actors, resulting also in public-private partnerships and a close form of networking for implementation among governmental and non-governmental actors. At the same time, there is no central, global network existent; thus the EU has an important focus on developing EU-internal policies and to bring these to other countries and organizations. There exists more competition and overlapping authority than in the networks concerned with anti-money laundering and terrorism financing. Moreover, the EU's activities in for instance GLACY(+) reflect that the international measures on cybercrime are increasingly connected to national security and that cybercrime governance is seen as an instrument for peace and stability, especially with regard to the protection of national infrastructures. While states have major concerns regarding cybercrime, major intergovernmental agreements that would restrict cybercrime or enhance international counter-crime cooperation have not yet been established. Networks of public and private actors thus represent an alternative, and currently the only available, form of governance.

Conclusions: It takes a network ... or many, or different ones

Dealing with the complexity of the global financial system and cyberspace, the European Union has reacted by establishing networks on different levels, ranging from global efforts to horizontal and vertical European networks. These networks are used to develop policies or regulatory ideas, to share information and data, or to ensure enforcement. Yet, there also exist important differences. While anti-money laundering and counter-terrorism financing efforts are globally coordinated by the FATF and the UN Security Council, there is only the Council of Europe's Cybercrime Convention comparable in the broadest sense in the field of cybercrime. In both cases, however, policy development rather takes place through members in international organizations outside the European Union. Guaranteeing effective implementation of global regulations in its member states, the European Union has nonetheless established important coordinative functions in internal and external networks, including contact with non-state actors.

This chapter has shown the large extent of networking that takes place to combat transnational crime. The application of the network approach to the case studies enabled the analysis of the EU's dynamic relationship with public and private actors on the regional and global level. The chapter has shown that EU activities take place on all levels, from being involved in networks that develop ideas and policies against crime to networks that implement and enforce laws nationally and transnationally. Networks against crime can be bilateral as well as multilateral; they often cross borders to non-EU states – even if linked to enforcement – and their number has grown over time. In all areas analyzed, private actors are involved in some, yet not all networks. This is particularly visible in cybercrime governance, where a large part of the infrastructure depends on private actors, but also in money laundering and terrorism prevention where banks and financial institutions play a key role in counter-efforts.

The analysis has shown that indeed, besides states, new actors have been empowered that complement inter-state politics. Concomitantly, with the empowerment of private actors, the power relations in global policy-making change from a stable attribute ascribed based on material, organization of ideational resources to a dynamic relation between actors based on coercion and the construction of meaning (see Godet and Orsini, Chapter 1). Insofar as the EU's networking supporting the theoretical conceptions that networks challenge state-centered approaches that conceive sovereignty as a rigid structure, it has been illustrated in this chapter that networks constitute a new form of governance, illustrating that national borders are rather a shared feature. While networks also constitute sites of exclusion by representing partial interests of non-elected members and thus can be seen as challenging principles of accountability and legitimacy, they have at the same time been established to provide tailored responses to the challenges of crime. In this regard, they serve as a flexible tool to increase efficiency in cases where specific expertise is required.

With regard to the governance of transnational crime, the European Union has reacted on two different levels of complexity – global and external as well as European and internal. Core challenges are the multifaceted nature of these crimes, as well as fragmentation of information and policies across member states. While the EU is a member of the global networks and established bilateral and multilateral cooperative efforts, it also needs to bridge across internal differences, including potential sovereignty concerns of member states. The EU's activities are most pronounced with regard to enforcement, guaranteeing that global and European rules against crime are effectively applied in member states.

It is not unlikely that the EU will ultimately change its networking efforts from an emphasis on internal implementation to presenting global policy proposals, given the loosening of the transatlantic partnership with the US. The weakening of the traditional Western alliance is likely to result in new divergences in crime policies, too. Facing this new complexity, and having established itself as a common European actor in the field of crime governance, it could be difficult for the EU to continue taking a back seat in developing global counter-crime policies.

References

Andreas, P. & Nadelmann, E. 2006. *Policing the Globe. Criminalization and Crime Control in International Relations*, Oxford: Oxford University Press.

Arquilla, J. & Ronfeld, D. (eds.) 2001. *Networks and Netwars: The Future of Terror, Crime and Militancy*, Washington: Rand.

Betti, S. 2001. The European Union and the United Nations convention against transnational organised crime. In: Union, E. (ed.) *Civil Liberties Eeries*. Brussels: European Parliament.

Biersteker, T.J. & Eckert, S.E. 2008. *Countering the Financing of Terrorism*, London: Routledge.

Block, L. 2007. Europe's emerging counter-terrorism elite: The ATLAS network. *Terrorism Monitor*, 5, 10–12.

Börzel, T.A. 1998. Organizing Babylon - On the different conceptions of policy networks. *Public Administration*, 76, 253–273.

Bures, O. 2012. Informal counterterrorism arrangements in Europe: Beauty by variety or duplicity by abundance? *Cooperation and Conflict*, 47, 495–518.

Christou, G. 2016. *Cybersecurity in the European Union. Resilience and Adaptability in Governance Policy*, Houndmills: Palgrave Macmillan.

Christou, G. 2018. The challenges of cybercrime governance in the European Union. *European Politics and Security*, 19, 355–375.

Commission on Crime Prevention and Criminal Justice 2013a. *Promoting Technical Assistance and Capacity-building to Strengthen National Measures an International Cooperation Against Cybercrime*. Resolution 22/8. United Nations.

Commission on Crime Prevention and Criminal Justice 2013b. *Strengthening International Cooperation to Combat Cybercrime*. Resolution 22/7. United Nations.

Council of Europe 2001. *Convention on Cybercrime*. European treaty series – No. 185. Budapest: Council of Europe.

Council of Europe 2016. GlobalAction on cybercrime extended (GLACY)+.

Council of the European Union 2004. *Working Structures of the Council in Terrorism Matters*. Options paper. 9791/04. Brussels: European Union.

Council of the European Union 2016. *Implementation of the Counter-terrorist Agenda set by the European Council*. 13627/16. Brussels: European Union.

De Hert, P., Parlar, C. & Sajfert, J. 2018. The cybercrime convention committee's 2017 guidance note on production orders: Unilateralist transborder access to electronic evidence promoted via soft law. *Computer Law & Security Review: The International Journal of Technology Law and Practice*, 2018, 1–10.

De Oliveira, I.S. 2018. The governance of the financial action task force: An analysis of power and influence throughout the years. *Crime, Law and Social Change*, 69, 153–172.

Den Boer, M., Hillebrand, C. & Nölke, A. 2008. Legitimacy under pressure: The European Web of counter-terrorism networks. *Journal of Common Market Studies*, 46, 101–124.

Doody, J. 2015. The institutional framework of EU counter-terrorism. In: De Londras, F. & Doody, J. (eds.) *The Impact, Legitimacy and Effectiveness of EU Counter-Terrorism*. London: Routledge.

Eurojust 2017. Third meeting of the EJCN.

European Commission 2001. *Communication from the Commission to the Council, the European Parliament, the European Economic and Social Committee and the Committee of the Regions*. Network and information security: Proposal for a European policy approach. COM(2001)298 final. Brussels: European Union.

European Commission 2007. Communication from the commission to the European Parliament, the council and the committee of the regions – towards a general policy on the fight against cyber crime. In: European Union (ed.) COM(2007) 267 final. Brussels.

European Commission 2010. *Communication from the Commission to the European Parliament, the Council, the European Economic and Social Committee and the Committee of the regions*. A digital Agenda for Europe. COM(2010) 245 final/2. Brussels: European Union.

European Commission 2012. *We Protect Global Alliance to End Child Sexual Exploitation Online*.

European Commission 2013. *Joint Communication to the European Parliament, the Council, the European Economic and Social Committee and the Committee of the regions*. Cybersecurity strategy of the European Union: An open, safe and secure cyberspace. JOIN(2013) 1 final. Brussels: European Union.

European Commission 2015. *EU Agenda on Security*. COM(2015) 185. Brussels: European Union.

European Commission 2017a. Commission staff working document impact assessment. Accompanying the document proposal for a regulation of the European parliament and of the council on enisa, the "Eu Cybersecurity Agency", and repealing regulation (eu) 526/2013, and on information and communication technology cybersecurity certification ("cybersecurity Act"). Swd(2017) 500 final. Brussels: European Union.

European Commission 2017b. *Communication from The Commission To The European Parliament, The European Council And The Council*. Eleventh progress report towards an effective and genuine security union. COM(2017) 608 final. Brussels: European Union.

European Commission. 2018. *NIS Cooperation Group's Guidelines for Implementing the NIS Directive and Addressing Wider Cybersecurity Policy Issues*. https://ec.europa.eu/digital-single-market/en/news/latest-nis-cooperation-group-guidelines-for-implementing-nis-directive [Accessed 09.04.2019].

European External Action Service 2014. 1st EU-US cyber dialogue.

European External Action Service 2016. *Shared Vision, Common Action: A Stronger Europe*. A global strategy for the European Union's foreign and security policy. Brussels.

European External Action Service 2018. Global action on cybercrime extended (GLACY+).

European Parliament & the Council 2004. Regulation (EC) 460/2004 of the European Parliament and of the council of 10 march 2004 establishing the European Network and Information Security Agency. No 460/2004. European Union.

European Parliament & the Council 2009. Directive 2009/140/EC of the European Parliament and of the Council of 25 November 2009 amending Directives 2002/21/EC on a common regulatory framework for electronic communications networks and services, 2002/19/EC on access to, and interconnection of, electronic communications networks and associated facilities, and 2002/20 EC on the authorisation of electronic communications networks and services. 2009/140/EC. Brussels: European Union.

European Parliament & the Council 2013. Directive 2013/40/EU of the European Parliament and of the Council of 12 August 2013 on attacks against information systems and replacing Council Framework Decision 2005/222/JHA. 2013/40/EU. Brussels: European Union.

European Parliament & Council of the European Union 2003. Regulation (EU) 526/2013 of the European Parliament and of the council of 21 May 2013 concerning the European Union Agency for Network and Information Security (ENISA) and

repealing Regulation (EC) No 460/2004. Regulation (EU) No 526/2013. Brussels: European Union.
European Parliament & Council of the European Union 2016. Directive (EU) 2016/1148 of the European Parliament and of the Council of 6 July 2016 concerning measures for a high common level of security of network and information systems across the Union. Directive (EU) 2016/1148. Brussels: European Union.
European Union 2012. Treaty on European Union and the treaty on the functioning of the European Union – consolidated version of the treaty on European Union. European Union.
Europol 2014. Joint Cybercrime Action Taskforce (J-CAT).
Europol 2018. *Website: Financial Intelligence Units. FIU.NET*. https://www.europol.europa.eu/about-europol/financial-intelligence-units-fiu-net, last access in May 2018.
FATF 2012. *International Standards on Combating Money Laundering and the Financing of Terrorism & Proliferation – the FATF Recommendations. Version February 2012*, Paris: FATF.
Gardner, K.L. 2007. Fighting terrorism the FATF way. *Global Governance*, 13, 325–345.
Haufler, V. 2009. The Kimberley process certification scheme: An innovation in global governance and conflict prevention. *Journal of Business Ethics*, 89, 403–416.
INTERPOL. 2019a. Cyber partnerships. https://www.interpol.int/en/Crimes/Cybercrime/Cyber-partnerships [Accessed 09.04.2019].
INTERPOL. 2019b. Investigative support for cybercrime. https://www.interpol.int/en/Crimes/Cybercrime/Investigative-support-for-cybercrime [Accessed 09.04.2019].
Irion, K. 2012. *The Governance of Network and Information Security in the European Union: The EUropean Public-Private Partnership for Resilience (EP3R)*. 27th European Communications Policy Research Conference (EUROCPR). Policies for the Internet.
Jakobi, A.P. 2013a. *Common Goods and Evils? The Formation of Global Crime Governance*, Oxford: Oxford University Press.
Jakobi, A.P. 2013b. Governing war economies: Conflict diamonds and the Kimberley process. In: Jakobi, A.P. & Wolf, K.D. (eds.) *The Transnational Governance of Violence and Crime: Non-State Actors in Security*. Houndmills: Palgrave.
Jakobi, A.P. 2015. Global networks against crime: Using the financial action task force as a model? *International Journal*, 70, 391–407.
Kahler, M. 2009. Networked politics: Agency, power and governance. In: Kahler, M. (ed.) *Networked Politics. Agency, Power and Governance*. Ithaca: Cornell University Press.
Kaunert, C. 2010. The external dimension of EU counter-terrorism relations: Competences, interests, and institutions. *Terrorism and Political Violence*, 22, 41–61.
Kaunert, C. & Della Giovanna, M. 2010. Post-9/11 EU counter-terrorist financing cooperation: Differentiating supranational policy entrepreneurship by the commission and the council secretariat. *European Security*, 19, 275–295.
Kingah, S. & Zwartjes, M. 2015. Regulating money laundering for terrorism financing: EU–US transnational policy networks and the financial action task force. *Contemporary Politics*, 21, 341–353.
Knoke, D. & Yang, S. 2008. *Social Network Analysis*, Los Angeles: Sage.
Levi, M. & Reuter, P. 2007. Money laundering. In: Tonry, M. (ed.) *The Oxford Handbook of Crime and Public Policy*. Oxford: Oxford University Press.
Lugna, L. 2006. Institutional framework of the European counter-terrorism policy setting. *Baltic Security & Defence Review*, 8, 101–127.

Mackenzie, A., Bures, O., Kaunert, C. & Léonard, S. 2013. The European Union counter-terrorism coordinator and the external dimension of the European union counter-terrorism policy. *Perspectives on European Politics and Society*, 14, 325–338.

Moneyval 2017. Committee of experts on the evaluation of anti-money laundering measures and the financing of terrorism. In: EUROPE, C.O. (ed.) *Committee of Experts on the Evaluation of Anti-Money Laundering Measures and the Financing of Terrorism*. Council of Europe.

Nance, M.T. 2018. The regime that FATF built: An introduction to the financial action task force. *Crime, Law and Social Change*, 69, 109–129

Reinicke, W.H. 1998. *Global Public Policy. Governing without Government?*, Washington: Brookings Institution.

Rosenau, J.N. & Czempiel, E.-O. (eds.) 1992. *Governance without Government: Order and Change in World Politics*, Cambridge: Cambridge University Press.

Scherrer, A. 2009. *G8 Against Transnational Organized Crime*, Farnham: Ashgate.

Scott, J. 2007. *Social Network Analysis. A Handbook*, Los Angeles: Sage.

Slaughter, A.-M. 2004. *A New World Order*, Princeton: Princeton University Press.

Tsingou, E. 2018. New governors on the block: The rise of anti-money laundering professionals. *Crime, Law and Social Change*, 69, 191–205.

United Nations 2011. *Resolution Adopted by the General Assembly on 21 December 2010*. A/RES/65/230.

UNODC 2002. *Results of a Pilot Survey of Forty Selected Organized Criminal Groups in Sixteen Countries*, Vienna: UNODC.

Welfens, B. 2016. Combating organised crime – the role of Eurojust. In: Töttel, U., Bulanova-Hristova, G. & Flach, G. (eds.) *Research Conferences on Organised Crime at the Bundeskriminalamt in Germany Vol. III*. Wiesbaden: Bundeskriminalamt.

Williams, P. 2001. Organizing transnational crime: Networks, markets and hierarchies. In: Williams, P. & Vlassis, D. (eds.) *Combating Transnational Crime*. London: Frank Cass.

12
CONCLUSIONS
Global complexity, networks, and the role of EU and European actors

George Christou and Jacob Hasselbalch

Introduction

This volume set out to address a central question: *How has increased regime complexity in the global order impacted on the ability of the EU and European actor networks to navigate, manage, and influence debates and policy?* To this end, complexity within the global order has been the independent variable, and our aim has been to utilize state-of-the-art literature on networks and complexity, in order to further our understanding of how such complexity impacts on the ability of EU and European actor networks to influence debates and policy across a multitude of areas.

That the world is complex and that we are living through uncertain times that necessitate reflection through a more sophisticated set of tools is an observation that has been increasingly confirmed by the dynamic and turbulent global environment within which we live and must navigate on a daily basis, whether in the form of challenges to democracy, economic and financial crises, or the increasingly salient climate problem. The shocks and crises that have permeated the European Union and Europe more broadly are integral and interconnected to this global complexity. Our cases have shown that the EU and European actor networks have been able to react, navigate, and manage global complex arenas and issues in a multitude of ways across and between different levels – macro, meso, and micro – with varying degrees of success. This concluding chapter offers thoughts and reflections on the theoretical and empirical implications of the analyses in this volume, and charts a way forward in relation to future research on complexity, networks, and the evolving global order.

Trends, networks, and complexity

The framing of the volume points to several trends. First, we confirm that the EU and European actors are facing a situation of increased governance complexity in all issue areas that were addressed by the volume. And this complexity is not a theoretical artifact conjured up by scholars but recognized as a fundamental condition by the actors being studied. Whether this complexity presents a broadened opportunity space or a constrained field of action depends on the case. And the degree to which the EU and European actors successfully manage and navigate this complexity also varies. Second, we confirm that the organizational model of the network is appreciated by EU and European actors as a useful tool in which to manage the complexity of global issues. In most cases, EU and European actors have been shrewd constructors and navigators of transnational networks, either by acting through them or by establishing the conditions under which the networks function. Third, whether or not policy coherence and effectiveness results from networked approaches to global issues cannot be determined solely from the abstracted properties of the network. However, if those properties are viewed in tandem with a rich, case-specific appreciation of the social context in which the network operates, our understanding of complex global issues increases. In other words, network perspectives, in all case studies, add to our understanding of the world and to the capacity for European actors to realize policy coherence and effectiveness.

The volume opens with three chapters that orient our discussion of networks on the Macro, Meso, and Micro level. Godet and Orsini set the stage for the volume by reviewing the evolution and current state of thinking on networks in the global order. They argue that networks do not build a new global order as much as they offer a new perspective on the classical inter-state Westphalian order. There are three different ways that this perspective adds to our understanding of global order. First, it bridges the state-centric view of a world defined by horizontal relations between sovereign states with the world society view of a global system that adheres to a set of socio-cultural norms. Second, the network perspective brings forward new actors: transnational networks comprised of, for example, NGOs, businesses, IOs, and sub-governmental bodies. Third, power is redefined as a relational property rather than an attribute. They end the chapter by questioning the capacity to control networks in a world defined by increasing complexity – a question that is taken up by Pattberg and Widerberg.

Pattberg and Widerberg view the increased complexity of global governance as a case of increasing institutional density, overlaps, interactions, unexpected and unintended consequences, and a proliferation of actors. Where they differ from other scholars is in taking complexity theory as a natural starting point for dealing with complex global governance. They argue that network theory is ideally placed to cope with the non-linear and emergent properties of complex systems, and they offer their thoughts on how to mobilize network thinking on different analytical levels, including the broader governance architecture, specific functional or organizational fields within a given regime complex, and between the institutions and organizations comprising the other levels.

In order to unpack interaction within network structures, Henriksen and Seabrooke conceptualize a space for action within complex systems in terms of multilevel networks involving professionals and organizations acting to control issues. They focus on the role of professional networks; how the expert professionals working on complex governance issues traverse their own peer networks; as well as the organizational networks formally and informally involved in governing issues. These "issue professionals" can make use of a range of strategies working with and through professional-organizational networks to exert control over issue areas, including decoupling, challenging, blocking, colonizing, mandating, and yoking.

In general, the opening theoretical chapters display the vast analytical breadth and flexibility of network thinking. The range of applications, the analytical level, the degree of formalization, the units of analysis, and the types of actions – can all be tailored to suit the analytical purpose of any given study. The empirical chapters draw on this rich menu of options to demonstrate the benefits of taking a network perspective on the EU and European actors in the global order.

The empirical chapters differ in how they relate to network thinking. Are networks predominantly understood theoretically, as a way to conceptualize or approach an empirical phenomenon or as a method of analysis that seeks to make relations between units tangible and legible? In their chapter, Godet and Orsini draw this distinction between network theories and network methods, which are frequently used together but may also be used independently. What they point to, then, is that applying network theory does not necessarily require using the method of social network analysis. Conversely, social network analysis as a method can be used in service of all manner of theoretical pursuits.

In this volume there is an equal concentration of empirical chapters that emphasize the method and the theory. The chapters by Beaumier, Dimmelmeier, Haagensen, and Valeriani all conduct social network analyses and draw on the figures and results from these analyses to generate novel insights and support their arguments. On the other hand, the chapters from Christensen, Dupont, Van Langenhove and Boers, and Jakobi and Kandt rely on the network concept to better describe features of their case studies that other concepts would not do equal justice to. One of the ambitions of the volume is to show that both of these routes to working with networks are productive and add value, including even more formal approaches that put greater emphasis on network measures and statistics; the latter are not covered substantively in this volume, but Dimmelmeier's chapter goes the furthest in this direction.

The levels of analysis: Macro, Meso, and Micro

The empirical chapters in the book each deal with networks and European actors on one or more of the Macro, Meso, and Micro levels.

The macro level

On the Macro level, Beaumier argues that private regulatory networks play an important role in the governance of the digital economy, and moreover, that these networks helped the EU export its own rules to the US. The EU was successful in seeking influence through private networks. In the case of climate and biodiversity governance, Dupont found that the importance of the EU as an actor in these networks depended on the EU's own internal performance and ambition to tackle these challenges. Coherence, in this case, follows from aligning internal and external goals. Jakobi and Kandt found that the EU was most active in enforcing and implementing global goals and practices internally in the cases of money laundering and cybercrime, but that the emphasis may shift more toward policy formulation as the transatlantic partnership with the US comes under increasing pressure. Van Langenhove and Boers shed light on the changing world order by characterizing it as a rejection of a unipolar model that has given way to a highly contested diffusion of power across multiple sites and types of actors. This runs the risk of leading to a confusing state of "diplomacy of everything".

In all these cases, policy actors are confronted with a situation of increasing complexity and "polycentricity", regardless of sector. This complexity is characterized by fragmentation of information and policies, multi-faceted issues that affect multiple societal sectors at once, and dramatic shifts in power relations between traditional (especially states) and new actors. The empowerment of new actors owes much to the fact that key infrastructure and resource is often held privately and not publicly: for example, banks, financial institutions, internet providers, social media, scientific expertise, and so on. This necessitates interaction between public and private actors as well as interaction among groups of private actors across national and regional divides.

The studies all demonstrate, albeit in a variety of ways, EU and European actors working with and through networks in order to achieve policy coherence and effectiveness. The range of tasks taking place within networks ranges from the development of ideas and policies to the implementation and enforcement of laws, and influence is sought by direct participation in the networks or by shaping their environment and goals. This puts a premium on flexibility and adaptive capacity, as policy actors have to remain responsive to sudden shifts within these networks. At the same time, it redefines policy coherence and effectiveness as the extent to which policies can capture, encompass, and remain sensitive to rapid developments in the sector they are targeting – developments that may originate in distant sites, but rapidly come to change conditions for everyone. As noted by Godet and Orsini, networks are thus bridging the state-centric and world society views of the international system, in both theory and practice.

The meso level

On the Meso level, Dimmelmeier charts the emergence of a transnational field of expertise and community of experts in sustainable finance, and finds that EU institutions are generally well integrated and their efforts to shape the field are cohesive. While this coherence seems to be indicative of EU success in influencing the field, Dimmelmeier suggests that too much coherence may also be risky: it can reinforce and empower incumbent actors and approaches, crowding out the novelty that exists on the periphery of the network. Broadening membership in the network may be beneficial here. In contrast, Haagensen finds that EU actors were not instrumental in the expert networks that came to define the issue of sovereign debt restructuring. Instead, legal experts exerted control over the appropriate solutions for dealing with sovereign debt restructuring, even in the face of competing institutional visions. These legal networks did not enable coherence and alignment between EU actors, given the complexity of the Economic and Monetary Union. Beaumier and Dupont also speak to the Meso level in dealing with how the EU accommodates and shapes complex regimes. For Dupont, this implies EU-internal climate and biodiversity initiatives, and for Beaumier, the interaction between the EU and European (as well as non-European), private actor associations in data protection.

In contrast to the more macro-oriented findings, the authors that engaged with networks and complexity on the Meso level were less concerned with how global reorientations in power and capacities impacted European actors, and more concerned with how complexity is managed and navigated in issue-specific settings defined by overlapping regimes (see Pattberg and Widerberg, Chapter 2). The role of expertise comes to the fore, here. While Dimmelmeier, Beaumier, and Dupont (in the case of climate change) found high degrees of coherence and effectiveness of EU and European actor networks, Haagensen and Dupont (in the case of biodiversity) found low degrees. The studies from Haagensen and Dupont suggest that EU-internal unity of vision is a key success factor for determining the effectiveness and international recognition of European policy leadership. Dupont introduces a very useful distinction between "output effectiveness" (where agreed actions align with stated goals) and "outcome effectiveness" (where agreed actions lead to an improved state of affairs). The chapters suggest that output effectiveness may lead to higher levels of coherence even when lacking outcome effectiveness. Aligning actions with stated goals may allow European actors to assume leadership positions in networks that may be leveraged toward outcome effectiveness at a later point in time.

The micro level

The cases that focus on the Micro level zoom in even further, opening up the networks to the scrutiny of the maneuvers and positions that actors take within them.

Christensen traces the evolution of European tax policy networks from a narrow, "embryonic" community marked by low levels of diversity, scope, and contestation, toward a much more open and adversarial network constellation that is heterogeneous in nature, consisting of unstable coalitions leading to unpredictable outcomes. This has been associated with a move from the OECD to the EU as the dominant forum for international tax issues today. Interestingly, the growth and opening of the network to more divergent actors and opinions was directly responsible for its increasing influence. Valeriani looks at networks of European voluntary service organizations, in order to probe the relationship between networks and their members. He argues that the third sector, civil society, is an especially apt environment in which to observe networked relations, due to resource scarcity, increased competition, and dependence on the public and private sectors. By taking an in-depth look at the Italian voluntary service organization Lunaria, he argues that agency within networks depends more on network position than on the material resources and constraints of an organization. He also notes the importance of values and missions as drivers of voluntary organizations. The chapters by Dimmelmeier and Haagensen also both speak to the Micro level of networks in their analysis of the positions of and connections between individual texts and persons in the fields of sustainable finance and sovereign debt restructuring.

These chapters all draw attention to the importance of professional-organizational interaction within networks, and how this may radically rework both the content and outcome of policy debates. We see this most dramatically in the chapter by Christensen, where the actions of limited groups of professionals succeeded in shifting the global forum for international tax policy issues. There is a parallel here to Haagensen, who also finds outside influence wielded by a select group of legal experts in the realm of sovereign debt restructuring. The question of whether or not the EU succeeds in seeking influence within networks on the Micro level can be found by paying attention to the selection of strategies suggested by Henriksen and Seabrooke in their chapter. For example, Christensen argues that it was due to a strategy of "challenging" established actors through parallel professional-organizational networks, that the EU was able to increase their influence. Similarly, Valeriani proposes that the strategy of "mandating" explains the embedding and agency of lead organizations within a network.

Concluding thoughts: Findings, limitations, and future directions

The chapters in this volume, it can be argued, demonstrate in a variety of ways the importance of focusing on network characteristics and interaction on each analytical level, macro, meso, and micro, as well as making evident the links connecting one level to the other. We see several chapters spanning the divide between macro, meso, and micro, showing how features of one level directly impact conditions on the others. Returning to the key research question of the volume, we offer some concluding remarks on the implications of the chapters overall in relation to two scenarios: (1) How EU and European actors have navigated and benefited from global complexity; and (2) The extent to which EU and European actors have been constrained by or struggled to navigate and order global complexity.

The case studies on data protection, sustainable finance, taxation, climate change, and voluntary service organizations all point to clear, strong roles for EU and European actors in the networks addressing these issues. In all these examples, increasing regime and global complexity presented an opportunity that EU and European actors successfully seized in order to strongly influence debates and policy. On the other hand, the case studies on biodiversity, money laundering, cybercrime, science diplomacy, and sovereign debt were less clear-cut when it comes to assessing the influence of European actors. In these case studies, EU and European actors were often limited in their potential and capacity to address and shape the governance of the issue, and were often reactive to developments and initiatives originating in areas outside of their sphere of influence and control.

It is difficult to say with certainty what separates the first group of case studies from the second group, but we can suggest some differences that may pave the way for future research to enable a better understanding of this. We would suggest that at least three different factors appear critical for European actors to navigate, manage, and influence complex global regimes with success. These are:

(1) A strong EU-internal unity of vision regarding the nature of the problem and ways forward. European action in some cases was hampered by a lack of agreement, for example, between member states or between different units or organizations within a network on how policy problems are defined and what kinds of solutions are deemed possible and favorable. As an example here, the case study on Science Diplomacy displays the difficulty of acting coherently when member states and EU institutions all develop their own policies and visions, leading to increased fragmentation.
(2) A strong record of action and leadership on the issue. European action often faces the constraint of working with a context of policy fragmentation and different levels of information across member states. This was clearly the case in transnational cybercrime and money laundering. Lack of progress on addressing biodiversity also exemplifies this point.
(3) Adaptive capacity. Finally, this relates to the capacity of EU and European actors to adapt and remain flexible in the face of rapidly changing regime and global conditions. An example of where European actors fell short on this measure comes from the case study on sovereign debt, where the institutional procedures of Eurozone reform struggled to keep up with the pace of change within the expert network of legal professionals. In contrast, the EU was quicker to adapt its role in global climate change governance, which has led to increased recognition of EU leadership.

Finally, then, what can we glean with regards to the limitations of the network approach in relation to our cases and more broadly. Importantly, what do our cases suggest with regard to future research directions in relation to the ability of actors to navigate what is undoubtedly a more complex global arena across a growing number of issues areas?

Some of these limitations were introduced in previous chapters, especially the three opening theoretical chapters. Network thinking runs the risk of limiting the overall field of vision: it may leave aside the history and social genesis of a network, glossing over the already-existing dynamics and potential tensions within the network (Pouliot 2013, p. 54). Also, it has been suggested that similar node positions within networks can obscure differences in behavior (White and Harary 2001). For both of these reasons, the chapters in this volume have stressed the importance of placing the network within its social, political, and economic context. What our cases demonstrate is that the balance of abstracting data for network models and retaining rich, empirical detail can be difficult to strike, and has to be assessed on a case-by-case basis. Furthermore, and as several chapters in the volume show, demonstrating the existence of an emerging network does not always allow more in-depth probing of why such a network is emerging or, indeed, the relative influence of actors within such a network (or indeed, those that have been excluded). As pointed to by Pattberg and Widerberg in Chapter 2, for this to be achieved, further conceptual and methodological innovation is needed to provide in-depth understanding and mapping of a network (Meso level) and enriched analysis of the motivations of actors within it (Micro level).

More broadly, there are issues that, whilst raised theoretically, have not been touched upon substantively through the cases in this volume but are, nevertheless, in our view, central to the study of networks and complexity going forward. The question of power and struggles for power within networks, for example, has been raised by various scholars (Minhas et al. 2017; Coburn et al. 2013; Gulati and Srivastava 2014; Morin et al. 2017). Whilst there has been an indication within this volume of how increasing complexity has empowered actors other than states within networks, further work needs to explore not only how networks may redefine the look and feel of a power struggle but also how they re-imagine or contest them. Indeed, networks may erase structural or hierarchical inequalities by placing qualitatively different actors on a similar, networked footing and seeing networks in such cases may imply changes solely to the form of governance, but not the function or the content (Hurrell and Woods 1999, p. 25). The question of how to deal with power as understood by the various traditions in EU studies and International Relations strikes us as a fruitful avenue of future research.

In cases where networks demonstrably change traditional forms of governance, we find further challenges. Even if networks are becoming the default response to global and transnational regime complexity, it is far from demonstrated that networks are the best way to solve global challenges. Indeed, as alluded to in this volume in relation to environmental governance, from an "outcome" perspective, we cannot conclude that actions taken in the relevant global networks that address this issue, or the EU's role therein, have been effective, even if there has been an exponential increase in actions. Furthermore, it may be that networks merely become new vectors for the proliferation of problems and reproduction of inequalities at a global scale (Toope 2000, p. 97). Networks may also undermine traditional bases of power, which can be welcome in some cases, but less so in others. What are, for example, the consequences of private sector actors becoming more powerful in global networks than third or public sector representativeness? How is the public interest upheld in global issue networks characterized by complexity? Finally, networks are also often criticized for lacking accountability, transparency, democracy, and representativeness (Papadopoulos 2007; Heretier 2003, p. 818; Jensen 2009, p. 4; Toope 2000, pp. 96–97). This begs further questions of how informal and formal governance practices within any such networks – the former which have proliferated in European and global cybercrime governance, for example – can be both accountable and effective in terms of process, action, output, and outcome.

In spite of these challenges, this volume has shown – at least in the diverse range of cases that have been explored – that for EU and European actors facing global complexity, networks are here to stay and are frequently associated with increased policy coherence and effectiveness. Moreover, we have demonstrated more broadly that across a number of issues areas, complex regimes have galvanized new connections and networks that include a range of stakeholders, with different expertise, motives, and levels of influence and control. In this way, we hope to have provided "a much wider panorama of vision" (Slaughter 2017, p. 4) in the study of networks and complexity, theoretically and empirically. This, in full knowledge that there is much more to be done to continue refining and nuancing research in this area in order to provide a richer understanding for academics and policymakers alike of network structures, designs and solutions in a political ecosystem increasingly characterized by complexity and a web worldview.

References

Coburn, Cynthia E., Mata, Willow S and Choi, Linda (2013) "The Embeddedness of Teachers' Social Networks: Evidence from a Study of Mathematics Reform", *Sociology of Education*, vol. 86, no. 4, pp. 311–342.

Gulati, Ranjay and Srivastava, Sameer B. (2014) "Bringing Agency Back into Network Research: Constrained Agency and Network Action", in Daniel J. Brass , Giuseppe (JOE) Labianca , Ajay Mehra , Daniel S. Halgin and Stephen P. Borgatti (eds.) *Contemporary Perspectives on Organizational Social Networks, Research in the Sociology of Organizations*, vol. 40, Bingley: Emerald Group Publishing Limited, pp.73–93.

Heretier, Adrienne (2003) "Composite Democracy in Europe: The Role of Transparency and Access to Information", *Journal of European Public Policy*, vol. 10, pp. 814–833.

Hurrell, Andrew and Woods, Ngaire (1999) *Inequality, Globalization, and World Politics*, Oxford: Oxford University Press.

Jensen, Thomas (2009) "The Democratic Deficit of the European Union", *Living Reviews in Democracy*, vol. 1, pp. 1–8.

Minhas, Shahryar, Hoff, Peter and Ward, Michael D. (2017) "Influence Networks in International Relations", Working Paper, Cornell University. https://arxiv.org/abs/1706.09072.

Morin, Jean-Frédéric, Louafi Sélim, Orsini Amandine and Oubenal, Mohamed (2017) "Boundary Organizations in Regime Complexes: A Social Network Profile of IPBES", *Journal of International Relations and Development*, vol. 20, no. 3, pp. 543–577.

Papadopoulos, Yannis (2007) "Problems of Democratic Accountability in Network and Multilevel Governance", *European Law Journal*, vol. 13, no. 4, pp. 469–486.

Pouliot, Vincent (2013) "Methodology: Putting Practice Theory into Practice", in: Rebecca Adler-Nissen (ed.) *Bourdieu in International Relations: Rethinking Key Concepts in IR*, Abingdon: Routledge, pp. 45–58.

Slaughter, Anne-Marie (2017). *The Chessboard and the Web*, New Haven: Yale University Press.

Toope, Stephen (2000) "Emerging Patterns of Governance and International Law", in: Michael Byers (ed.) *The Rule of Law in International Politics*, Oxford: Oxford University Press, pp. 91–108.

White, Douglas R. and Harary, Frank (2001) "The Cohesiveness of Blocks in Social Networks: Node Connectivity and Conditional Density", *Sociological Methodology*, vol. 31, no. 1, pp. 305–359.

INDEX

Page numbers in "*italic*" indicate a figure and page numbers in "**bold**" indicate an illustration.

AAAS 192
actor-network theory 22
actors 214; in complex governance systems 51; influence in a network 27; measuring the structural position of 40; popularity of 40; role of in rules adoption 72; traditional state 22; understanding positions of 37
adaptive capacity 219
Adshead, M. 5
Africa 205
Alliance network, mapping of *172*
Alliance of European Voluntary Service Associations/Organizations 163–164, 168; mixed method approach and mapping of 168–172; *see also* Lunaria
American Medical Association 53
American private actors 72, 83, 85; European private actors and 72
Amsterdam, Treaty of 188
anti-money laundering and terrorism financing 207; laundering efforts 198; regime 201
anti-terrorism activities 200
Asia-Pacific 205
Asmussen, Jörg 133, 137
assemblages 35
ATLAS network 203
Atta, Mohammed, use of centrality from network analysis 40

Bach, David 75, 79
banking secrecy 198
Bank of International Settlements 201
Bayern LB (Germany) 133
Beaumier, G. 215–217
Bellini, N. 5
Best, H. 4
betweenness centrality 40, 44, 46
Biermann, F. 38
Big Data 86n2
bilateral and multilateral trade agreements 71
biodiversity network, international 154–157
biofuel governance, in a European Union (EU) context 52
biofuel issues 21
Bitonti, A. 5
BNP Paribas (France) 133
Boers, E. 215, 216
book, the: aims of 6–8; objectives of 7–8; structure of 8–12
boomerang effect 166
border protection 200
borders, blurring of 25, 27
Bottom-up networks 188
Bourdieusian "field" methods 60
Boussebaa, M. 63
Bradford, Ann 76
Braithwaite, John 76

Brexit campaigners 2
bricolage 35
brokerage 40
Brussels' effect 76, 81, 82, 85
Brussels European "bubble" 192
Brussels institutions, permanent representations and 189
Brussels Maastricht, Treaty of 188
Buchheit, Lee 136, 139, 140
Bulgaria 5
Bush administration 113
business actors, cooperation with 206
business associations 71
Byrne, D. 36

California effect 86n1
Callaghan, G. 36
Cambridge Analytica scandal 193
Canada 75
Capital Markets Union (CMU) 90
Capra, F. 37
carbon accounting 39, 40; climate change governance regime complex and 46
carbon emissions 39
Caribbean 205
CDM 40
centrality 19; betweenness 40, 44, 46; closeness 40, 46; conceptualizations of 40; degree 40; eigenvector 40, 46; in a network 40
centralization, degree of 38
centralized network structure 203
Centre for International Governance Innovation (CIGI) 140
CFSP (Common Foreign and Security Policy) 190
change, trajectory of 62
Chessboard and the Web, The (Slaughter) 3
Chinese regulatory commission 90
Christensen 215, 217, 218
civil society 187; civil society networks 6; empowering 6; networks and 164–168
Civil Society Organisations (CSOs) 22, 163–165
classical diplomacy 183
classical foreign policy analyses 74
classical neoliberal regime theory 34
classical state-centric international system 18; network approaches and 25
Clean Development Mechanism 39, 92
Cleary Gottlieb 140, 142
Clifford Chance 136
climate and biodiversity networks, European Union (EU)'s role in 150
Climate Bonds Initiative (CBI) 93, 99

climate change 2, 34; governance arena 34; governance regime complex 46
climate governance, organizational fields and 39
closeness centrality 40, 46
clustering coefficient 39, 40
cluster level (clustering) 38–40; organizational fields and 46
clusters, in a network 39–40
COCOP (Working Party on the Application of Specific Measures to Combat Terrorism) 202
cohesion 28, 51, 55–56, 63, 105
Cold War 35, 113
Collective Action Clauses 129–130
Commerzbank (Germany) 133
Committee of Eminent Persons 61
Common Foreign and Security Policy (CFSP) 190
communication 199; diplomacy and 183; networks and 167
communication technologies 20, 206
community detection 19–20
complex actors, network approaches and 25
complex adaptive systems 3; biological understanding of 3
complex entity, EU legal order and 5
complex global governance systems 46
complex governance systems 35; actors in 51
complex interdependent world, rule-setting in 73–77
complexity 35, 51, 214; concept of 6; global order and 213; intra-European perspective and 5; management of 198; meso level networks and 217
complexity approaches 5
complexity theory 35, 44, 214; complex regimes and 107; complex systems and 35–37
complex regimes 217
complex systems 3–4, 36, 215; complexity theory and 35–37
computer-based crimes 205; *see also* crimes
computer networks, taking over 204
computer-related crimes 204
concept network *104*
Conference of the Parties COP15 152, 153
conflict diamonds, criminalization of 199
Cooperation Group 206
co-publication network 96
co-publication network by degree, TOP 10 texts of **98**

COREPER 189, 192
corruption 200
COTER (dealing with international aspects) 202
Council of Better Business Bureau (BBB) 81
Council of Europe 164, 200, 201; Council of Europe Convention 205
Council Working Group on Terrorism 203
counter-terrorism policing, in the European Union (EU) 5
country-by-country reporting (CBCR) 111, 117–121
crime 197
crime governance 200
Crockett, Andrew 61
cross-border cooperation, European Union (EU) and 6
cross-border crimes 203
CSIRTs Network 206
cybercrime 197–198, 216; EU networking against 204–207
Cybercrime Convention 205; eight priority countries and 205
cybercrime governance 198, 205; complexity of 207
Cyber Fusion Center 204
cybersecurity 206; networks and enforcement in 207
Cybersecurity Strategy 205

Dallara, Charles 133
data and espionage, illegal access to 204
data protection 198, 200; American and European approaches to 73; EU and American agreements over 85; number of active private codes of conduct 80; private actor associations and 217; rules, categories of 89; rules, EU 72; transatlantic private regulatory networks on 83; transatlantic regulation of 77–80
Data Protection Directive (DPD) 75–80, 82, 84
data transfer, networks for 203
degree centrality 40
Denmark 193
Deutsche Bank (Germany) 133
Digital Agenda, EU's 207
digital ambassador, to stateless private sector 193
digital diplomacy 182
digital disinformation challenges 192
digital economy 85

digital technologies, impact of on diplomacy 182
Dimmelmeier, A. 215–218
Dingwerth, K. 38
diplomacy 181–182, 194; complexity in 182; principles of 191; world networks and 182
diplomacy of everything 216
diplomatic activities, impact of social media on 187
diplomatic environment 181
diplomatic epistemic networks 195
diplomatic networks 181
Directorate General of Research, Technology, and Development 193
DOLFINS project, of the Horizon 2020 funding 95
domestic regulatory systems 73
DPD *see* Data Protection Directive
Dupont, C. 215–217

Eagleton-Pierce, M. 63
Earth Day (2017) 191
Earth Summit 155
EC3 (European Cybercrime Center) 206–207
economic adjustment program 127
Economic and Monetary Union 217
economic development, cooperation and 5
economic nationalism, Donald Trump and 2
Egmont Group 203
eigenvector centrality 40, 46
elements 51
elites, in Europe 5
embeddedness 20
emergence 94
emergent properties 36
ENP *see* European Neighborhood Policy (ENP)
entrepreneurial authority 76
environmental agreement 21
environmental issues 147–148
environmental networks, European Union (EU)'s role in 148–150
Environmental Protection Agency 22
epistemic arbitrage 62
epistemic authority 63
epistemic communities 21, 22, 114
EU and European actors *134*; adaptive capacity and 219; and global complexity 218; global complexity and 221
EU Commission 57

EU data protection rules 72
EU direct tax reforms 114
EU environmental legislation 155
EU green bond label 90
EU institutions: publications of and sustainable finance 106; selected documents commissioned **97**
EU-internal climate and biodiversity initiatives 217
EU-internal cooperation 200
EU-internal unity of vision 217, 219
EU leadership 219
EU LIFE grants 95
Eurochambres 82
Eurocommerce 81
Eurojust 203, 206, 207
Europe: governance in 190; multi-level governance 188–189; multi-level governance dynamics in 52; regional integration and 188; in relation to others 5–6
European actor networks 217; and influence on debates and policy 213
European actors 1; changing trends and 214; networks and 215, 216; *see also* EU and European actors
European Administrative Space 4
European Bank for Reconstruction & Development 132
European Chiefs of Police 203
European Commission (EC) 85, 90, 114, 115, 117–119, 149; DPD and 79, 85; eEurope 2005 and 84; the EU structure and 189; FATF and 202; GDPR and 86; task force on financial risk 133
European Council 200; working groups on counter-terrorism legislation 202
European Cybercrime Center (Europol) 206
European data privacy rules, United States of America (USA) and 72
European data protection approach 81–85
European diplomatic actors 182
European External Action Service (EEAS) 188, 193, 205
European Financial Stability Facility (EFSF) 135–136
European governance networks, people who populate the 4–5
European Institute 190
European integration, attitudes toward 5
European Judicial Cybercrime Network 206

European macro-regions, cooperation between 5
European Neighborhood Policy (ENP) 6
European networks 2–6
European order, the 18
European policies, externalization of 73
European policy leadership 217
European private actors 72, 83; American private actors and 72; *see also* EU and European actors
European Public-Private Partnership for Resilience 206
European regional policy 5
European regulation and governance, network approaches to 4
Europeans, as actors in global networks 5; *see also* EU and European actors
European Science Diplomacy initiatives 193
European Stability Mechanism (ESM) 137; Treaty of 142
European Task Force of Chiefs of Police 203
European tax policy networks/systems 110, 217
European Union (EU) 1, 51, 164; actors 217; as actors in global networks 5; biofuel governance in 52; "complexity" of European affairs and 4; counter-terrorism policing in the 5; against cybercrime 204–207; Digital Agenda 207; Economic and Financial Committee (EFC) 142; European External Action Service (EEAS) and 188; food standards of 72; global complexity and 213; global environmental regimes and 157–158; global financial system and cyberspace 207; global market regulation and 72; as an intergovernmental machine 18; international tax policy and 114–117; involvement in transnational policy networks 6; legal order 5; money laundering and terrorism financing 201–204; networked actors in 23; as a networked form of governance 18; and networks against crime 199–200; networks and 26, 216; policies within 64; political and institutional infrastructure of 189–190; regime complexes and 3; regulatory capacity of the 4; role of in global market regulation 72; *sui generis* case of 188–190; transformation of governance in 4; UK leaving the 2

European Union Counter-Terrorism
 Coordinator 200
European Union's Emission Trading
 scheme 39
European Union's FLEGT program 34
European voluntary service organizations,
 networks of 218
Europol 200, 203, 205–207
Euroregions 5
Eurozone reform 219
Eurozone sovereign debt crisis 127
EU-sponsored research 96; sustainable
 finance and 104, 106
EU-US cooperation 205
EU–US Cyber Dialogue 205
EU Wildlife Trade Regulations 156
evaluating power relationships 19
exemplary implementer 202
expert networks, Greek debt
 restructuring and 138–143
experts, importance of 5

fake news 191, 192
Farrell, H. 74
Farrow, R. 181
FATF (Financial Action Taskforce) 201
Federal Trade Commission (FTC) 78
Federation of European Direct and
 Interactive Marketing (FEDMA) 81
Fernandez, Ramon 133
Financial Action Taskforce (FATF) 201
Financial Markets Law Committee's
 Sovereign Bond Scoping Forum 140
financial sector, climate change within 98
Financial Stability Board's Task Force on
 Climate Related Financial Disclosures
 (FSB-TCFD) 91
financial system, sustainable 90
"Financing a sustainable European
 economy" (HLEG) 102
Fletcher, Tom 184, 185
Food and Agriculture Organization
 International Treaty meetings 24
Foreign Sovereign Immunities Act
 (FSIA) 128
forest governance architecture 35
forest governance domain 42–44
Forest Law Enforcement, Governance and
 Trade action (FLEGT) 156
forestry regime complex 46
formalization 215
fragmentation 35, 38, 216
Framework for Global Electronic
 Commerce (White House) 79

France 192–193
French bank BNP Paribas 132
Frontex 200
functional fields 46, 215

G7 197, 200–202
G20 17, 22, 200, 202; critique of the
 184; Green Finance Study group 91;
 summits 188
Gates Foundation 187
GATF (Global Action Task Force) 171
GDPR (General Data Protection
 Regulation) 73, 78
Gelpern, Anna 139, 140, 142
General Data Protection Regulation
 (GDPR) 73, 78
Generation Y's leaders 187
Georgakakis, D. 4
GLACY 205
GLACY+ 205, 207
Global Action Task Force (GATF) 171
Global Alliance 205
Global Business Dialogue on
 e-Commerce (GBDe) 81
global climate change governance 219
global complexity: EU and European
 actors and 218–219, 221; European
 networks and 2–6
global crime governance 197, 198;
 networks and 198–201
global cybercrime governance 221
global economy, regulations and 71
global environmental governance
 147–148; complexity of 157–158
global environmental regimes, role of the
 European Union (EU) in 157–158
global financial crisis 110
global forest governance 35, 46; triangle 43
global governance 1, 34, 44, 46; analyzing
 complexity in 44, 46; complexity of 35,
 37, 38, 214; complex system approach
 36; networks in 29; regime complexes
 and 40
globalization 184; alternative to 22;
 Europe under 5
global leadership, lack of 194
global market regulation, European
 Union (EU) and 72
global networks 1
global order 214; limit of network
 approach to 27–29; networks and 18;
 regime complexity in 213; relevance of
 state competition in 2; role of networks
 in 2; transnational networks and 20–24

Global South 127
Godet, C. 72, 163, 197, 214–216
Goldmann, Matthias 140
Google, Apple, Facebook, and Amazon (GAFA) 193
Goss, Leland 139
Gottlieb, Cleary 142
governance 184–186; approaches 34; hybrid fields of 52; multi-level governance in Europe 188–189; networked forms of 18, 29; networked organization of 192; networks and 23; transformation of 4
governance actors, transnational networks as 23
governance architectures: fragmented 44; network approaches and 46
governance complexity 35; conceptualizing 35; in the European Union (EU) 214
governance networks 4, 23, 198
governmental actors 199; *see also* actors
governmental and non-governmental networks 23
governmental diplomacy 181
governmental organizations 195
governmental or non-governmental actors 22
government networks, international politics as 2
Gray, Robert 133, 139
Greek debt restructuring 127–129; case of 132–138; expert networks and 138–143
Green, J.F. 39, 40, 76
Green Bond Principles 93
green credit 90
Green Finance Study group, G20's 91
Greylock Capital (USA) 133
Group of Trustees (GoT) 128, 131–133, 135–138, 141–143
Gulati, Mitu 142
Gulf Cooperation Council 201

Haagensen, N. 215, 217, 218
Haas, Peter 21
Hafner-Burton 37
Hagan, Sean 139
Harary, F. 28
hard boundaries 2
Harmful Tax Competition 113
harmonizing networks 76
Harris, P. 5
Heinz, Otto 141
Heller, Ben 139
Henriksen, L. 8, 9, 129, 215, 218
hierarchies 27
high tech crime 200
Hildebrand, C. 5
Hilpert, U. 5
Horizon 2020 funding programme 95, 190
horizontal networks 200
HSBC (UK) 133
humanitarian military interventions 21
human trafficking issues 24
Humes, Hans 133
hybridity/hybrid fields 52, 53
hybrid two-level networks 59–61

ICAN (International Campaign to Abolish Nuclear Weapons 21
IMF (International Monetary Fund) 114, 117, 128, 139; ICMA and 139; SDRM and 130, 133, 135–136, 140
individual level 40, 46
individual regimes 3
industrial public-private partnerships 6
influence 40
influence and soft power 191
influence networks 21, 22, 178
information: fragmentation of 216; global access of 183
information systems, attacks against 205
Institute for climate economics (I4CE) 98
Institute of International Finance (IIF) 135
institutional complexity 38
institutional diversity 38
institutional expansion 4
intergovernmentalism: liberal 4; sovereign 1
Intergovernmental Panel on Climate Change (IPCC) 151
Intergovernmental Platform on Biodiversity and Ecosystem Services 27
intergovernmental politics 21, 23, 24
international actors, networks of 17
international biodiversity network 154–157
International Campaign to Abolish Nuclear Weapons (ICAN) 21
International Capital Market Association (ICMA) 93, 139
international cause, lobbying and TANS 21
International Chamber of Commerce (ICC) 81

international climate change network 150–154
International Conference of Data Protection and Commissioners (ICDPPC) 76
international cooperation 112, 190, 193, 195, 199, 204, 205
International Environmental and Scientific Affairs 22
international institutions, overlapping and non-hierarchical regimes and 3
international issues, within "regime complexes" 24
International Labor Organization 24
International Law Association's Sovereign Bankruptcy Study Group 140
International Monetary Fund 61
International Organisation of Legal Metrology (IOLM) 52
International Organization for Migration (IOM) 24
International Organization for Standardization (ISO) 52
international organizations (IO) 128, 197, 200; and connection to knowledge organizations 6; network alliances and 6
international police network (Europol) 200
international politics 2
international regimes 18, 23–24
international regulatory environment, creating a 71–72
international relations (IR) 198, 220; centrality and 19; complexity and 4; and concepts of networks 199; network analysis and 37; network approaches and 2, 17–18, 29, 194; organizing principle of 24; transnational advocacy networks (TANs) in 20, 21
International Standards Organisation (ISO) norms 74
international system 2, 72, 86, 164, 216
international tax policy 112–114; European Union (EU) and 114–117; progressive reform in 113
international tax policy issues 218
internet 3, 77, 186–187, 198, 216
Interpol 200, 204, 205
Interpol-Europol Cybercrime Conference (2013) 204
inter-state politics 23, 208
Intesa San Paolo (Italy) 133
intra-EU and extra-EU tax policy 114

intra-European affairs, networks and 5, 6
intra-European work, regime complexity and 4
intrepid brokers 60
ISO 14064-1 40
issue control 53, 62, 115, 121, 129, 136, 141; network 170; trajectories of 61–64; transnational 132
issue entrepreneurs 60, 61
issue professionals 52–54, 60, 61; concept of 53
issue professionals in a hybrid network 59
Italian CSO (*Lunaria*), and the European network 163
Italian National Statistic Institute (Istat) 163

Jakobi, A. P. 215, 216
J-CAT (Joint Cybercrime Action Task Force) 206
Johnson, Boris 2
Joint Committee on Strengthening the Framework for Sovereign Debt 136–138
Joint Cybercrime Action Task Force (J-CAT) 206

Kahler, M. 37; *Networked Politics* 3
Kandt, J. 215, 216
Karlsrud, J. 63
Kavalski, E. 36
Keck, M. E. 21, 37, 166
Keohane 21
Keohane, Robert O. 74
Kimberly Process 199
Kingah, S. 6
knowledge organizations, international organizations and 6
knowledge society 194
Koch-Weser, Caio 133
Krebs, study of 40
Krossa, A.S. 5
Kyoto Protocol 152

Lamarche, Michele 135
Larosière, Jacques de 132, 133
Latin America 205
Latin American 127
Latin American countries, sovereign debt restructurings 127
Lavenex 85
Lavenex, S. 75, 76, 86
League of Nations 111
Lemierre, Jean 133, 135, 139

liberal intergovernmentalism, versus neofunctionalism 4
Liikanen, I. 6
linear systems 36
Lisbon, Treaty of 188
literature review 2–6
local activism 21
Lunaria 11, 163, 167, 168, 218; Alliance of European Voluntary Service Organization and 169–171; case of 172–177; centrality and 172
LuxLeaks 115, 116

macro level networks 7, 143, 164, 216
mafia-style model 199
mapping relationships 19
March for Science initiatives 191
Marcussen, M. 4
Markets in Financial Instruments Directive (Mifid II) 90
Martinico, G. 5
Mathieu, E. 4
Melissen, J. 188
meso level networks 7, 8, 38, 39, 91, 94, 164, 216–217
methodological individualism 26
Mexico 130, 139
micro level networks 8, 18, 94, 121, 143, 164, 214, 217–218
mixed method approach, Alliance of European Voluntary Service Associations 168–172
modeling networks 41–42
Moldova 6
money laundering 2
money laundering and terrorism financing 2, 197–198, 200, 216, 219; EU networking against 201–204
Montreal Protocol 21
Moravscik, A. 18
Morocco 6, 90
Mühlen-Schulte, A. 63
Müller, Klaus-Peter 133
multilateral agreements 38
multilateralism, era of 182
Multilateralism 1.0 183–184
Multilateralism Mode 2.0 184–186
multi-level, multi-actor diplomacy *189*
multi-level networks 51
multi-level policy interactions 54–59
Multinational Corporations (MNCs) 164
multiple insiders 56
Murphy, Elaine 133

Nagoya Protocol 24
national borders, permeability of 25

national economies, opening of 71
nationalism 2, 194
neofunctionalism 4
network
network alliances, of international organizations 6
network analysis 3, 18, 19, 37; as an analytical instrument 199; concept of 19–20; driver of political outcome and 26; regime complexes and 39
network analysis toolkit 46
Network and Information Security (NIS) Public-Private Platform 206
network approaches 2; challenge to classic state-centric perspective 25; complex actors and 25; conceptualize the international scene and 24; groups' behavior and 26; international relations and 18; levels of application of 46; limitations of 219–220; limits of 27–29, 46; to multi-level European regulation and governance 4; power and 25; relations between units and 26; Science Diplomacy and 194; social environments and 27
network data, actual interpretation of 46
networked actors 22
Networked Politics (Kahler) 3
networks 17, 200, 214, 220–221; analysis of 3; behaviors and 22; centrality in 40; challenges and network solutions **168**; characteristics and interactions of 218–221; civil society and 164–168; concept *104*; and creating new world order 23; European 2–6; European Union (EU) and 207–208; European voluntary service organizations and 218; between experts and elites 5; global crime governance and 198–201; governance 23; hybrid two-level 59–61; influence 22; International Relations (IR) research and 199; levels of analysis and 215–218; macro level 215; mapping of 220; meso level 216–217; multi-level 51; as as new systems 23; nodes on 18–20, 28, *45*; organizational 53; as an organizational form 22; parallel-existing 197; policy outcomes and 163; polycentricity paradigm and 27; professional 53; professional-organizational interaction and 218; relatioship with members of 177–178; *see also* Lunariarole of in global order 2; social network analysis (SNA) and 3; solving global problems and 197; state competition and 2; as a tool to study

cooperation 5; transgovernmental 21, 72; transnational 72, 214; transnational advocacy networks (TANs) 21; types 198
network theories 55, 57, 215; applying 6; definition of 18–19; global governance systems and 34; measuring regime complexes and 38; transitivity in 40
new anarchy 35
new interdependence approach 74
Newman, Abraham L. 72, 75, 79
new medievalism 35
A New World Order (Slaughter) 2, 3
NGOs' organizational structures 27
Nice, Treaty of 188
9/11 terrorist attack 40, 201, 203
NIS Directive 206
Nobel Peace Prize 21
nodes: on networks 18–20, 28, 40, 45; the number of connections of 40, 96–97
non-EU-sponsored research 96
nongovernmental organizations (NGOs) 71
non-governmental or governmental actors 22
non-humans, policy networks and 22
non-linear relationships/systems 36–37
non-state actors, cooperation with 206
Norway 203
nuclear weapons, treaty to ban the use of 21
Nye 21
Nye, Joseph S. 74

OECD 71, 110–114, 201, 218; international tax policy issues and 114–115; tax networks 112–113
online child abuse, combatting/ exploitation 204, 205
online fraud 204
organizational action 59
organizational characteristics 65
organizational fields 38–39, 46, 215
organizational forms, characteristics of 64–65
organizational hierarchy, mafia-style model of 199
organizational networks 53, 54, 215
organizational professional competencies 61
Organization of Economic Co-operation and Development (OECD) *see* OECD
organizations, networked modes of 6
Organization Studies 54
organized crime 1, 24, 197, 200, 203
Orsini, A. 72, 163, 197, 214–216

Ostrom, Elinor 148
overlapping and non-hierarchical regimes, international institutions and 3
Oxfam 63, 187
ozone layer 22; protocol on 21

Panama Papers 115, 116
Paradise Papers 115, 116
Parag Khanna 181
parallel-existing networks 197
Paris Agreement 23, 34, 90, 152
Pattberg, P. 8, 38, 129, 131, 165, 214, 220
peer networks 51, 54, 188, 215
peer recognition 52, 132
people, influencing the opinion of 187–188
permanent representations 192; Brussels institutions and 189
Poland 5
policing power 198
policy actors 6, 72, 192, 216
policy cohesion 53, 55, 132, 135, 137
policy networks, non-humans and 22
policy outcomes, networks and 163
political and economic elites 5
political ecosystem 221
political networks, modeling **41**
polycentric governance 158
polycentricity paradigm, networks and 27, 216
Posner, E. 72
post-Communist transition 5
postwar international liberal order, threat to 1
power 25, 40, 181, 214, 220; de-territorialization of 25
prestige 40, 54, 61
Principles Consultative Group (PCG) 131, 132
"Principles for Stable Capital Flows" 130
Principles on Promoting Responsible Sovereign Lending and Borrowing 142
privacy statement, data protection and 81
private actors 199, 202, 204; associations 217; role of in transatlantic regulation of data protection 77–80; *see also* actors
private banks, global networks of 201
private regulatory networks 9, 71–73, 77, 79, 80, 85, 216; data protection and 81–86; European data protection approach and 81–85
private sector actors, importance of 192
problems and policy recommendations **103**
professional characteristics 64, 65
professionalization 52
professional networks 51–53, 64

professional-organizational interaction, networks and 53, 121, 218; nexus 54–59; two-level network *56*
protectionism 194
public and private actors, interaction between 4, 199, 204, 206; *see also* actors
Public Diplomacy 188, 191, 192, 194; social media and 187–188
public policy 191
public-private partnerships, cybersecurity and 207
public standards 40

Radaelli, Claudio 110, 114, 115
rational process 76
regime complexes 3, 23, 35, 38, 215; clusters in 39; European Union (EU) and 3; global governance and 40; network approaches to 44; organizational fields and 46
regime complexity 35; intra-European work and 4
Regling, Klaus 137
regulations, global economy and 71
regulatory interdependence 73
related methodologies 37
relational ontologies 37
RELEX (Working Party of Foreign Relations Counselors) 203
Research and Innovation policy 190
resultant regimes 1
Romania 5
Rome (1957), Treaty of 188
Rowell, J. 4
Royal Society 192
rule-makers, and rule-takers 71; rule-making authority 72
Russia 6

Saccomanni, Fabrizio 133
Safe Harbor agreement 72, 75–77, 79–82, 84
Schengen areas 200
Schoenman, R. 5
Schwartz, Paul M. 76
science and innovation 190
science and technology: community 193; policy domains and 190
science diplomacy 182, 190, 219; case of 190–191; with networks 192–194; new agenda for 191–192; praxis of 192–194
science diplomats 191
Scott, J.W. 6

Seabrooke, L. 8, 9, 129, 215, 218
security issues 191
selected documents commissioned EU institutions **97**
Setser, Brad 139
Sikkink, K. 21, 166
Single Market 4
Slaughter, Ann-Marie 2, 21, 26–27, 37, 40, 182, 186, 192, 195; *Chessboard and the Web, The* 3; *A New World Order* 2, 3
Sobel, Mark 138
social actors 20
social cohesion 55
social contract, science society 191
social environments 27
social media 187–188
social network analysis (SNA) 2–4, 28, 37, 215; theory 18
social systems 51
society: digitalization of 182; as a network 25
socio-cultural norms 24
soft power 190
sovereign debt restructuring 127–129, 217–219; literature review 129–132; main legal professionals embedded *141*
Sovereign Debt Restructuring Mechanism (SDRM) 130
Sovereign Debt Workout Institution (DWI) 140
sovereign intergovernmentalism 1
sovereign single-mindedness 2
sovereign states, Westphalian model of 184
sovereignty 25
Standby Action Taskforce 64
state-centric approaches 24; state-centric world 24
state-centrism, power from 25
state competition, networks and 2
stateless private sector, digital ambassador to 193
state sovereignty, challenge to 25
state to state diplomacy 182–183
Stone, D. 6
structural holes 58
structuralism 26
"Study on the potential of green bond finance" (DG ENV) 102
Sub-Committee on EU Sovereign Debt Markets 142
superposition principle 36
Suranyi, Gyorgy 133
sustainability management 53

Sustainable Development Goals (SDGs) 90
sustainable finance 90–92, 216, 218; European Union (EU) and 94–96; findings from the three networks 104–106; historical context of 92–93
sustainable financial system (UNEP Inquiry) 90
system level 38; regime complexes and 46

TANs (transnational advocacy networks) 21
tax haven leaks 115
tax policy discussions, European Union (EU) and 110
terrorism 2
Thomas, Gerassimos 137
Timber Regulations 156
Top 10 documents by overall citations **99**
TOP 10 texts of co-publication network by degree **98**
Torfing, J. 4
track-one diplomacy 191
trade agreements 71, 156
trading up phenomenon 73, 75
traditional state actors 22
trafficking in human beings 200
Tran, Hung 139
transatlantic partnership, United States of America (USA) and 216
transgovernmental networks 17, 21, 72
transnational actors 72
transnational advocacy networks (TANs) 21
transnational crime 197–198, 200, 201, 219; governance of 208
transnational governance 61, 64
transnational issue 54
transnationalization 20
transnational networks 17, 18, 72, 214; actors and 25; global order and 20–24; as governance actors 23
transnational organized crime *see* transnational crime
transnational policy network 6; EU's involvement in 6
transnational regime complexity 220
transnational terrorism 202
Treaty of Amsterdam 188
Treaty of Brussels Maastricht 188
Treaty of Lisbon 188
Treaty of Nice 188
Treaty of Rome (1957) 188
Treaty of the European Stability Mechanism (ESM) 142

Treaty of the European Union, and combatting organized crime 200
Trichet, Jean-Claude 132, 133
Trump, Donald 1
TRUSTe (now TrustArc) 81
Turkey 6
two-level network 64

UN Convention 201
unconventional diplomacy 194
UN Development Programme 153
UN Fiscal Commission 113
United Nations Charter 183
United Nations Children's Fund 24
United Nations Conference on Trade and Development's (UNCTAD) report 139
United Nations Department of Economic and Social Affairs (UNDESA) 140
United Nations Environment Programme's Emissions Gap Report 148
United Nations Environment Programme's Inquiry, sustainable financial system (UNEP Inquiry) and 90
United Nations Framework Convention on Climate Change (UNFCCC) 34, 39, 151
United States of America (USA) 1–2, 22; EU foods standards and the 72; transatlantic partnership with 216
United States of America (USA) and, European data privacy rules 72
UNODC 204
UN Security Council 184, 201
US hegemony, erosion of 184
US. Private regulatory networks 77
US State Department's Bureau of Oceans 22
US Treasury's Sovereign Debt Roundtable 140

Valeriani, M. 11, 215, 218
Van Langenhove, L. 193, 215, 216
Van Middelaar, L. 189
Vogel, David 73

Waibel, Michael 140
web worldview 2, 221
Westphalian order 214
White, D. R. 28
White House, Framework for Global Electronic Commerce 79
Widerberg, O. 8, 38, 41, 77, 129, 131, 165, 214, 220

Wieser, Thomas 136, 137
Working Group on Terrorism 202
Working Party of Foreign Relations Counselors (RELEX) 202–203
Working Party on the Application of Specific Measures to Combat Terrorism (COCOP) 202
World Bank 93, 114, 128, 153
World Intellectual Property Organization Committee, on genetic resources 24
world order: changes in 184; disruptions of 184; networks and 20
world politics 44; as a system of complex systems 46; transformation of 35
World Social Forum 22
world society perspective 25
World Trade Organization (WTO) 63, 71

Yearbook of International Organizations *165*

Zandstra, Deborah 139, 140

Printed in the United States
by Baker & Taylor Publisher Services